A PLEASURE TO MEASURE

Tasks for Teaching Measurement in the Elementary Grades

By

Jeffrey Barrett
Illinois State University
Normal, Illinois

Diana Behnke
Normal, Illinois

Craig Cullen
Illinois State University
Normal, Illinois

David Klanderman
Trinity Christian College
Palos Heights, Illinois

NATIONAL COUNCIL OF
TEACHERS OF MATHEMATICS

www.nctm.org/more4u
Access code: PTM14782

Copyright © 2017 by
The National Council of Teachers of Mathematics, Inc.
1906 Association Drive, Reston, VA 20191-1502
(703) 620-9840; (800) 235-7566; www.nctm.org

Library of Congress Cataloging-in-Publication Data

Names: Barrett, Jeffrey Edward.
Title: A pleasure to measure : tasks for teaching measurement in the
    elementary grades / by Jeffrey Barrett, Illinois State University, Normal,
    Illinois [and three others].
Description: Reston, VA : National Council of Teachers of Mathematics, [2016]
Identifiers: LCCN 2015049347 (print) | LCCN 2016009347 (ebook) |
    ISBN 9780873537629 (pbk.) | ISBN 9780873538954 ()
Subjects: LCSH: Mathematics—Study and teaching (Elementary)
Classification: LCC QA465 .P575 2016 (print) | LCC QA465 (ebook) |
    DDC 372.35--dc23
LC record available at http://lccn.loc.gov/2015049347

The National Council of Teachers of Mathematics supports
and advocates for the highest-quality mathematics teaching
and learning for each and every student.

Printed in the United States of America

CONTENTS

Chapter 2

Grade 1: Motivation to Measure

Chapter 3

Grade 2: Comparing and Understanding Measures

Chapter 4

Grade 3: Length, Area, and Angle Measurement

Chapter 5

Grade 4: Length, Area, Volume, and Angle Measurement 169

Chapter 6

Grade 5: More Length, Area, Volume, and Angle Measurement 211

References 245

Children's Books Cited 246

Accompanying Materials Available at More4U

To download and print the following materials, go to NCTM's More4U website (http://www.nctm.org/more4U) and enter the code shown on this book's title page.

INTRODUCTION

We have all had the unsettling experience of discovering flaws in our carefully planned approaches to teaching particular topics in mathematics. One of this book's authors, Jeff Barrett, offers a personal account of one such experience related to teaching measurement:

> Early in September I was co-teaching a series of lessons with an experienced classroom teacher (Barrett et al. 2003). We had taught many measurement lessons together the previous year with another group of second graders. Now, as we addressed a new group of students, we came to our first day of learning measurement. We pulled out our rulers and some classroom objects to measure. Before we started, I reminded students of five important steps in measurement, which I recorded on the board:
>
> 1. Lay your ruler down in front of you with the inches marked on the top.
>
> 2. Place the object to be measured along the top of the ruler.
>
> 3. Align the object to be measured with the left end of the ruler.
>
> 4. Read the number that is under the right end of the object from the ruler.
>
> 5. Remember to include your units!
>
> After we reviewed the steps, I encouraged students to measure the length of several preselected objects—a pen, a chalkboard

eraser, a box of chalk, and a tape dispenser—and to record their measurements in a simple chart.

Our students quickly got to work aligning objects with rulers and reporting measures. As we circled the room, we had to remind some students of step 5 by asking "What is your unit?" Aside from needing these few reminders, students successfully completed the measuring tasks, and I was satisfied that they had met the goals of our lesson. That is, they could correctly measure the lengths of objects. I felt confident as I reflected on the way students handled those tasks.

Soon after that, while reading Principles and Standards for School Mathematics (National Council of Teachers of Mathematics [NCTM] 2000), I came across a classroom episode: "The teacher observed that Mari's hand slipped as she was aligning her ruler with the pencil. Mari made no comment but recorded this measurement as 12 inches also" (p. 106). I stopped to think about my own experiences with those second graders. Surely they would not have made the mistake of disregarding step 3—"Align the object to be measured with the left end of the ruler"—right? Mari reported, "The book is longer, but they are both 12 inches" (p. 106). Why was she willing to say that the book was longer than the pencil but that they had the same measure? How would other second graders react in this situation? What does Mari's analysis mean about what she understands, or doesn't understand, about linear measurement? What did my students really learn when I taught them to follow those five measurement steps?

Later in my career, I set out to try to get answers to some of my questions. Rather than wait for the right measurement situation to arise naturally, I posed some related tasks to make it happen. I created a worksheet with images of measuring tools paired with line segments to be measured (fig. 0.1). Drawing the line segments directly on the page prevented the students from aligning them with the left end of the ruler (the essential third step in measurement).

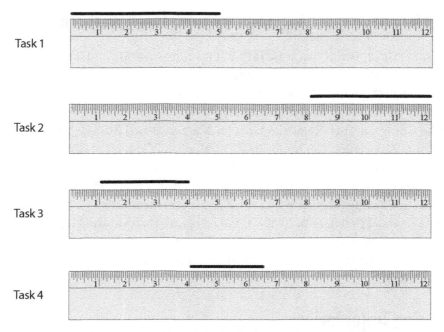

Task 1

Task 2

Task 3

Task 4

Fig. 0.1. Tasks 2–4 on this worksheet were designed to prevent students from aligning the left end of the ruler with the object to be measured.

Before reading ahead, take some time to think about how your students might respond to the tasks in figure 0.1. We have observed that this kind of exercise often reveals a variety of thinking strategies. Table 0.1 shows some measurement approaches that students used to complete the tasks. For a more complete discussion of this task and other related tasks, see chapter 3.

Table 0.1. Second graders' strategies for completing measurement tasks

Strategy	Likely responses			
	Task 1	Task 2	Task 3	Task 4
Right-hand endpoint	5 inches	12 inches	4 inches	6 inches 6.5 inches 7 inches
Left-hand endpoint	0 inches*	8 inches	1 inch*	4 inches
Counting tick marks	5 inches 6 inches	5 inches	4 inches	3 inches 4 inches
Correct (counting intervals)	5 inches	4 inches	3 inches	2.5 inches**

* These responses are included in the table for completeness, but we do not anticipate that students will use this strategy for this task.

** We may also consider 2 or 3 inches to be correct, depending on the student's ability to deal with partial units.

Standards for Teaching and Learning Measurement

The primary purpose of this book is to improve the teaching and learning of measurement in kindergarten through grade 5. We draw on two main sources for measurement topics in this grade band: the measurement content standards from *Principles and Standards for School Mathematics* (NCTM 2000) and the Common Core State Standards for Mathematics (CCSSM; National Governors Association Center for Best Practices and Council of Chief State School Officers [NGA Center and CCSSO] 2010). These publications not only provide specific content standards but also detail the ways in which we engage students in learning. These are described as Process Standards by NCTM and as Mathematical Practices in CCSSM. We recognize that coordinating these demands from two sources is challenging; but it is also worthwhile, especially in preparation for the high-stakes tests that will be used to assess and document student learning.

Learning Trajectories: A Framework for Measurement Activities

We hope to help teachers improve student learning by offering activities that help reveal student thinking. Because activities in isolation are of limited value, we also provide frameworks called *learning trajectories* (Barrett, Clements, and Sarama 2017) to support teaching and learning with these tasks. Each learning trajectory (LT) consists of three main parts: (1) a description of successively more complex strategies, (2) researchers' interpretations of students' thinking and reasoning, and (3) a collection of tasks designed as both formative assessments and catalysts for students' growth as they move from using less complex strategies to more complex strategies. In this book, we discuss three different but related LTs for measurement: length, area, and volume.

Applying Standards and Learning Trajectories in the Classroom

In the following example, we show how the length LT can be used to facilitate interpreting student thinking, making instructional decisions, and preparing classroom activities. Similar examples using the area and volume LTs appear in subsequent chapters. Here, we address a measurement and data standard for grade 1 from CCSSM:

> Express the length of an object as a whole number of length units, by laying multiple copies of a shorter object (the length unit) end to end; understand that the length measurement of an object is

the number of same-size length units that span it with no gaps or overlaps. (1.MD.A.2)

Below is a possible assessment task related to the standard:

Give students three 1-inch strips of paper and a 5-inch object to be measured. Ask the students to use the 1-inch strips to measure the length of the object.

We anticipate that although there will be some variety in your students' responses, most will fit into two or three categories. We expect that some grade 1 students—let's call them group A—will say that they cannot complete the measurement task because they do not have enough 1-inch strips to span the length of the object. Others—we'll call them group B—may take the three 1-inch strips and space them out so that they start and end at the left and right ends of the object (fig. 0.2) and report a measure of "3" or "3 inches." Still other students—group C—are likely to take the three 1-inch strips, lay them end to end starting from the left end, and then move two of the strips to the end of the collection (fig. 0.3) and report an answer of 5 inches.

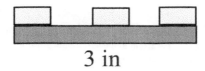

3 in

Fig. 0.2. An incorrect measurement technique: spacing out the strips provided

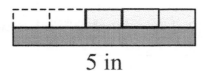

5 in

Fig. 0.3. A correct measurement technique: iterating strips

At this point, teachers will have to decide how to move forward in the lesson. How should we make this decision? Should all students be treated the same? Do we need to treat every student individually? An LT can be helpful in answering these questions. See table 0.2 for a brief excerpt from the length LT that can help us analyze the three hypothetical student responses from the task above. A summary of all levels for the length, area, and volume LTs is available at http://www.childrensmeasurement.org/learning-trajectories.html.

Table 0.2. Excerpt from the length learning trajectory (Barrett, Clements, and Sarama 2017)

LT level	Thinking and strategies	Instructional tasks to motivate growth to next LT level
End-to-End Length Measurer Lays units end to end to create measures for comparison. Can produce a meaningful measure when given all the objects but may struggle to do so when given fewer objects than needed to span the object to be measured.	Develops an initial understanding that an object can be measured by repetitions of shorter-length units. Begins to understand the need to use equal-size units and to avoid gaps between units. When provided with fewer unit pieces than needed to span a length, may assign a numerical value to the length by moving the pieces along the length while counting.	Provide more than enough unit pieces than needed to span the length of an object. Pause the activity before students align the object with all the unit pieces needed. Ask them to predict how many units would be needed to span the object. Allow them to check, if needed. Use relatively large objects as units to create a measuring tool (e.g., pen lengths). Challenge students by providing fewer than the total number of unit objects needed to lay end to end along the object to be measured.
Length Unit Relater and Repeater Iterates a single unit to measure. Relates size and number of units, at least intuitively: "If you measure with centimeters, not inches, you'll need more because each one is smaller." Can add two lengths to obtain the length of the whole.	Can maintain an image of each placement while moving the physical unit to the next iterative position and counting it. Begins to anticipate that fewer numbers of larger units would be needed to span an object. Iterates a single unit, sometimes with mistakes, to find how many would stretch end to end.	Lay a ribbon above a long measuring tool without aligning the ribbon with either endpoint. Cover a portion of the long measuring tool with dark construction paper or fabric. Ask students to find the length of the ribbon. Ask students to draw and measure sequences of segments that are decreasing by length using only one unit object or a ruler.
Consistent Length Measurer Measures straight paths consistently. Aware of the need to use identical units when measuring, relationship between different units, partitions of unit, zero point on rulers, and accumulation of distance. Can resolve broken (or covered) ruler tasks effectively. Iterates a single length unit without gaps or overlaps along a straight path.	Able to use rulers well because he or she sees the ruler as a collection of iterated units. Sees that a length is a ratio comparison between the unit object and the measured object and begins to work with partitions of units, such as halves and quarters. May make errors when considering the length of a bent path as the sum of its parts.	Ask students to predict lengths of objects in a room and then allow them to check with a measuring tool. Provide students with bent paths. Ask them to determine the total length of the paths and to extend the path to a given target length.

We can see that the students in the three groups described in the example fit into one of two levels: End-to-End Length Measurer or Length Unit Relater and Repeater.

In groups A and B, students were not able to resolve the task correctly when they did not have enough 1-inch strips to span the length of the object. Given the age of these students and their difficulties with this task, we anticipate that they are operating at the End-to-End Length Measurer level. To verify this, we suggest trying a similar task in which students are given more than enough 1-inch strips to span the object. If the students report the correct answer in this case, we would conclude that they are in fact operating at the End-to-End Length Measurer level because they demonstrated an ability to *lay units end to end to create measures for comparison* but were unable to *iterate a single unit to measure*. We would then select an instructional task from the third column of the table in the End-to-End Length Measurer row to prompt students' growth to the next level of the LT, Length Unit Relater and Repeater.

In group C, students demonstrated their ability to *iterate a single unit to measure* when they placed the 1-inch strip in the first position and again in the third, thus counting an empty space as a 1-inch strip. Before we conclude that these students are operating at the Length Unit Relater and Repeater level, we need to verify that they are not operating at the next higher level, Consistent Length Measurer. This can be done by repeating the task above with a longer object to be measured and fewer 1-inch strips, or a single 1-inch strip. If students successfully complete these modified tasks, we could check their ability to resolve a broken (or covered) ruler task, as described in the Length Unit Relater and Repeater row of the table. Assuming that students are unable to resolve this task correctly, we would conclude they are in fact operating at the Length Unit Relater and Repeater level because they have demonstrated an ability to *iterate a single unit to measure* but cannot yet *resolve a broken ruler task*. Finally, we would select an instructional task from the third column of the table in the Length Unit Relater and Repeater row to prompt reflection and reorganization of their thinking, supporting a shift to the next level of the trajectory, Consistent Length Measurer.

Although we believe the LTs are helpful tools for the teaching and learning of measurement, we also recognize the potential complexities that come with adding another resource. Keeping this in mind, we provide a crosswalk linking the CCSSM content standards for measurement, the NCTM content standards for measurement, and the length, area, and volume learning trajectories (see table 0.3). We anticipate that this crosswalk will help you connect the content standards to the LTs, which provide insight into student thinking and strategies along with instructional tasks.

Table 0.3. Measurement content standards and related learning trajectories

CCSSM	NCTM Measurement Standards	Length learning trajectory	Area learning trajectory	Volume learning trajectory
K.MD.A.1: Describe measurable attributes of objects.	*Understand measurable attributes of objects and the units, systems, and processes of measurement*	(2) Length Quantity Recognizer	(2) Area Simple Comparer	(1) Volume Quantity Recognizer
K.MD.A.2: Directly compare objects with a measurable attribute.	**Expectations:** In prekindergarten through grade 2 all students should—	(3a) Length Direct Comparer		
K.MD.B.3: Classify objects into categories; count and sort.	• recognize the attributes of length, volume, weight, area, and time;	(2) Length Quantity Recognizer		
K.G.B.4: Analyze and compare two- and three-dimensional shapes.	• compare and order objects according to these	(3a) Length Direct Comparer—Mental		
1.MD.A.1: Order three objects by length; compare the lengths of two objects indirectly by using a third object.	attributes;	(3b) Indirect Length Comparer (3c) Serial Orderer to 6 +		
1.MD.A.2: Express the length of an object as a whole number of length units, by laying multiple copies of a shorter object (the length unit) end to end; understand that the length measurement of an object is the number of same-size length units that span it with no gaps or overlaps.	• understand how to measure using nonstandard and standard units; select an appropriate unit and tool for the attribute being measured.	(4) End-to-End Length Measurer		
2.NBT.A.1, 2.NBT.A.1a, 2.NBT.A.1b: Understand that digits of a three-digit number represent amounts of hundreds, tens, and ones.	*Apply appropriate techniques, tools, and formulas to determine measurements*	(6) Consistent Length Measurer		
2.NBT.A.2: Count within 1,000; skip-count by 5s, 10s, and 100s.	**Expectations:** In prekindergarten through grade 2 all students should—	(6) Consistent Length Measurer		
2.NBT.A.3: Read and write numbers to 1,000 using base-ten numerals, number names, and expanded form.		(6) Consistent Length Measurer		

Table 0.3. continued

CCSSM	NCTM Measurement Standards	Length learning trajectory	Area learning trajectory	Volume learning trajectory
2.NBT.B.5: Add and subtract within 100 using strategies based on place value, properties of operations, and/or relationships.	• measure with multiple copies of units of the same size, such as paper clips laid end to end;	(6) Consistent Length Measurer		
2.NBT.B.6: Add up to four two-digit numbers using strategies based on place value and properties of operations.	• use repetition of a single unit to measure something larger than the unit, for instance, measuring the length of a room with a single meterstick;	(6) Consistent Length Measurer		
2.NBT.B.7: Understand that in adding or subtracting three-digit numbers, one adds or subtracts hundreds and hundreds, tens and tens, ones and ones; and (de)composes tens or hundreds.		(6) Consistent Length Measurer		
2.MD.A.1: Measure the length of an object by selecting and using tools such as rulers, yardsticks, meter sticks, and measuring tapes.	• develop common referents for measures to make comparisons and estimates.	(5) Length Unit Relater and Repeater (6) Consistent Length Measurer		
2.MD.A.2: Measure the length of an object twice, using length units of different lengths; relate to the size of the unit chosen.		(5) Length Unit Relater and Repeater		
2.MD.A.3: Estimate lengths using inches, feet, and (centi)meters.		(7) Conceptual Ruler Measurer		
2.MD.A.4: Measure to determine how much longer one object is than another; express the difference in terms of a standard unit.		(4) End-to-End Length Measurer		
2.MD.B.5; 2.OA.A.1: Use addition and subtraction within 100 to solve word problems involving lengths that are given in the same units, e.g., by using drawings (such as drawings of rulers); use addition and subtraction within 100 to solve one- and two-step word problems involving situations of adding to, taking from, putting together, taking apart, and comparing, with unknowns.		(5) Length Unit Relater and Repeater (6) Consistent Length Measurer (8) Integrated Conceptual Path Measurer		

Table 0.3. continued

CCSSM	NCTM Measurement Standards	Length learning trajectory	Area learning trajectory	Volume learning trajectory
2.MD.B.6: Represent whole numbers as lengths from 0 on a number line diagram with equally spaced points.		(4) End-to-End Length Measurer (5) Length Unit Relater and Repeater		
2.MD.D.9: Measure lengths of several objects to the nearest whole unit, or by making repeated measurements of the same object. Show the measurements by making a line plot.		(5) Length Unit Relater and Repeater		
2.OA.C.4: Find the total number of objects arranged in rectangular arrays with up to 5 rows and up to 5 columns.			(7) Area Row and Column Structurer	
2.G.A.2: Partition a rectangle into rows and columns of same-size squares and count to find the total number of them.			(5) Area Unit Relater and Repeater (6) Partial Row Structurer (7) Area Row and Column Structurer	
3.NF.A.1: Understand a fraction $1/b$ as the quantity formed by 1 part when a whole is partitioned into b equal parts.	_Understand measurable attributes_ of objects and the units, systems, and processes of measurement.	(6) Consistent Length Measurer		
3.NF.A.2, 3.NF.A.2a, 3.NF.A.2b: Understand a fraction as a number on the number line; represent fractions on a number line diagram.		(6) Consistent Length Measurer		
3.NF.A.3, 3.NF.A.3a, 3.NF.A.3b, 3.NF.A.3c, 3.NF.A.3d: Explain equivalence of fractions, and compare fractions.		(6) Consistent Length Measurer		

Table 0.3. continued

CCSSM	NCTM Measurement Standards	Length learning trajectory	Area learning trajectory	Volume learning trajectory
3.MD.A.2: Measure and estimate liquid volumes and masses of objects by using standard units of grams (g), kilograms (kg), and liters (l). Use drawings (e.g., beaker with a measurement scale).	**Expectations:** In grades 3–5 all students should— • understand such attributes as length, area, weight, volume, and size of angle and select the appropriate type of unit for measuring each attribute; • understand the need for measuring with standard units and become familiar with standard units in the customary and metric systems; • carry out simple unit conversions, such as from centimeters to meters, within a system of measurement; • understand that measurements are approximations and how differences in units affect precision;			(5) Capacity Relater and Repeater
3.MD.B.4: Generate measurement data by measuring lengths using rulers marked with halves and fourths of an inch. Show the data using units—whole numbers, halves, or quarters.		(5) Length Unit Relater and Repeater (6) Consistent Length Measurer		
3.MD.C.5, 3.MD.C.5a, 3.MD.C.5b: Recognize area as an attribute of plane figures and understand concepts of area measurement.			(4) Primitive Coverer	
3.MD.C.6: Measure areas by counting unit squares (square cm, square m, square in., square ft., and improvised units).			(5) Area Unit Relater and Repeater	
3.MD.C.7: Relate area to the operations of multiplication and addition.			(7) Area Row and Column Structurer (9) Array Structurer (8) Area Conserver	
3.MD.D.8: Solve real-world and mathematical problems involving perimeters of polygons, including finding the perimeter given the side lengths, finding an unknown side length, and exhibiting rectangles with the same perimeter and different areas or with the same area and different perimeters.		(7) Conceptual Ruler Measurer (8) Integrated Conceptual Path Measurer (9) Coordinated and Integrated Abstract Measurer with Derived Units		

Table 0.3. continued

CCSSM	NCTM Measurement Standards	Length learning trajectory	Area learning trajectory	Volume learning trajectory
3.OA.A.1: Interpret products of whole numbers, e.g., interpret 5 × 7 as the total number of objects in 5 groups of 7 objects each.	• explore what happens to measurements of a two-dimensional shape such as its perimeter and area when the shape is changed in some way;		(9) Array Structurer	
3.OA.A.3: Use multiplication and division within 100 to solve word problems in situations involving equal groups, arrays, and measurement quantities, e.g., by using drawings.	• understand the need for measuring with standard units and become familiar with standard units in the customary and metric systems.		(7) Area Row and Column Structurer (9) Array Structurer	
3.OA.A.4: Determine the unknown whole number in a multiplication or division equation relating three whole numbers.				
3.G.A.2: Partition shapes into parts with equal areas. Express the area of each part as a unit fraction of the whole.				
4.OA.A.2: Multiply or divide to solve word problems involving multiplicative comparison, e.g., by using drawings; distinguish multiplicative comparison from additive comparison.	*Apply appropriate techniques, tools, and formulas to* determine measurements	(7) Conceptual Ruler Measurer		
4.NBT.B.5: Illustrate and explain multiplication by using rectangular arrays, and/or area models.	**Expectations:** In grades 3–5 all students should– • develop strategies for estimating the perimeters, areas, and volumes of irregular shapes;	(8) Integrated Conceptual Path Measurer		
4.NF.A.1: Explain why a fraction a/b is equivalent to a fraction $(n \times a)/(n \times b)$ by using visual fraction models, noticing that the number and size of the parts differ but the fractions are the same.				
4.NF.B.4a, 4.NF.B.4b: Apply and extend previous understandings of multiplication to multiply a fraction by a whole number.				

Table 0.3. continued

CCSSM	NCTM Measurement Standards	Length learning trajectory	Area learning trajectory	Volume learning trajectory
4.MD.A.2: Use the four operations to solve word problems involving distances, intervals of time, liquid volumes, masses of objects, and money, including problems that require expressing measurements given in a larger unit in terms of a smaller unit.	• select and apply appropriate standard units and tools to measure length, area, volume, weight, time, temperature, and the size of angles; • select and use benchmarks to estimate measurements; • develop, understand, and use formulas to find the area of rectangles and related triangles and parallelograms; • develop strategies to determine the surface areas and volumes of rectangular solids.	(5) Length Unit Relater and Repeater (6) Consistent Length Measurer		
4.MD.A.3: Apply the area and perimeter formulas for rectangles.		(6) Consistent Length Measurer	(9) Area: Array Structurer	
4.MD.C.5, 4.MD.C.5a, 4.MD.C.5b: Recognize angles as two rays sharing a common endpoint; understand angle measurement.		(8) Integrated Conceptual Path Measurer		
5.NBT.B.5: Fluently multiply multidigit whole numbers using the standard algorithm.				
5.NBT.B.6: Illustrate and explain division by using equations, rectangular arrays, and/or area models.				
5.NBT.B.7: Add, subtract, multiply, and divide decimals to hundredths, using concrete models or drawings.				
5.NF.A.1: Add and subtract fractions with unlike denominators by replacing given fractions with equivalent fractions.		(8) Integrated Conceptual Path Measurer		
5.NF.A.2: Solve word problems involving addition and subtraction of fractions referring to the same whole, including cases of unlike denominators, e.g., by using visual fraction models.		(8) Integrated Conceptual Path Measurer		

Table 0.3. continued

CCSSM	NCTM Measurement Standards	Length learning trajectory	Area learning trajectory	Volume learning trajectory
5.NF.B.4, 5.NF.B.4a, 5.NF.B.4b: Multiply a fraction or whole number by a fraction.				
5.MD.A.1: Convert among different-sized standard measurement units within a given measurement system (e.g., convert 5 cm to 0.05 m), and use these conversions in solving multistep, real-world problems.		(6) Consistent Length Measurer		
5.MD.C.3, 5.MD.C.3a, 5.MD.C.3b: Recognize volume as an attribute of solid figures and understand concepts of volume measurement.				(6) Volume/Spatial Structuring: Partial 3-D Structurer
5.MD.C.4: Measure volumes by counting unit cubes, using cubic cm, cubic in., cubic ft., and improvised units.				(6) Volume/Spatial Structuring: Partial 3-D Structurer
5.MD.C.5, 5.MD.C.5a, 5.MD.C.5b: Relate volume to the operations of multiplication and addition and solve real-world and mathematical problems involving volume.				(9) Volume/Spatial Structuring: 3-D Array Structurer

How This Book Is Organized

The following chapters offer numerous examples of activities connected to grade-specific content standards. Each activity can be linked to NCTM's *Principles and Standards for School Mathematics* (2000), CCSSM, and the relevant length, area, and volume LTs, as shown in table 0.3 and summary tables within each chapter. (NCTM has produced supporting resources for *Principles and Standards for School Mathematics*, including a set of frequently asked questions, a Quick Reference Guide that outlines standards and expectations by grade band, and a CD that assists those interested in exploring the ten standards and learning more about them. In addition, the *Principles and Standards for School Mathematics* Navigations Series translates NCTM's Principles and Standards into action in the classroom and highlights major mathematics content areas in grade-band-specific volumes.)

Within each grade-level chapter of this book, we present activities to address key ideas as identified in CCSSM for that grade. We explain how to prepare for each activity, detail necessary materials and specific tasks within the activities, discuss anticipated student responses, and offer suggestions for extensions. The activities are structured as follows:

- **Essentials:** Gather necessary materials and prepare for the activity.

- **Engage:** Pose a problem or a situation based on a work of literature or art or using technology tools.

- **Explore:** Invite students to begin, and involve them in the measuring tasks.

- **Expect:** Anticipate, assess, and interpret students' thinking. Look for successes and struggles with the activity.

- **Extend:** Do more to help students build on the key measurement ideas presented in the activity.

- **Enrich:** Connect this concept to literature, relevant websites, or real-life situations; help students relate measurement ideas to people and their careers, such as Olympic athletes, chefs, or musicians.

Reproducible materials for a number of activities from throughout the book are available as classroom-ready PDF files at NCTM's More4U site. For access to these resources, readers should go to http://www.nctm.org/more4U and enter the access code on the title page of this book.

Although we have included references to children's literature in many of the sections labeled **Essentials** and **Enrich**, we expect that most of our activities can be adapted by replacing the suggested story or context with a different introduction to set the challenge or topic. Telling a story about your own experiences or posing a problem directly will work just as well.

We hope you and your students find it a pleasure to measure!

CHAPTER 1

KINDERGARTEN:
ATTRIBUTES TO MEASURE

Big measurement ideas identified in CCSSM: This chapter focuses on students' noticing and identifying attributes of objects and sets of objects. We want to help students understand what an attribute is and help them use attributes to sort and order objects. We also want to help them expand their vocabulary of comparison words while we enable them to distinguish between measurable and nonmeasurable attributes.

Learning trajectory levels in this grade: Two levels of measurement understanding are relevant to this grade with regard to length, area, and volume. During the kindergarten year, students are likely to recognize attributes including length, area, and volume. Kindergartners tend to demonstrate understanding that fits the Pre-Length Quantity Recognizer or Length Quantity Recognizer level for length measurement. Similarly, these students tend to fit the descriptions that Barrett, Clements, and Sarama (2017) provide for the Area Quantity Recognizer and Volume Quantity Recognizer levels. As students progress beyond identifying attributes, they compare directly and indirectly in ways that are consistent with the Length Direct Comparer level. These ideas are echoed in the measurement standards from the CCSSM for kindergarten: K.MD.A.1, K.MD.A.2, and K.MD.B.3.

Table 1.1 provides an overview of the activities in this chapter. Each activity is linked to the relevant CCSSM standard and levels from a learning trajectory on measurement. The activities are divided into three groups. Activities 1–4 focus on describing and sorting objects by attributes, activities 5–9 focus on comparing objects by length, and activities 10–14 focus on comparing objects by attributes.

Table 1.1. Kindergarten activities matched with Common Core State Standards and learning trajectory levels

General CCSSM	Learning activities	Activity-specific standards	Learning trajectory levels
Describing and sorting by attribute K.MD.A.1: Describe measurable attributes of objects K.MD.A.2: Directly compare objects with a measurable attribute K.MD.B.3: Classify objects into categories; count and sort	**Activity 1: Right on the Button!** Key idea: Describing and sorting by attributes	K.MD.A.1 K.MD.A.2 K.MD.B.3	Length Quantity Recognizer Area Quantity Recognizer
	Activity 2: What's Bugging You? Key idea: Ordering three objects by size	K.MD.A.1 K.MD.A.2 K.MD.B.3 1.MD.A.1	Length Comparer (Direct, Indirect)
	Activity 3: Goats, Trolls, and Bridges Key idea: Identifying and comparing by attributes	K.MD.A.1 K.MD.A.2 1.MD.A.1	Length Quantity Recognizer Length Comparer (Direct)
	Activity 4: Big, Small, Short, Tall? Key idea: Comparing to order objects	K.MD.A.1 K.MD.A.2 1.MD.A.1 2.MD.A.1 2.MD.A.2 2.MD.A.4	Length Quantity Recognizer Length Comparer (Direct) Length Unit Relater and Repeater Area Quantity Recognizer
Comparing by length K.MD.A.2: Directly compare objects with a measurable attribute	**Activity 5: Which Is the Shortest of All Your Toes?** Key idea: Comparing by length	K.MD.A.2	Length Comparer (Direct)
	Activity 6: Faster, Slower, Higher, Lower! Key idea: Expand students' vocabulary for comparing objects	K.MD.A.1 K.MD.A.2	Length Comparer (Direct)
	Activity 7: Reach for the Stars! Key idea: Relating age, height, and reach	K.MD.A.1 K.MD.A.2	Length Comparer (Direct) (Exploring, Conversion) Length Unit Relater and Repeater
	Activity 8: On the Other Hand . . . Key idea: Counting up units of length using a hand as a unit	K.MD.A.1 K.MD.A.2 1.MD.A.2	End-to-End Length Measurer (Exploring) Length Unit Relater and Repeater
	Activity 9: Watch Out for the Big Guy! Key idea: Comparing things to parts of our bodies	K.MD.A.1 K.MD.A.2	Length Quantity Recognizer Length Comparer (Direct, Indirect)

General CCSSM	Learning activities	Activity-specific standards	Learning trajectory levels
Comparing by attributes K.MD.A.2: Directly compare objects with a measurable attribute	**Activity 10: She Swallowed a What?** Key idea: Comparing volume and length	K.MD.A.1 K.MD.A.2 1.MD.A.1	Length Quantity Recognizer Length Comparer (Direct) Volume Quantity Recognizer
	Activity 11: "Just Right!" Key idea: Comparing three objects by size and order	K.MD.A.1 K.MD.A.2 1.MD.A.1	Length Quantity Recognizer Length Comparer (Direct) Area Quantity Recognizer Volume Quantity Recognizer
	Activity 12: Inch by Inch Key idea: Measuring length by repeating inch units	K.MD.A.1 K.MD.A.2 1.MD.A.2 2.MD.A.1	Length Quantity Recognizer Length Comparer (Direct) End-to-End Length Measurer Length Unit Relater and Repeater
	Activity 13: Which One Fits? Key idea: Capacity with envelopes and cards	K.MD.A.1 K.MD.A.2 1.MD.A.1 K.G.B.4	Length Quantity Recognizer Length Comparer (Direct) Area Quantity Recognizer
	Activity 14: Fill It to the Top! Key idea: Noticing volume as a measurable attribute	K.MD.A.1 K.MD.A.2 2.MD.A.2	Length Quantity Recognizer Length Comparer (Direct, Indirect) Area Quantity Recognizer Volume Quantity Recognizer Volume Filler Volume Quantifier

Activity 1: Right on the Button!

Key idea: Describing and sorting by attributes
Learning trajectory level: Length Quantity Recognizer; Area Quantity Recognizer

Essentials

Collect at least 20 buttons of different sizes, shapes, and colors for each table or group of students.

Engage

Read *The Button Box* by Margarette S. Reid (Dutton 1989). Colorful illustrations and simple text invite the reader to sort, classify, sequence, and count buttons.

Explore

Discuss some of the sorting methods used in the book. After students have had time to play with the buttons at their table, have them sort the buttons by color and then by shape or size. Have them shift to another collection of buttons for more practice if needed.

Expect

- It is OK if a set contains only one button.

- Students may mix buttons together, using more than one strategy without applying the same strategy to all the buttons. For example, they might sort some buttons into two stacks of red and not-red buttons but then sort the rest of the buttons into stacks of large and small buttons so some red buttons show up in those stacks.

- Are students able to support their sorting strategy by using appropriate descriptive words?

- Can students sort their buttons into sets based on an attribute (such as number of holes, shank or no shank, shiny or not) and have you guess their strategy?

Extend

- Read "A Lost Button" from *Frog and Toad Are Friends* by Arnold Lobel (Scholastic 1970). Toad and Frog set out on a walk that is spoiled by the loss of Toad's button. The button is found after a search that includes help from their friends. Have students describe the buttons in the text and match them to buttons in their collection.

- Use the collection of buttons that students have sorted to build patterns. Begin by sharing a pattern, say A, B, A, B. . . . Next, have students make and share a pattern with others, such as small button, large button, small button, large button. . . .

- Have students sort collections of objects such as keys, coins, pebbles, bolts, or jar lids. Ask students about the sorting work of their classmates: "Can you guess which attribute was used to sort these?"

- Students can also use these objects to form patterns in artistic designs. You can begin a classroom discussion about their artwork to emphasize the attributes and the grouping of similar objects.

Enrich

Read *Sorting* by Henry Pluckrose (Children's Press 1995). Objects are sorted in various real-life situations.

Other possibilities include *Play with Sorting!* by Joyce Markovics (Rourke Educational Media 2013), which presents sorting situations using a range of attributes, and *Comparing with Cats* by Tracey Steffora (Heinemann Library 2014), which distinguishes between defining attributes and nondefining attributes (like color or orientation in space).

Activity 2: What's Bugging You?

Key idea: Ordering three objects by size
Learning trajectory level: Length Comparer (Direct, Indirect)

Essentials

Gather scrap materials like pipe cleaners, packing peanuts, tape, beads, lids, ribbon, wire, cans, juice boxes, or buttons.

Engage

Read *The Best Bug Parade* by Stuart J. Murphy (HarperCollins 1996). In this imaginative story, a variety of different bugs talk among themselves to compare their relative sizes while marching in a parade.

Explore

Have each student construct a "bug" from scrap materials. Students are likely to create a variety of bugs, some small and some large. Select from the small bugs a set of three and have their creators sort those bugs into small, smaller, and smallest. Then select from the big bugs a set of three and have students sort them into big, bigger, and biggest. Reconfigure the groups of bugs and repeat the activity at least two more times. (Ideally, no bug will fall into the same spot in the ordering each time.)

Expect

- Students naturally will want to order any set of three objects by size by identifying the small one, the big one, and then the middle-sized one. This activity is meant to develop vocabulary that is more definitive, introducing the comparison words *smaller* and *smallest* (and likewise *bigger* and *biggest*). When you ask students to sort a set of small bugs, you might suggest that they begin by finding the smallest one. Similarly, it may be easiest for them to find the biggest of the three big bugs. To challenge students, ask them to find the bigger bug in a set of three bugs before identifying the biggest bug. Two bugs will be bigger, and then, of those two, one will be the biggest.

- Watch and listen to learn which dimensions students use to determine size. Was it necessary to establish length or height as the criterion?

- Discuss why a student's bug might have been the big one in one group, while in another group it was the bigger one and in yet another the biggest (see fig. 1.1). Could the same scenario have happened with small, smaller, smallest?

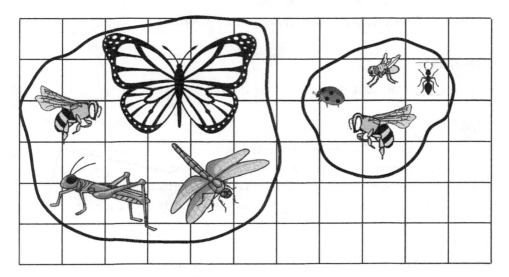

Fig. 1.1. A bumblebee is smallest in the group of insects on the left, although it is the largest insect in the other grouping.

Extend

Have students order all the bugs for one big bug parade. It may be worthwhile and less confusing to build the parade one bug at a time. Identify the smallest and the largest bugs first, allowing plenty of space between those two bugs for other bugs to join the parade. Each placement of a new bug promotes students' comparison skills.

Enrich

Read *A Garden Full of Sizes* by Simone T. Ribke (Children's Press 2004). A garden offers many size comparison opportunities. For example, pumpkin seeds are small, while radish seeds are tiny. Apples grow on thin branches; the trunk of the apple tree is thick.

Activity 3: Goats, Trolls, and Bridges

Key idea: Identifying and comparing by attributes
Learning trajectory levels: Length Quantity Recognizer; Length Comparer (Direct)

Essentials

Provide a space for students to act out the story.

Engage

Read *The Three Billy Goats Gruff*, illustrated by Stephen Carpenter (Scholastic 1998). Three different-sized billy goats have to deal with a mean, ugly troll who lives under the bridge that they need to cross to get to greener pastures on the other side. The different sizes of the goats also reflect their different ages.

Explore

Choose four students to act out the parts of the goats and the troll. The remaining students can make the sounds of the bridge crossings at increasing levels of loudness to indicate older, heavier, and larger goats. Voice volume should indicate increasing age and size of the goats. Ask the "goats" to switch roles (e.g., the smallest, youngest goat now plays the largest, oldest goat), and have them repeat the play. Have each "goat" explain how his or her part was different for the second performance.

Expect

- Students may think of size in different ways. Some students may need encouragement to use words other than *big* and *little*. Others may use words like *taller, heavier, shorter*, and *wider* to describe the goats.

- You can use this story to help students connect five ideas: (1) the ordinal words, (2) the goats' ages, (3) height or width, (4) weight, and (5) the volume of their voices. For example, the first goat is the youngest, the smallest, the lightest in weight, and has the smallest voice. The other two goats' attributes differ accordingly.

- Ask students to name ways in which the last goat to cross the bridge is different from the first goat.

- Do students mention more than one attribute when explaining how one goat differed from the next? Look for specific attributes of size such as height, length, width, horn thickness, or beard length.

Extend

- Point out that the size of the printed words in the book describing the sounds—TRIP, TRAP, TRIP, TRAP, TRIP, TRAP!—get bigger with each goat shown to indicate loudness and to correspond to the increasing size of the goats.

- Have students illustrate the events of the story in sequential order. Encourage students to use their illustrations to retell the story to a friend or family member.

Enrich

Read *Big, Bigger, Biggest* by Marilyn Deen (Capstone Press 2012), and check out the world's big, bigger, and biggest animals.

Activity 4: Big, Small, Short, Tall?

Key idea: Comparing to order objects
Learning trajectory levels: Length Quantity Recognizer; Length Comparer (Direct);
    Length Unit Relater and Repeater; Area Quantity Recognizer

Essentials

Gather an amaryllis bulb or a Wisconsin Fast Plant, dirt, a planting pot, and Unifix cubes. Scout out the school's neighborhood to find appropriate trees and buildings for an extended walking activity.

Engage

Read *Titch* by Pat Hutchins (Macmillan/McGraw Hill 1971). Titch is the smallest of three students and has the smallest of everything until he plants a seed.

Explore

Discuss the story. Titch wants a kite that flies higher than that of his sister and brother. Where might it fly? Titch also wants a musical instrument bigger than his sister's trumpet and his brother's drum. What could it be?

Have students look at the instruments shown on page 20 of *Titch* and decide which is larger. How do they know? Titch wants a tool bigger than a hammer or saw. Ask students for ideas about bigger tools. Look at the two tools on page 24 and ask students to say which tool is larger. How do they know?

Pete has a big spade, Mary has a fat flowerpot, and Titch has a tiny seed. Ask the students how Titch might feel about this.

Ask students to estimate the height of the plant as shown on pages 30–32. Imagine that Titch is 3 feet tall (see page 32), his sister is 4 feet tall, and his brother is 5 feet tall. How tall must the plant be? You may expect students to say the plant is 7 or 8 feet tall. Ask them to defend their answers, especially ones that vary greatly from 7 or 8 feet.

Expect

- Expect students to say that the drum is bigger than the trumpet, but encourage them to be more specific about attributes of the two instruments: height, width, distance around, area of the drumhead, or even loudness.

- As students consider the plant's growth from page 30 to page 32, they may mention the height or the number of leaves or branches.

- For the discussion of the story of Titch, find out whether students can identify attributes beyond the size words *big* and *small*. For example, tools can be compared by noticing differences in length, area, volume, or weight. Listen for words and phrases like *wider*, *fatter*, *thinner*, *covers more space*, or *takes up more space*.

Extend

- Plant an amaryllis bulb (or a Wisconsin Fast Plant) in a pot. Do not show students any packaging with a picture of the plant. Ask the students to make a series of drawings to show what they expect the plant to look like and how tall they expect it to be after one week, two weeks, or three weeks. How many days will it take to grow to be 6 inches tall, or 12 inches tall? (Once it sprouts, it will grow fast enough to measure the growth daily.)

- Stack up Unifix cubes to show how much the plant has grown. Change the color of the cubes each week to show how much it grew during that week. Eventually, the accumulation of cubes will reflect the plant's growth rate each week.

- Take a walk and look for a tall tree (or building), then a taller tree (or building), and then the tallest tree (or building). Have students fold a sheet of paper in thirds horizontally and mark the folds to indicate the heights of the tall, taller, and tallest trees or buildings they saw on the walk.

- If a neighborhood walk is not an option, read *Jack and the Beanstalk* by Paul Galdone (Clarion 1974). Have students fold a sheet of paper in thirds, as described above, and draw a picture of the beanstalk with Jack climbing it. Ask students to think of a plant that is taller than a dandelion but not as tall as the enormous beanstalk in the story and show this comparison in their drawing (see fig. 1.2 on the following page).

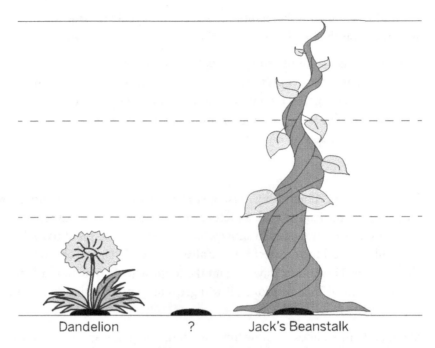

Dandelion   ?   Jack's Beanstalk

Fig. 1.2. What plant is taller than a dandelion but not as tall as the beanstalk?

Activity 5: Which Is the Shortest of All Your Toes?

Key idea: Comparing by length
Learning trajectory level: Length Comparer (Direct)

Essentials

Gather fabric ribbon pieces of varying lengths (or lengths of twine, but avoid yarn or other stretchy materials).

Engage

Read the following poem:

Which Is Longer?

Which is longer,
A car or a block?
Which is longer,
A shoe or a sock?
Which is shorter,
A tree or a flower?
Which is shorter,
A minute or an hour?

Which is longer,
A bike or a frog?
Which is longer,
An ant or a dog?
Which is the shortest
Of all your toes?
And who has the very
Shortest nose?

—Anonymous

Explore

Read the poem again and have students answer each question posed by it. Ask how they can tell which is longer or shorter.

Can students substitute other objects to compare in the poem? For example, they might replace "a tree or a flower" with "a bush or a dandelion." Encourage them to stay in the same category of objects for each pairing, but do not stress the need for the words to rhyme.

Expect

- Are students thinking and talking about length, or are they merely considering overall size?

- Are students able to place new ribbons into the collections in the right place to keep the order?

- Do students include all the ribbons in their drawing?

- Can students identify ribbons of the same length?

Extend

Give each student a ribbon.

- Have students find and record three objects in the classroom that are shorter than their ribbon, three that are longer, and a few items that are about the same length.

- Ask students to order the ribbons at their table from shortest to longest.

- Place the ordered sets of ribbons from two tables next to each other. Ask one student to add his or her ribbon in the correct place to the ordered set from the neighboring table. Continue combining sets across tables until every ribbon is included in the classroom set and ordered by length.

- Share what you notice about the collection of ribbons. Have students view the collection from different sides of the table. Each student should then make a record of the set of ribbons on paper.

Enrich

Read *Long and Short: An Animal Opposites Book* by Lisa Bullard (Capstone Press 2006). Brief text introduces the concepts of long and short, comparing some of the world's longest animals with animals that are short.

Activity 6: Faster, Slower, Higher, Lower!

Key idea: Expand students' vocabulary for comparing objects
Learning trajectory level: Length Comparer (Direct)

Essentials

Gather chart paper, a marker, and paper for "ME books" (described in Extend).

Engage

Read *Slower Than a Snail* by Anne Schreiber (Scholastic 1995). Comparisons in the story help students expand their vocabulary beyond *big* and *little*. Make a list of the size words used in the book on chart paper, and post this chart in the classroom for future reference. Or read *Fast and Slow: An Animal Opposites Book* by Lisa Bullard (Capstone Press 2006). Brief text introduces the concepts of fast and slow, comparing some of the world's fastest animals with animals that are slow.

Explore

Have students move in the room to stand next to an object that is smaller than they are, and then ask them to move again to stand next to something that is bigger, narrower, wider, lighter, heavier, or shorter than they are. They should stand next to a new object each time.

Expect

- Students should realize that *bigger* does not necessarily mean that an object is heavier; for example, a pillow is bigger (wider, taller) than a brick.

- Students who struggle to think of comparison items may need help describing the criteria (speed, height, weight, width) for the comparison.

Extend

- Reread *Slower Than a Snail* and stop to allow students to think of substitutions for the comparisons. Say, "The little girl said she was smaller than an elephant. You are too. What other animals are you smaller than?"

- Ask students to make "ME books" composed of comparison sentences that might include:

  — I am smaller than a _____.

  — I am bigger than a _____.

  — I am narrower than a _____.

  — I am wider than a _____.

  — I am lighter than a _____.

  — I am heavier than a _____.

  — I am shorter than a _____.

  — I am taller than a _____.

  — I am faster than a _____.

  — I am slower than a _____.

Ask students to illustrate their comparison sentences, as shown in figure 1.3.

Fig. 1.3. Sample ME book pages

Enrich

Read *Big and Small: An Animal Opposites Book* by Lisa Bullard (Capstone Press 2006). Brief text introduces the concepts of big and small, comparing some of the world's biggest animals with animals that are small.

Activity 7: Reach for the Stars!

Key idea: *Relating age, height, and reach*

Learning trajectory levels: *Length Comparer (Direct); (Exploring, Conversion)*
   Length Unit Relater and Repeater

Essentials

Make a chronological list of birthdays for the class and a bulletin board display of 12 calendar pages arranged as a clock face, as shown in figure 1.4.

When is your birthday?

January
   9-Ted
February
   7- Jeanne
   20 -Jackie
March
   9-Jan
   9-John
April
   13-Gus
   20-Diana
May
June
   15-Jackson
   20-Camden
July
   18-Mary
August
   17-Becky
September
   5-Michael
October
   13-Gary
November
   28-Trisha
December
   12-Sandy

Fig. 1.4. Sample birthday list and calendar pages arranged like a clock face

Attach a cloth tape measure to a doorframe in your classroom. Use markers to color strips of masking tape, and place the strips of tape along the tape measure to indicate 6-inch intervals. It is important that each piece of tape be a different color. Place the zero on the tape measure at floor level.

Engage

Read *Happy Birthday, Sam* by Pat Hutchins (Penguin 1985). On his birthday, Sam is still not tall enough to reach the door handle, light switch, or taps at the sink, but Grandpa's present solves his problem.

Explore

Have students recall and share things they could not reach when they were four years old or younger. Ask them to suggest objects in the classroom or at home that they still cannot reach, and make a class chart. Ask students, "Are there things that you can reach now but could not reach a year ago?"

Expect

- When using the birthday graph to discuss ages, dates, and months of birthdays, ask students whether they really become a whole year older on their birthday. Aren't they really only one day older?

- For the extension activities, be mindful that some students may think that they failed at estimating if their guess was not exact. It may be helpful to have them work in pairs to estimate the reach of a partner.

- Were students able to estimate their reach within a foot? That is a reasonable margin of estimating for this age. Did their estimation change after several tries?

- Could students identify the highest mark reached by *any* classmate? The highest mark reached by *everyone* in the class? The mark that *the most* students were able to reach?

- Repeat the reaching activities at least four months later, if possible, to focus on changes in students' reach.

Extend

- Have students guess how far up the wall they think they can reach while standing flatfooted on the floor. Ask them, "Which color on the doorframe do you think you can reach?" Have them check their guess by reaching to the highest color they can on the doorframe. Encourage them to notice the corresponding number on the tape measure.

- Using the same routine with the markings on the doorframe, ask students how far they can reach if they stand on tiptoes or on a chair (have a reliable person hold the chair to assist). Discuss differences in students' reach. Was the tallest student able to reach the highest? How much higher can students reach when they jump up?

- Have students ask at home to figure out their age in months alone. For example, a kindergartener who is 5½ years old is 5 years and 6 months old, or 66 months old. He or she may be very surprised to be 66 anything!

Activity 8: On the Other Hand . . .

Key idea: Counting up units of length using a hand as a unit
Learning trajectory levels: End-to-End Length Measurer; (Exploring)
Length Unit Relater and Repeater

Essentials

Clear off at least one table so that it is ready to measure.

Engage

Show the drawing below (fig. 1.5; available at More4U), and explain how people have long used the human hand as a measurement for horses. For this purpose, a *hand* is the standard unit of measurement of equine height and is equivalent to 4 inches. A horse or pony is measured from the ground to the top of the shoulder. Ponies, for example, measure about 14.2 hands, or 56.8 inches.

Horses are measured in hands. A pony is about 14 hands high.

Fig. 1.5. How to measure a horse using hands

Explore

Ask students to measure the length of a table by using their hands and then measure the table's height and width in the same way.

Record their findings about the length of the table in hands, and list the numbers on a poster without ordering them or graphing them at first. Ask them, "What do these numbers tell us about the table's length?" Help students notice the range and frequency of some of the numbers.

Expect

- Students will probably not get the same result. If they do not, can they explain why not? Do the differences mean that some did the activity correctly and others did not? Have several students demonstrate how they used their hands. Point out that using different features of their hands (palm width versus wrist-to-fingertip length) will produce different measures for the same object.

- Are students consistent in using the same hand lengths, hand widths, or handspans when they measure? Are their fingers spread apart each time or kept together when using hand widths? Do they measure without overlaps or gaps?

Extend

- Have students repeat the hand measurement of the table's length. Ask them to report and discuss the results, including any variations from their first result.

- Have students find the distance from their own toe to their knee. Find another student whose toe and knee were the same distance apart.

- Have students measure parts of the room by using their hands. What is the distance from their own table to the teacher's desk? What is the width of the floor of the classroom? What is the width of the ceiling? This may be a challenge, so help them realize that the floor and the ceiling are usually the same width. What is the length of the diagonal across the floor?

Enrich

Read *Actual Size* by Steve Jenkins (Houghton Mifflin Harcourt 2004), which Illustrates the hands of the gorilla and the pygmy mouse lemur.

Activity 9: Watch Out for the Big Guy!

Key idea: Comparing things to parts of our bodies
Learning trajectory levels: Length Quantity Recognizer; Length Comparer (Direct, Indirect)

Engage

Read *Watch Out! Big Bro's Coming!* by Jez Alborough (Scholastic 1997). Terror spreads through the jungle—rough, tough Big Bro is coming to visit his brother the mouse.

Explore

Review the story. The mouse shows the size of his "Big Bro" to the frog by spreading his arms out wide. The frog passes the message along to the parrot, and then the parrot to the chimpanzee. Each animal shows the size of Big Bro by spreading his own arms out "as wide as they could go." The difference between the span of the mouse's outstretched arms and the chimpanzee's outstretched arms is great. The humor in the story grows as each successively larger animal's arm span makes Big Bro seem bigger and bigger.

Expect

- What if the chimpanzee had shown the elephant the actual width of the mouse's outstretched arms? The mouse's arm span might be 3 inches wide, while the chimpanzee's might be 72 inches. Help the students understand that the reference unit matters a great deal. The mouse uses himself as a reference unit to describe Big Bro, but only later does the chimpanzee realize that Big Bro is really only a mouse's arm span in size—small in comparison to the chimpanzee himself.

- Can students explain why using arm spans, hands, or feet to measure can sometimes be a problem?

Extend

- Have students compare their own arm span (fingertip to outstretched fingertip) with that of others in the class. Can they find a classmate with an arm span that is about the same?

- Students may also suggest other comparisons: foot length, length of stride, hand span, hand width, arm length, the length of fingertip to elbow, leg length, the measurement from floor to knee or floor to waist, or the circumference of their head (hat size). Explain that measurements based on these types of comparisons have often been useful throughout history. For example, a horse's height has been measured in "hands" for a long time, and a "foot" was originally based on the length of an average man's foot: 11 to 14 inches (see fig. 1.5).

Enrich

Read *A Big Guy Took My Ball!* by Mo Willems (Hyperion 2013). Piggy is devastated when a big guy (a blue whale) takes her ball. Her best friend, Gerald (an elephant), is big too, but is he big enough to help Piggy talk with the whale?

Activity 10: She Swallowed a What?

Key idea: Comparing volume and length
Learning trajectory levels: Length Quantity Recognizer; Length Comparer (Direct);
Volume Quantity Recognizer

Essentials

For each group of students, make a set of pictures of the animals that appear in the traditional story "There Was an Old Lady Who Swallowed a Fly," as shown in figure 1.6 (available at More 4U).

Fig. 1.6. Pictures of animals from *There Was an Old Lady Who Swallowed a Fly*

Engage

Read *There Was an Old Lady Who Swallowed a Fly* by Simms Taback (Scholastic 1997), a favorite American folk poem in which an old lady swallows a succession of creatures beginning with a fly and finishing with a final gulp of an entire horse.

Explore

Give each group of students a set of labeled pictures of the animals swallowed by the old lady, and ask them to put the animals in the order in which they appear in the story. Ask students to talk about how they ordered the animals. Listen for comparisons of the animals according to their length, width, and height.

Expect

- Are students aware that the animals that the Old Lady swallows get bigger as the story unfolds?

- Find out whether students see the differences from one animal to the next as changes in length, height, weight, or volume. Or are they focusing on another trait related to the increasing size of the animals? Determine whether students can identify specific attributes (height, weight, volume, or length) that help in understanding size differences.

Extend

Have students look through nonfiction animal books to find an insect smaller than a fly. Can they find an animal larger than a horse? How do they describe the differences in the sizes of these animals? Do they notice differences in height, weight, volume, or length?

Enrich

Read *Size* by Henry Pluckrose (Children's Press 1995). Photographs and text introduce the concept of size through comparisons.

Another possibility is *Life-Size Zoo* by Teruyuki Komiya (Seven Footer Kids 2009). This book shows life-size photographs of various animals with fold-out pages and charts of interesting facts about each animal.

Activity 11: "Just Right!"

Key idea: Comparing three objects by size and order
Learning trajectory levels: Quantity Recognizer (Length, Area, and Volume);
    Length Comparer (Direct)

Essentials

Gather chart paper; each student will need a stuffed animal, markers, and drawing paper.

Engage

Read *Goldilocks and the Three Bears,* illustrated by Paul Galdone (World's Work 1983). Goldilocks visits the house of the three bears, and, after sampling their porridge, chairs, and beds, she falls asleep in Little Bear's bed because it is "just right."

Explore

Organize students in groups of three, and give each group a tall, a middle-sized, and a short stuffed animal. Ask the students to put the stuffed animals in order of height, draw them, and then draw corresponding bowls, chairs, and beds for each member of their animal "family."

Expect

- What if someone has a stuffed dolphin—an animal that is long, not tall? Where would it go in the order? Students may need to decide which measurements to use when considering an animal's size. One way to compare is to find the greatest dimension of each animal.

- Do students describe and compare bowls, chairs, or beds by using overly general terms like *bigger* or *smaller*? Encourage them to describe differences among the objects in their drawings by comparing heights or widths.

- Are the animals, bowls, chairs, and beds in students' drawings proportioned to show size comparisons?

- Watch for one-to-one matching of objects to "family" members.

- Can students sequence the main events in the story?

Extend

- This story lends itself to talking about what happened first, next, and last. Have students work in pairs to retell the story in sequence.

- Make a class chart to collect describing words and phrases from pairs of students after they finish retelling the story. Entries on the chart could include *hot*, *cold*, *hard*, *soft*, and *just right*.

- Review the describing words and phrases on the chart, and ask if any of these could be used to compare two stuffed animals. Help students realize that size words are best for comparing because they can be measured. Highlight or circle words and phrases that indicate measurable attributes. If the chart does not have very many, encourage students to suggest words such as *bigger*, *smaller*, *about the same*, *lighter*, *heavier*, *wider*, or *narrower*.

- Show your own stuffed animal to the class and ask students to describe it. They might say it has blue eyes, it is tan, it is small, and it looks furry. Write those describing words on the chart. Encourage students to list such attributes as height, width, weight, or thickness.

- Choose a student to show his or her stuffed animal to the class. As students offer describing words about the animal, add them to the class chart.

- Have pairs of students compare their animals by using a word from the chart. Have them write and illustrate the comparison. For example, John's bear is wider than Jill's dog, or Jill's dog is shorter than John's bear.

- Have students compare their stuffed animals with other items in the classroom. For example, ask them to name an object that they estimate to be shorter than their stuffed animal. Then have the class watch as a student compares his or her animal with the object. Repeat, with different students comparing different attributes. Then ask students to look for objects that are about the same height, width, and so forth, as their animal. Challenge: Ask students to look for an object that is taller *and* lighter than their stuffed animal.

- Can students line up the stuffed animals at their table in order from shortest to tallest? Ask them to combine their animals with another table's animals, recreating the height order, and then have the whole class arrange their animals in height order.

Activity 12: Inch by Inch

Key idea: Measuring length by repeating inch units
Learning trajectory levels: Length Quantity Recognizer; Length Comparer (Direct);
   End-to-End Length Measurer; Length Unit Relater and Repeater

---

Essentials

Gather orange pattern block squares for each student and enough clay for each student to make a worm.

Engage

Read *Inch by Inch* by Leo Lionni (Astor-Honor 1960). Various birds make use of an inchworm's ability to measure, and all goes well—until the hungry nightingale's request.

Explore

Discuss what the birds in the book wanted the inchworm to measure: the robin's tail, the flamingo's neck, the toucan's beak, the heron's legs, the pheasant's tail, and the whole hummingbird. Finally, the nightingale asks the inchworm to measure its song. What is different about the nightingale's request? This is a good opportunity to review measurable and nonmeasurable attributes. After protesting, the inchworm agrees to measure the song. But does the inchworm really do that?

Help students search through a variety of bird books and other animal books or online resources that include measurements of birds. Ask them to record the lengths of different birds and share the information with the group. Then compile the size facts into a class book with extra pages so that students can add more facts throughout the year.

Expect

- Help students focus on determining a beginning point or an endpoint when measuring a bird. Are beaks included in the bird's length? Where does the inchworm start measuring, and how does he know when to stop counting?

- Some students may overlap or leave gaps when they imprint the square edges along the worms in the extension activities or when they measure with the clay worm. In these exploratory activities, the emphasis is on identifying length as an attribute that helps in making comparisons.

- Students might report that the robin's tail is "5." Others might say it is "5 inches." Still others could say it is "5 inchworms long." We want to encourage them to notice the attribute of length, and using words like *inch* or *inchworm* helps emphasize length as well as the concept of the unit as essential information in a measurement.

Extend

- Give each student a handful of orange pattern block squares. Tell them that each side of the square is an inch long. Can they line them up to measure a pencil, a book's height and width, a crayon, and so on?

- Have each student roll out a clay worm. Demonstrate how to imprint the edge of the orange square repeatedly along the clay worm to make a "measuring worm." It might be best for students to do this activity in pairs so they can help each other.

- When students have made imprints along the entire length of their clay worm, they can carry it around to measure objects in the room. Demonstrate how to figure out the length of an object by counting the square imprints that match up to the object when the measuring worm is placed alongside it with one end of the worm lined up with one end of the object. Encourage students to start by measuring objects shorter than their worm. Be sure to introduce the word *about* because students' measurements won't be exact, and encourage students to give inches as the unit, saying, for example, "My pencil is about 6 inches long."

- Show students a ruler, a yardstick, and a cloth measuring tape. Indicate the inch units along the entire length of all three tools, dragging your finger along as you count aloud together (as opposed to merely pointing to the numbers). This demonstration is not just about counting: you are emphasizing the continuous aspect of length. Ask whether a ruler, a yardstick, or a measuring tape would be best for measuring the robin's tail, the heron's legs, and so on.

Enrich

Consider any of the following books and online resources:

- *What in the World Is an Inch?* by Mary Elizabeth Salzmann (ABDO 2009). Shows use of length-measuring tools in several situations.
- *National Audubon Society First Field Guide: Birds* by Scott Weidensaul (Chanticleer Press 1998). Lengths of birds are easy to identify in the information given for each bird.

- *Audubon Online Bird Guide*: http://www.birds.audubon.org/birdid/ quick-guide. Browse by common bird names.

- *Everybody's Everywhere Backyard Bird Book* (North American edition) by editors of Klutz Press, 1992.

- National Wildlife Federation website: www.nwf.org

Activity 13: Which One Fits?

Key idea: Capacity with envelopes and cards
Learning trajectory levels: Length and Area Quantity Recognizer; Length Comparer (Direct).
(Note that calling students' attention to the attributes of length and width at the same time introduces them to the idea of surface area. In this activity, coordinating the two dimensions for the envelopes or cards provides a basis for comparing areas of flat spaces.)

Essentials

Gather at least four greeting cards and matching envelopes in various shapes and sizes (one small, one large, one wide, and one tall and narrow), construction paper, and scrap paper.

Engage

Display cards on one side of the board and envelopes on the other. Read "The Letter" from *Frog and Toad Are Friends* by Arnold Lobel (Scholastic 1970). Toad is sad because he never gets any mail, so Frog sends his friend a letter.

Explore

The object is for students to match the cards visually to the envelopes that they came in when you bought them. Suggest to students that they begin with the largest card and find the envelope that fits it and then work down in size. Once they think they have made the matches, talk about how they knew by looking that a given card and envelope went together. Put the cards in their corresponding envelopes to show students whether their choices were correct. Talk about the two dimensions of height and width and which one was more useful to determine each match.

Expect

Some students may try to argue that the smallest card could fit in more than one of the envelopes. That may be so, but you need to show them that the remaining cards would then be unmatched. Suggest that they put all four cards inside matching envelopes at the same time.

If the envelopes are colored to match the cards, students will be able to avoid using visual estimation of area by attending to color, so try to find cards with similar-colored envelopes, or perhaps all white.

Extend

Have students make a card and an envelope to hold it. Suggest three ways to make envelopes: a simple "hamburger" fold (like a hamburger bun), a "hot dog" fold (like a hot dog bun), or a modified trifold with diagonals, as shown in figure 1.7. Students are likely to explore more possibilities if you provide scrap paper to use for the envelope construction.

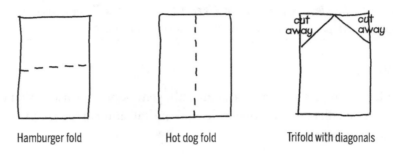

Hamburger fold   Hot dog fold   Trifold with diagonals

Fig. 1.7. Ways to fold paper to make envelopes

Activity 14: Fill It to the Top!

Key idea: Noticing volume as a measurable attribute

Learning trajectory levels: Quantity Recognizer (Length, Area, and Volume);
    Length Comparer (Direct, Indirect); Volume Filler; Volume Quantifier

Essentials

Arrange desks into clusters of four or five, or have students work at tables in groups of four or five. For each group, prepare a clear plastic box (approximately the size of a shoebox) with sand, about an inch in depth. Alternatively, you could use birdseed, rice, dried beans, split peas, or colored water. Prepare a box of the same size for your own use, filling it with sand to a greater depth, about 2 inches. Prepare a second box for your use, this time with a much smaller base, and fill it with sand to a depth of about 2 inches (any small, clear rectangular plastic box will suffice). Also have two additional empty clear shoebox-size containers.

For the extension activity, you will need at least four clear glasses of different shapes.

Engage

Read *When This Box Is Full* by Patricia Lillie (Greenwillow Books 1993). Each month a child adds something to an empty box, including a paper heart shape for February and a shell with sand for July.

Explore

Ask students, "Is the box in the story really full at the end of the year, or could the child add more sand?"

Ask students to compare the amount of sand in the teacher's box with the amount of sand in their own box. Which container has more sand? How do you know?

Expect

- Most students will immediately guess that the teacher's box contains more sand because the level of sand in the box is twice as high as the sand in their own box. Their explanations might focus only on the attribute of height (and miss the attribute of volume). To test students' understanding, show them the smaller clear rectangular box of sand. Once again, ask students to compare the amount of sand in their box with the amount in your box. If students incorrectly guess that your box contains more sand because they looked only at the height of the sand, you can help them by asking one group of students to transfer the sand (carefully!) from their shoebox to an empty one while you do the same. This should cause them to reconsider their first guess. Can students talk about the differences in height and width at the same time and how both are related to the volume of sand?

- Students should eventually (by fifth grade) realize that volume comparisons generally require attention to three different dimensions. Holding two of these dimensions constant allows for a comparison along the remaining dimension. The activities here provide opportunities for kindergartners to make direct comparisons of volume and capacity. We want students to attend to these attributes in contrast to such attributes as height, weight, or length.

Extend

Perhaps on another day, students can compare the height of water in differently shaped glasses (some short and wide, some tall and narrow). Use colored water to make it easy to see the height of the liquid in the glasses. Can the students support their comparisons as in the sand exercise?

Provide an empty container to check students' initial guesses. Start by pouring the water from one glass into this container. Mark the height of the water on the side of the container with a piece of tape. (You will need to pour the water back into its glass after recording the height and before pouring in the next glass.)

Enrich

Read *Measure It!* by Joyce Markovics (Rourke Educational Media 2013). Photographs present measures of weight, length, time, and temperature.

CHAPTER 2

GRADE 1:
MOTIVATION TO MEASURE

Big measurement ideas identified in CCSSM: Begin by establishing quantity. Count a complete set of units spanning an object and report that number as the measure of the length of the object. For example, a book might be nine paper clips long. Help students relate that practice to using a ruler. After using complete sets of units to span the object to be measured, use only a few iterated units to span the object (by "leapfrogging" the units).

Learning trajectory levels in this grade: Students move from direct comparison and indirect comparison that do not require counting to end-to-end length measurement, which does require counting. For example, students using end-to-end strategies might arrange a set of straws in a line to span the entire length of a table and report the number of straws as the length (see activity 1). Also, students should begin to work with Length Unit Relater and Repeater strategies, using just a few units to measure the length of an object by repeating the units in a leapfrog manner. Table 2.1 shows the learning trajectory levels for length, area, and volume for this grade.

Table 2.1. Learning trajectory levels by grade and topic

Grade	Length LT levels	Area LT levels	Volume LT level
1	End-to-End Length Measurer Length Unit Relater and Repeater	Physical Coverer and Counter Complete Coverer and Counter Area Unit Relater and Repeater	Volume Filler

Rulers show us a careful and practical record of stepping or repeating units, as we might illustrate with rows of paper clips or sticks. An informal pre-assessment length measurement activity is included at the end of activity 1 and a post-assessment at the end of activity 7 (length measurement is the focus of the first eight activities).

Table 2.2 provides an overview of the activities in this chapter. Each activity is linked to the relevant CCSSM standard and levels from a learning trajectory on length measurement. The activities are divided into four groups. Activities 1–5 focus on comparing and ordering objects by length or height, activities 6–8 focus on measuring length with a shorter object, activities 9 and 10 focus on using operations to compare length, and activities 11–14 focus on recognizing measurable attributes and comparing objects by these attributes.

Table 2.2. Grade 1 activities matched with Common Core State Standards and learning trajectory levels

General CCSSM	Learning activities	Activity-specific standards	Learning trajectory levels
Comparing and ordering 1.MD.A.1 Order objects by length; compare the lengths of objects indirectly	**Activity 1: The Line Up Book** Key idea: Comparing lengths and distances by using nonstandard units	1.MD.A.1 1.MD.A.2 2.MD.A.2	End-to-End Length Measurer
	Activity 2: A Very Big Bunny Key idea: Ordering by height	1.MD.A.1	Length Comparer (Direct, Indirect)
	Activity 3: Measuring with Monkeys Key idea: Comparing by length, jump distance, and speed	1.MD.A.1 1.OA.A.1 2.MD.A.1 2.MD.A.4	Length Comparer (Direct, Indirect) End-to-End Length Measurer
	Activity 4: Much Bigger Than Key idea: Comparing height/reach and age	1.MD.A.1 1.OA.A.1 2.MD.A.1 2.MD.A.4	Length Comparer (Direct, Indirect) End-to-End Length Measurer
	Activity 5: Let's Fly a Kite Key idea: Symmetry	1.MD.A.1 1.G.A.1 4.G.A.3	Length Comparer (Direct) End-to-End Length Measurer Physical Coverer and Counter

General CCSSM	Learning activities	Activity-specific standards	Learning trajectory levels
Measuring with whole number lengths 1.MD.A.2 Report whole number lengths using multiple copies of a shorter object laid end to end	**Activity 6: Measuring Puppies and Kittens** Key ideas: Nonstandard units; comparing lengths	1.MD.A.1 1.MD.A.2 1.OA.A.1	Length Comparer (Direct, Indirect) End-to-End Length Measurer
	Activity 7: Super Sand Castle Saturday Key ideas: Nonstandard units; comparing lengths	1.MD.A.1 1.MD.A.2 1.OA.A.1	Length Comparer (Direct, Indirect) End-to-End Length Measurer Length Unit Relater and Repeater
	Activity 8: Twelve Snails to One Lizard Key idea: Benefits of using tools marked with standard units	1.MD.A.1 1.MD.A.2	End-to-End Length Measurer Length Unit Relater and Repeater
Coordinating number and length 1.OA.D.7 Use equations to model length 1.OA.D.8 Use equations to model and solve length tasks	**Activity 9: Elevator Magic** Key idea: Modeling subtraction as movement along a vertical number line	1.OA.A.1 1.OA.D.7 1.OA.D.8	Length Unit Relater and Repeater
	Activity 10: Ready, Set, Hop! Key idea: Applying addition or subtraction to compare lengths	1.MD.A.1 1.MD.A.2 1.OA.A.1 1.OA.D.7 1.OA.D.8	Length Comparer (Direct, Indirect) End-to-End Length Measurer Length Unit Relater and Repeater (Exploring) Consistent Length Measurer

Table 2.2. continued

General CCSSM	Learning activities	Activity-specific standards	Learning trajectory levels
Recognizing and comparing by attributes, especially area and volume K.MD.A.1 Recognize measurable attributes K.MD.A.2 Compare by measurable attributes	**Activity 11: The Grouchy Ladybug** Key idea: Comparing by measurable attributes	K.MD.A.1 K.MD.A.2 1.MD.A.1 1.MD.B.3	Length Quantity Recognizer Length Comparer (Direct, Indirect) Area Quantity Recognizer Volume Quantity Recognizer
	Activity 12: Mighty Maddie Key ideas: Comparing by weight; volume as an attribute	K.MD.A.1 K.MD.A.2 1.G.A.1 3.MD.A.2 (Explore)	Volume Quantity Recognizer Volume Quantifier (Comparing)
	Activity 13: A House for Birdie Key idea: Capacity as an attribute	K.MD.A.1 K.MD.A.2 5.MD.C.3 (Explore)	Length Comparer (Direct, Indirect) Volume Quantity Recognizer Volume Filler Volume Quantifier
	Activity 14: The Mitten Key idea: Capacity as an attribute	K.MD.A.1 K.MD.A.2 5.MD.C.3 (Explore)	Length Comparer (Direct, Indirect) Volume Quantity Recognizer Volume Filler Volume Quantifier

Activity 1: The Line Up Book

Key idea: Comparing lengths and distances by using nonstandard units
Learning trajectory level: End-to-End Length Measurer

Essentials

Gather blocks, books, toys, pencils, straws, markers, cotton swabs, crayons, toothpicks, and other small objects.

Engage

Read *The Line Up Book* by Marisabina Russo (Greenwillow 1986). Sam lines up blocks, books, boots, toys, cars, and other objects all the way from his room to his mother in the kitchen.

Explore

Review the pictures in the book. What did Sam use when he ran out of blocks, books, toys, and shoes?

Ask students how far it is from Sam's room to the kitchen. Do they count all the objects along the path?

Count all the objects Sam placed along the path. Does the count tell us the length of the path? What if he had used only blocks? Would the answer be the same number?

Expect

- Sam leaves gaps between the objects that he uses to measure the distance. Is this a problem? What else does he do that might make the total length inaccurate? (He uses a variety of different-length units and counts them: books, boots, blocks, cars, etc.) Discuss what happens when Sam uses several objects of different lengths. Note that his measurement is unrepeatable. He himself would be unlikely to space the same objects in the same order to find the same measure again.

- What if Sam's mom noticed the gaps and placed a spoon in each gap? There would be more objects along the path, so the total number of objects would change. Did the length of the path actually change just because the number of objects changed? (Some students may say that it did.)

- In the first extension activity, check whether students leave gaps or overlap objects when they measure distances in the classroom. At first, students entering the end-to-end level of reasoning often leave gaps or overlap; it may help if you suggest closing up gaps or fixing overlaps and recounting to find the length.

- When students are estimating and measuring in the gym (the third extension activity), observe whether they use the information about the distance from the free-throw line to the baseline to make estimates of the other measures of the court. Students are not likely to use exact proportional reasoning, but some may correctly attempt to double their estimates.

- Students were asked to measure with straws and with cotton swabs, which are much shorter. Did they begin to realize that there is an inverse relationship between the size of the measuring units and the number of units needed to measure a length?

Extend

- Give students opportunities to measure distances between objects in the classroom. For example, have them measure the distance between their desk and the teacher's desk and between their desk and the door to the hallway. Provide enough objects (such as markers) to span the entire distances. Which distance is longer? (It is best if students use the same unit of measure to compare these distances.)

- Next, have students choose a path to measure with two different units, and then have them compare those totals. For example, they might first use straws and then cotton swabs. Have the students record both measurements. Suppose that a path measures 4 straws long and also measures 12 cotton swabs long. Point out that the measure increased with the shorter units.

- Measure distances in the gym. In *The Line Up Book*, Sam lies down on the floor to measure distance. Ask how many students lying down would be needed to span the distance from the free-throw line to the baseline. Alternatively, have students measure by counting arm spans or foot lengths. Next, ask students to estimate and measure the distance from midcourt to the baseline and the distance from one baseline to the other (full court length).

Enrich

Read *Length* by Henry Pluckrose (from the series MathCounts; Children's Press 1995). Photographs and descriptions support the concept of length through comparisons.

Pre-assessment for length

- Preassemble seven towers of Unifix cubes as follows: one tower made of three red cubes, one of four black, one of five white, one of six yellow, one of seven orange, one of eight green, and one of nine blue. Hide the orange seven-cube tower. Scramble the order of the other six towers and lay them down on a table. Tell the student whom you are assessing, "Put these towers in order from shortest to tallest." Make note of the result. Next, give the student the orange tower and say, "Where will this one fit in your lineup?" *Note:* If students struggle to put all six towers in sequence, have them arrange fewer towers first.

- Provide each student with a sheet of paper showing the outline of a ruler (a rectangle at least 8 inches long by 1 inch high). Be sure that rulers are not available or visible to students. Hand the student whom you are assessing a pencil and tell him or her, "Add what you need to make this look like a ruler." *Note:* A range of responses should be expected, with some students using only numerals to show spacing along the rectangle and others placing evenly spaced tick marks and using numerals to label the tick marks.

Activity 2: A Very Big Bunny

Key idea: Ordering by height
Learning trajectory level: Length Comparer (Direct, Indirect)

Essentials

Gather adding machine tape, scissors, washable markers, masking tape, cloth measuring tapes, and chart paper.

Engage

Read *A Very Big Bunny* by Marisabina Russo (Schwartz & Wade Books 2010). Amelia is so big that none of the other students will play with her, but a new classmate teaches her that size is not always the most important thing.

Explore

Ask students to share attributes that describe Amelia. She is the tallest, has the biggest feet, and is the heaviest. Have them contrast those with attributes that describe Susannah. Talk about their solution to balance the seesaw.

The teacher in the story likes to line up the class in size order, and Amelia is always last. Ask the tallest student and the shortest student in your class to stand up, and one at a time, have the students find their place in line by height.

Demonstrate how to cut a piece of string or adding machine tape equal to the height of one of your students. Direct the student to stand up straight with his back as close as possible to the wall and use a washable marker to indicate the student's height. After he moves away from the wall, have the student hold the adding machine tape or string against the wall, starting at the mark. After it unrolls, hold it taut, crease it where it hits the floor directly under the mark and then cut along the crease. Have the other students work in pairs to do the same thing. Label the lengths of adding machine tape or string with their names.

Display five or six of the strips on a table. Have the students arrange the strips in length order, using one edge of the table as a baseline against which they should align one edge of the strips, as in figure 2.1.

Heights of Students in Our Group

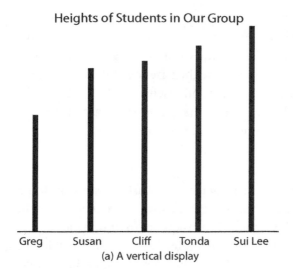

Greg   Susan   Cliff   Tonda   Sui Lee

(a) A vertical display

Heights of Students in Our Group

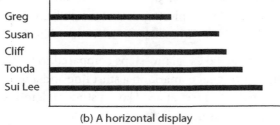

(b) A horizontal display

Fig. 2.1. Examples of ribbon displays (from *Navigating through Measurement in Prekindergarten–Grade 2* [Dacey et al. 2003, p. 26])

Expect

- Students may not realize that they need to place their tapes along a common baseline. Discuss this with them.

- Students may not yet be capable of transitive reasoning. A student may need to compare her or his own height to the height of each person individually, instead of reasoning that because she or he is taller than Bobby, and Bobby is taller than Amy, she or he must be taller than Amy.

- In the extension activity, you can expect students to measure their tape to the nearest inch in most cases. Suggest that students double-check their measure by having their partner measure the same tape again.

- While students are working with the height strips laid out on tables, ask them to look at the strips from two adjacent sides of the table, viewing the strips vertically and then horizontally. From the first vantage point, it may seem more natural for the students to use the word *height* (the strips are tall or short). From the other vantage point, it may be more natural to use the word *length* (the strips are long or short). For a challenge, ask students to stand opposite the baseline of the display (where the ends of the strips are all aligned) and discuss whether they would compare them differently. Do they think that all the strips are the same length because they reach the same edge of the table?

Extend

- Provide cloth measuring tapes, and ask the students to find about how tall they are by measuring their strip. Have them write their height in inches on their strip. Next, ask them to draw a picture to show the strips displayed on the table, including the name and height of each student. Then gather and display all the strips representing students' heights on one table, stacking strips of the same length on top of one another. It may be helpful to have one student at a time come and add his or her strip into the collection. Take a photograph of the collection of strips, or make a poster as a data display to relate all the students' heights.

- In the story, Amelia takes "giant" steps compared to Susannah's "baby" steps. Using masking tape, mark off a start line and a finish line on the floor, approximately 10 feet apart. Have a student demonstrate a giant step and then count as he or she takes giant steps from the start line to the finish line. Have the same student demonstrate baby steps, placing his or her feet heel to toe, and count those from start to finish. Record the results on a chart that shows each student's name alongside columns in which you will list the number of baby steps, giant steps, and natural walking steps it takes for each student to travel from start to finish (see fig. 2.2). Have students speculate about whether they will need to take more or fewer walking steps than baby steps. Ask why. Did their predictions pan out?

Students	Measure in baby steps	Measure in giant steps	Measure in walking steps
Brooke			
Cal			
...			

Fig. 2.2. Recording sheet for measuring a distance in baby steps, giant steps, and walking steps (adapted from *Navigating through Measurement in Prekindergarten–Grade 2* [Dacey et al. 2003, p. 33])

Activity 3: Measuring with Monkeys

Key idea: Comparing by length, jump distance, and speed
Learning trajectory levels: Length Comparer (Direct, Indirect); End-to-End Length Measurer

Essentials

Gather string, rulers, yardsticks, at least one balance scale, and objects to weigh on the scale.

Engage

Read the book *Measuring with Monkeys* by Tracey Steffora (Heinemann Library 2014). Monkeys are compared by measuring how long their tails are, how far they can jump, how much they weigh, how fast they run, and how warm their climate is.

Explore

Follow the Teaching Notes on page 24 of the book. First, play a questioning game in which students are challenged to make comparisons between themselves and various animals by weight, length, and speed.

Next, demonstrate the use of the balance scale by weighing various pairs of objects. Be sure to have students predict which object will be heavier first, and then use the scale to check the prediction.

Finally, use rulers to cut lengths of string to represent the three different tail lengths shown for the monkeys on pages 10 and 11 of *Measuring with Monkeys*.

Expect

- Students may notice that the picture of the tail of the vervet monkey measures about $2^{1}/_{2}$ inches long—not 24 inches as labeled. Help students understand that the image was reduced to fit on the page.

- The ratio of the tail lengths of the two monkeys shown on page 10 of the book is correctly reported as 2:1 (or 24:12). However, the representations of the tail lengths of the spider monkey and the tamarin shown on page 11 do not reflect the labeled 3:1 (36:12) ratio. The white line segments do not capture the full length of the monkeys' curved tails. Suggest that students watch while you use strings to measure the entire curved length of each of the monkeys' tails. Then compare the length of the strings. These measurements will reflect the 3:1 ratio more closely.

- Check to see whether students can explain why two tamarin tail lengths equal a vervet tail length, or three tamarin tail lengths equal one spider monkey tail length.

- Do students mention that a measurement of 12 inches or 1 foot is *about* the length of a tamarin tail? Do they realize that the tail of an actual tamarin might be longer or shorter than 12 inches?

Extend

- Ask students to use the lengths of string that represent the actual tail lengths of the tamarin (about 12 inches long), the vervet (24 inches), and the spider monkey (36 inches) to find objects in the room that are the same length. They should begin by predicting and recording their predictions about which objects will be about the same length as each of their three string pieces. They should then check their predictions and record their findings.

- Review the data on pages 10 and 11 about the monkeys' tail lengths. Ask students to explain to a partner how they know that the vervet's tail is twice as long as the tamarin's tail. Point out to the students that a standard 12-inch ruler is the same length as the tamarin's tail, so they can use more than one ruler to measure the length of the other two monkey tails. Some may notice that one tamarin tail length and one vervet tail length combine to match the length of a spider monkey tail.

Enrich

Sample other books in the 2014 Animal Math series by Heinemann Library, including *Adding with Ants, Comparing with Cats, Shapes with Snakes, Skip Counting with Meerkats,* and *Taking Away with Tigers.*

Activity 4: Much Bigger Than

Key idea: Comparing height/reach and age
Learning trajectory levels: Length Comparer (Direct, Indirect); End-to-End Length Measurer

Essentials

Fasten a cloth tape measure vertically along a doorframe or on a wall. Fasten a set of seven 12-inch rulers, arranging them end to end vertically on the opposite side of the doorframe (see fig. 2.3).

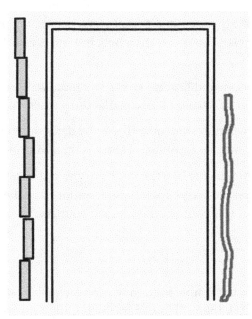

Fig. 2.3. Arrangement of rulers and tape measure alongside doorframe

Engage

Read *Much Bigger Than Martin* by Steven Kellogg (Deal 1976). Having a brother who is bigger is not always easy. Little brother Henry's attempts at growing much bigger than his brother don't really change things, but he does come up with a temporary solution for shooting baskets.

Explore

Discuss the typical height for a person at birth, at age 6, at age 20, at age 30, and at the age of grandparents. Have the students collect data by asking familiar adults about their heights. Ask the students to report back and discuss their findings. Combine their findings in a chart or table to show typical heights for humans at different ages (at least at 0, 6, 20, and 30).

Prompt students to write by saying: "List some good things and some bad things about being the tallest (or shortest) person in your family." Students may enjoy illustrating their writing.

Expect

- Students may reason that height and age are directly related (i.e., if you are older, you must be taller). The data they gather may help them dispel this misconception.

- Students may not grasp the fact that the difference between two people's heights can be expressed in different ways, depending on the choice of units (e.g., Jim is 1 foot taller than Bob, but Jim is also 12 inches taller than Bob).

- In the story, Mom and Dad make marks on the wall to record the heights of their two sons. What do those marks show when you compare them?

- Check to see whether students can use the dates on the wall by the marks to figure out how much younger Henry is than Martin.

- Do students notice that Martin and Henry were the same size in 1974 and in 1976, respectively? This is also mentioned in the text; Dad says, "When Martin was your age, he was just your size" near the end of the book.

Extend

- Have students guess how high they can reach while standing flatfooted on the floor. Ask them, "How many inches high can you reach this way?" Have them check their guess by reaching and touching the highest inch marker possible on the doorframe. Report that measurement as their standing reach. Next, ask them how far they can reach if they stand on tiptoe or on a chair (have a reliable person hold the chair to assist).

- Discuss differences in students' reach. Was the tallest student able to reach the highest? How much higher can students reach when they jump up than when they stand flatfooted?

- Find the typical standing reach for the entire class, and compare this with the typical standing reach for students in a different class. How much difference is there between the typical reach of students in one class and that of students in the other?

Enrich

Read *Measure It!* by Joyce Markovics (Rourke Educational Media 2013; teacher notes are available at http://rem4teachers.com). One-foot-long rulers stacked end to end make it obvious that an ostrich is 6 feet tall.

Activity 5: Let's Fly a Kite

Key idea: Symmetry
Learning trajectory levels: Length Comparer (Direct); End-to-End Length Measurer;
Physical Coverer and Counter

Essentials

Gather enough paper, scrap paper, scissors, markers, sequins, lace, pompons, craft glue, and pipe cleaners for the class. Cut a kite shape out of paper for each student and fold each one in half vertically.

Engage

Read *Let's Fly a Kite* by Stuart J. Murphy (HarperCollins 2000). Two squabbling siblings learn about symmetry when their babysitter helps them build and fly a kite.

Explore

Have students name all the objects in the book that are symmetrical (the sandwich, backseat, and beach blanket). Talk about what makes them symmetrical. If you fold the blanket down the middle, are both sides exactly the same?

The sides of the blanket in the story are the same, but the halves are too skinny, so how do Hannah and Bob solve that problem? (They fold it vertically instead of horizontally.)

Expect

- Students may need encouragement to look for more than one line of symmetry (the blanket, for example, has both vertical and horizontal symmetry). Note that students may use concepts such as *perpendicular* and *line of symmetry* before being able to define or explain the terms.

- Did students make sure that both sides of their decorated kites would match exactly (with regard to colors, patterns, and decorations) if folded along the midline (line of symmetry)?

Extend

- Ask students to find and list objects in the classroom that are symmetrical. Then ask them to look for symmetrical objects at home (e.g., quilts, wallpaper, pillows, and clothing) and in nature (e.g., leaves, flowers, and insects).

- Fold a piece of paper (scrap paper is fine) in half and then in half again, and cut out small shapes along the folds. Unfold it: it's a "snowflake." (Making a genuine snowflake shape requires a more complicated folding to give it six sides.) Find all the ways that it is symmetrical.

- Ask students to list any numerals or capital letters that are symmetrical.

- Provide each student with a paper kite shape that is folded vertically, and ask students to decorate only one half, using the markers and craft materials. Then tell them to trade kites with a partner, and finish the partner's kite to make it symmetrical. First, have students use a pencil to indicate where they think one detail should go (using "eyeball estimation"). Next, demonstrate how to use a ruler to find matching points across the line of symmetry and have students try to measure across the line of symmetry (see fig. 2.4).

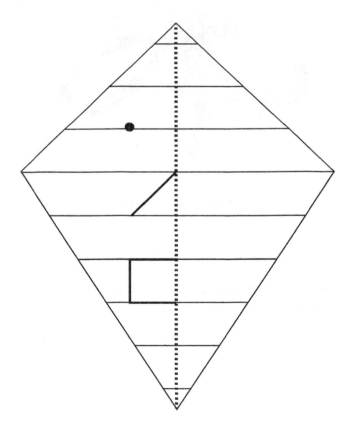

Fig. 2.4. Students can measure across the line of symmetry to decorate the kite symmetrically.

- Next, working in pairs, students should make another kite that is decorated in an asymmetrical fashion. The first partner should decorate only half of the kite, and then the partners should trade partially decorated kites and finish them. Which one was easier to make, the symmetric or the asymmetric kite? Why?

- Have students use a variety of colors of pipe cleaners to form a symmetrical butterfly, as shown in figure 2.5.

Fig. 2.5. Symmetrical butterfly

Enrich

Read *Seeing Symmetry* by Loren Leedy (Holiday House 2011). Several examples demonstrate and explain line symmetry (reflective symmetry) and point symmetry (rotational symmetry).

Activity 6: Measuring Puppies and Kittens

Key ideas: *Nonstandard units; comparing lengths*

Learning trajectory levels: *Length Comparer (Direct, Indirect); End-to-End Length Measurer*

Essentials

Gather stuffed animals, rulers and yardsticks (or metric measuring tools), leashes, water bowls, pet toys, and pieces of yarn.

Engage

Read *Measuring Puppies and Kittens* by Patricia J. Murphy (Enslow Elementary 2007). Learn to measure length, height, and width of animals with nonstandard units such as blocks, hands, and paper clips, as well as standard inch units on rulers and yardsticks.

Explore

How much taller is Tuffy the dog than his doghouse door? How much higher does Rocky the kitten jump than Muffin the kitten? Which animal has the widest paw—Jack, Max, or Buddy? Ask students to share their reasoning.

Expect

- The three pictures on pages 6 and 7 of *Measuring Puppies and Kittens* show the same puppy next to a stack of 5 cubes, 11 paper clips, and 3 handspans. Ask students to explain why the same puppy is said to be 5, 11, and 3 units tall. Can they explain why choosing smaller units (the paper clips) requires using more units than choosing larger ones (cubes or handspans) does?

- On pages 8 and 9, Pal is measured with both a blue and a yellow yardstick. If Pal had been measured once more with a red yardstick, how tall would he be?

- The book's illustrations show scaled, rather than actual-size, images of the animals. This allows the reader to see the entire animal on one page. Still, students may wonder why they cannot measure a picture and get the actual measure of the animal (e.g., the puppy is 34 inches tall, as shown on page 8, but the image of the puppy and the ruler really measures about 5 inches). Can students explain why we cannot measure the real puppy by measuring the photograph of the puppy?

- Students may answer the measurement questions with numbers alone, instead of including units. The book stresses labeling measurements with the unit of measure.

Extend

- The measurement situations lend themselves to further comparisons through subtraction. If Muffin's jump is 6 inches high and Rocky's is 9 inches high, it might be obvious that Rocky jumps higher, but can students figure out how many inches higher Rocky jumps than Muffin?

- Have students work in small groups to compare two or three stuffed animals by measuring different parts of the animals with rulers. Encourage the students to measure and record the length and width of each animal's nose, ears, head, paws, arms, hips, feet, and toes.

- Ask students to work with a partner to measure various aspects of their own bodies, such as their forearms, handspans or foot widths, head width, and shoulder breadth. This is a good time to explain to students that long ago, people used their bodies to measure things, as discussed on pages 6 and 7 of the book. They used the width of their hands, finger length, elbow-to-fingertip distance (called a *cubit*), and the distance from fingertip to fingertip across the span of their outstretched arms (called a *fathom*).

Enrich

Select other books in the same series: *Adding Puppies and Kittens, Counting Puppies and Kittens, Subtracting Puppies and Kittens, Telling Time with Puppies and Kittens* by Patricia J. Murphy (Enslow Elementary 2007).

Activity 7: Super Sand Castle Saturday

Key ideas: Nonstandard units; comparing lengths
Learning trajectory levels: Length Comparer (Direct, Indirect); End-to-End Length Measurer;
  Length Unit Relater and Repeater

Essentials

Gather at least two sizes of spoons and shovels, construction paper, pencils, and scissors.

Engage

Read *Super Sand Castle Saturday* by Stuart J. Murphy (HarperCollins 1999). Three friends compete in a sand castle contest to build the tallest tower, the deepest moat, and the longest wall. They measure with spoons, shovels, and bare feet until the lifeguard supplies a tape measure for them to use.

Explore

Demonstrate the iteration method shown in the book (measuring with just one unit by scooting it along without gaps or overlaps). For example, line up several markers along the ledge of the board at the front of the classroom, and ask students about the length of the board. Would it be possible to find the length of the board by using only two markers? Check whether students can imitate the iteration method used by the characters in the story, who measure the castle wall without leaving gaps or overlapping units. Next, challenge them to measure the board length with just one marker. See whether your students find the same answer as when you measured the board by lining up a collection of markers.

Help students notice that more short shovels and fewer long ones are needed when the friends measure the height of the castle. The same goes for the spoons when they measure the depth of the moat. The children in the story use their feet to measure the length of the castle wall.

Expect

- Like Juan, Sarah, and Laura in the story, your students may also assume that if more smaller units are needed to measure an object, it must be larger than another object that can be measured with fewer larger units.

- What could the characters in the book have used if the lifeguard had not had a tape measure? Do students realize that they could have chosen any of the tools as the consistent unit to measure all the sand castles? For example, if the friends had used the smallest unit, the black spoons, they could have made reasonable comparisons of all the objects. Of course, they would need to have had several spoons to stack or line up unless they scooted one spoon along to measure.

- Can students explain why it is helpful for everyone in a community to use the same measuring system?

Extend

- Have students trace and cut out their footprint to use in measuring the length of their desk, the whiteboard, a table, the width of a door, or other parts of the classroom. You might want to emphasize that students must measure without leaving gaps or overlapping by showing them how to place a footprint at the end of the table and then marking its length with a finger before sliding the footprint down to use again. Have students record their measures as follows: "The table is 7 Bobby's feet long."

- Read *How Big Is a Foot?* by Rolf Mullar (Dell 1991). A king wants a bed made so many feet long, but his foot is bigger than the carpenter's. Discuss the dilemma of the carpenter. Assign various students to trace around the right feet of adults at school and find which one is closest to the size of the king's foot by comparing each to a ruler. It helps if the students write a note to ask if they can trace the foot of each adult, so they don't interrupt any classes. Choose a student to practice on you while the others watch. Students must label the footprints after they are cut out because they will look very similar. Have them predict which adult will win (i.e., have the foot closest to the size of the king's foot). Were their predictions correct?

Enrich

Read *What in the World Is a Foot?* By Mary Elizabeth Salzmann (ABDO 2009). Rulers, yardsticks, and tape measures are used to measure the height of people, depth of a pool, length of a slide, and distance.

Post-assessment

Have students create their own ruler. Start by asking, "What does this rectangle need to make it a ruler? Draw in whatever is needed to show a ruler."

Activity 8: Twelve Snails to One Lizard

Key idea: Benefits of using tools marked with standard units
Learning trajectory levels: End-to-End Length Measurer; Length Unit Relater and Repeater

Essentials

Gather orange pattern blocks (1-inch squares), rulers, yardsticks, cloth measuring tapes, adding machine or cash register tape, enough clay for each student to form a small snail, string, and drawing paper.

Engage

Read *Twelve Snails to One Lizard: A Tale of Mischief and Measurement* by Susan Hightower (Simon & Schuster 1997). Milo needs to measure a log to patch the hole in the beaver dam. When inch-long snails, foot-long lizards, and a yard-long boa constrictor do not work, he finds that a yardstick is easiest to use.

Explore

The author chose to use snails in this story because the garden-variety ones are about 1 inch long, iguanas are pretty close to 12 inches long, and boa constrictors grow to about 36 inches when they are around 18 months old. Have the students draw and label a snail, an iguana, and a boa constrictor on adding machine tape, drawing each animal on separate strips. Encourage students to use inch squares, a ruler, and a yardstick as references. Finally, have each student make a 1-inch-long snail out of clay.

Expect

- Do students realize that the length of the curving trails of snails cannot be measured by merely finding the distance between the two endpoints? Encourage students to trace the shape of the trail with string and then straighten it out along a ruler to find the entire length. Help them notice that the original curved trail is the same length as the straightened trail. Next, ask them to measure the distance between the endpoints. Which distance is greater? How much greater?

- Keep in mind that although students may obtain the correct numeric answer when measuring with inch squares, a ruler, or a yardstick, they may not understand what the measure actually means. For example, suppose that a log measures 4 feet long. Students may not immediately connect this measure to the length of four iguanas placed end to end, even if they know that each iguana measures 1 foot in length. They may need to check the length of the log, using their paper strip showing the length of an iguana.

Extend

- Be sure that each student's snail measures about an inch long. Have students draw a meandering trail for their snail to follow on a sheet of paper. Students should then move their snail along the trail from beginning to end (they may want to illustrate items found in a garden along the trail). Provide students with square pattern blocks, string, rulers, and cloth measuring tapes. Give them a second sheet of paper, and challenge them to draw a different-shaped trail that is about as long the first snail trail.

- Share illustrations in *Actual Size* by Steve Jenkins (Houghton Mifflin Harcourt 2004). The book shows that an Atlas moth is 12 inches across, as is a goliath birdeater tarantula and the eye of the giant squid. A goliath frog is 36 inches with its legs extended, and a giant Gippsland earthworm is a yard long as well. Discuss how best to measure a long, curved animal like a worm.

Enrich

Read *What in the World Is an Inch?* by Mary Elizabeth Salzmann (ABDO 2009). This book demonstrates the use of rulers, yardsticks, and tape measures and includes measurement scenarios involving mixed units—for example, both feet and inches are needed to measure a table that is 2 feet 6 inches long.

Activity 9: Elevator Magic

Key idea: *Modeling subtraction as movement along a vertical number line*
Learning trajectory level: *Length Unit Relater and Repeater*

Essentials

For each student, make a copy of the elevator keypad shown in figure 2.6 (template without floor numbers available at More4U), and gather enough drawing paper for the class.

Engage

Read *Elevator Magic* by Stuart J. Murphy (HarperCollins 1997). The story brings the concept of subtraction to life through rhyming text about a descending elevator. Changing from one floor to another floor in an elevator can be measured in units that we call *floors*. We can measure our progress up and down the building by subtracting or adding floors.

Explore

Give students a copy of an elevator keypad with ten buttons drawn but not labeled. Have them write the number 10 next to the top button to indicate the tenth floor and then write the numbers of the remaining floors (see fig. 2.6).

Reread the story, and have students label each floor that is mentioned as you go through it (floors 8, 5, 4, and 1) in another way, this time it by what it is used for (e.g., floor 8 is Mom's office, floor 5 is the bank).

Once again, read through the story, and have students pretend to be Ben and move their fingers along their own paper keypad.

Write an equation to fit each change of floors. Encourage students to follow the example of using subtraction equations, as Ben did, to show downward movement in the elevator. For example, if Mom and Ben want to go to the bank, which button should they press on the elevator? They are starting at Mom's office on floor 8, and Mom knows the bank is 3 floors down. Now, write an equation: $x = 8 - 3$. We can solve for x or count down floors on the elevator keypad (the template).

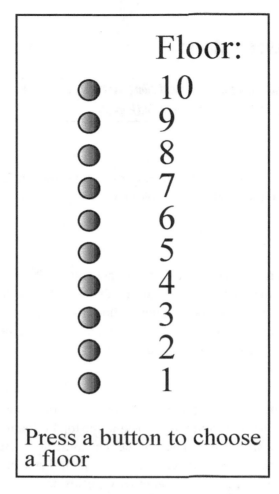

Fig. 2.6. Elevator keypad template

Expect

- Students may not have had much experience using subtraction equations to show something other than a take-away situation. Emphasize that subtraction may indicate downward motion between floors, as when Ben finds out which floor is three floors down from floor 8. Subtracting may also represent the number of gaps between specific floors, as when Ben figures out how many floors he needs to go down to move from 4 to 1.

- Watch the students' hand motions to see whether they correspond to the appropriate number of floors moved in each scenario and whether they go in the right direction. Check whether their equation matches the change in floors. The first extension activity will present opportunities for this assessment.

- When students draw the extension to the keypad (see Extend), check to determine whether they space the buttons equally and whether they make the upper ten buttons span the same distance as the lower ten buttons. Do they write the numbers without omitting any and without confusing tens and ones positions (e.g., writing 31 instead of 13)?

- Note that this activity does not easily support the idea of partial units. Students may not think about an elevator that stops partway between floors. What would students say if asked what button to push to move $2^1/_2$ floors down from floor 8? Would they say you have to go all the way down to floor 5? Students will learn more about partial units in subsequent grades.

Extend

- There are five unlabeled floors. Have students decide as a class what to name the other floors and label them accordingly (e.g., Toys, Electronics, Furniture, Clothes, and Shoes). Subsequent tasks will be simpler if everyone uses the same name for each floor. Next, have students work with a partner to tell another story that involves moving from the tenth floor down to the first floor with at least three stops on the way down. Recall that Ben mentions the following three steps each time he thinks about which button to press (page 7 of the book):

  > We are on floor 10.
  >
  > 2 floors down.
  >
  > $10 - 2 = 8$

  Accordingly, Ben chooses the button for floor 8. Have students explain a new scenario to their partner and record what Ben might say in that scenario. Include his current floor number, the number of floors he will move down, and the equation. While students talk about each change, ask them to use sweeping motions to indicate the number of floors that he will move.

- Give students a blank sheet of paper (same size as the keypad sheet) to draw the extension of the keypad that would be needed for a building twice as tall. Help them attach this sheet above their original sheet to extend the drawing of the elevator keypad to include the new floors (11 through 20). After some discussion, students should understand that the top floor is the 20th floor and that the next floor after the 10th is the 11th. (If students ask what is on these ten upper floors, you can tell them to assume that they are apartments, so each floor only needs a number label.)

Activity 10: Ready, Set, Hop!

Key idea: Applying addition or subtraction to compare lengths
Learning trajectory levels: Length Comparer (Direct, Indirect); End-to-End Length Measurer;
Length Unit Relater and Repeater; (Exploring) Consistent Length Measurer

Essentials

Make a walk-on number line (for example, draw a vertical line on an old plastic tablecloth or window shade and write number labels along it) and tape it down.

Engage

Read *Ready, Set, Hop!* by Stuart J. Murphy (Scholastic 1996). Two frog friends compete to see who needs to take fewer hops to win. Counting the hops and then comparing them provides opportunities to build equations for adding and subtracting.

Explore

Reread the story to the students, and have them describe what is happening in each picture. Point out that the information to solve the equations appears in the story itself. Pose additional questions like the following for students: If Moe took eight hops to reach the pond, but Matty hopped ten times to reach the pond, how many more hops did Matty need to get there? We might write an equation to show this problem: $10 - 8 = d$. Now suppose that Moe took four hops to reach a rock. How many hops would you expect Matty to take to reach the same rock?

Expect

- Did students pick up on the use of the words *more, plus, fewer,* and *less* to help them distinguish between adding and subtracting?

- Students may not realize the underlying assumption that the two frogs in the story hop the same distance each time they hop, but they hop differently from each other.

Extend

- Read the story a third time and have the students tally the jumps that Moe and Matty take. Does their answer match the summary at the end of the story? What's so special about the ending of the story?

- Have the students make up and illustrate other jumping situations for Moe and Matty. Have one frog hop two spaces along the number line each time, while the other frog hops three spaces each time. The students may benefit from acting out the hops on the walk-on number line (be sure it is numbered at least to 20, with arrows placed at both ends).

- Provide an empty number line (just a line with arrows drawn at both ends), and have students show hops along the top of the number line. Ask students to write numbers to indicate where each hop begins and ends. Ask students to predict the number of hops needed to reach the number 20 on a number line if a frog hops two spaces each time. Select a color and mark these hops, finding the total number of hops. Next, use another color to show what happens if the frog hops four spaces each time. Finally, show (with a different color) what happens if the frog hops five spaces with each hop.

- Give each student a ruler, and ask the students to show a partner two different ways to hop from 0 to 6 along the ruler, just like two frogs with different-sized hops. Next, have them demonstrate different ways to get from 0 to 12.

Related assessment

Combining sticks and writing number sentences: Work to find missing parts of bars of length 10 or less, given a single part. This activity reinforces measures of length as compositions of parts that make a longer whole.

Prepare materials for this assessment

Provide students with a complete set of ten numbered integer-length paper strips ranging from 1 unit long to 10 units long. Also, prepare integer-length paper strips from 11 to 18 units long.

Activity

Choose one strip and ask which strip needs to be paired with it for the two strips to be as long as the 10-unit strip. For example, lay down a strip that is 10 units long and another strip that is 7 units long. Ask which of the other strips would be needed to pair with the 7-unit strip to make a strip as long as the 10-unit strip. After students make predictions by matching strips with the 7 to make a 10, have them record their work by writing the number sentence as $10 = 7 + 3$. (The order in which the number sentence is written is important: We are saying that 10 consists of a 7-unit length and a 3-unit length.)

Next, show them the 10-unit strip, place the 7-unit strip below it (see fig. 2.7), and ask, "If we cut the longer strip and took away as much as this 7-unit strip from it, what length strip would remain?" This is modeled by $10 - 7 = 3$.

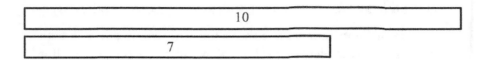

Fig. 2.7. A 7-unit strip placed under a 10-unit strip

Next, present students with any strip longer than 3 units and shorter than 19 units and ask them to build the equivalent of that long strip by using exactly two smaller strips.

Cuisenaire rods can be effective for this activity, but they will be measured in centimeters rather than inches, since they range from 1 cm unit cubes to 10 cm rods. If you use Cuisenaire rods, different-colored rods can represent various integers as lengths. Students may use the rods to represent addition or subtraction if they find out the unit length and then translate all the colors into integer values (e.g., purple rods are 4 centimeters long, and yellow rods are 5 centimeters long; so a purple rod and a yellow rod together are as long as the blue rod, which is 9 centimeters long). This would be an advanced level of challenge!

Activity 11: The Grouchy Ladybug

Key idea: Comparing by measurable attributes
Learning trajectory levels: Quantity Recognizer (Length, Area, and Volume);
*   Length Comparer (Direct, Indirect)*

Essentials

Gather chart or graph paper, markers, and a demonstration clock.

Engage

Read *The Grouchy Ladybug* by Eric Carle (Harper Trophy 1977). A ladybug spends the day (shown hour by hour) looking for an animal big enough to fight.

Explore

Go through the story a second time, this time listing the animals that the ladybug challenges to a fight. (In order, they are a yellow jacket, a stag beetle, a praying mantis, a sparrow, a lobster, a skunk, a boa constrictor, a hyena, a gorilla, a rhinoceros, an elephant, and a blue whale.) Do students notice that even the area of successive pages increases as the size of successive animals increases?

Expect

- The boa constrictor doesn't really seem to fit into the graduated-size theme. Why not? What attributes help us compare these animals? Have the students list attributes such as height, weight, width, overall length, or surface area (how big is each animal's skin?).

- What animal that is bigger than a skunk and smaller than a hyena might have been substituted for the boa constrictor? Students can consult nonfiction material on animals' sizes to help them answer this question. Talk about the real measurements that you would expect for a boa constrictor. Perhaps it would be 8 feet long and 4 inches in diameter. How would a zoo veterinarian measure a snake?

- Determine whether students can identify specific attributes of the creatures in the book, such as length or height, that can help explain the progression in their size.

- Can they find an animal that is larger than the skunk and smaller than the hyena and explain why it fits sizewise between the two? Listen for comparisons of the animals according to their length, width, weight, and height.

Extend

- Use the clocks on each page of *The Grouchy Ladybug* showing hourly intervals between 6 a.m. and 6 p.m. (half of a day) to talk about the need to use each number on the clock twice during one full day.

- It takes the ladybug one hour to get from animal to animal but 15 minutes to get from the front of the whale's head to its fin, then another 15 minutes to get from its fin to its tail, and 15 minutes after the slap of the tail to return home. What does this indicate about the size of the ladybug and the size of the whale?

- As a link to social studies or language arts, have students write a class book that would include advice to the grouchy ladybug on how to be friendlier.

Enrich

Read *More Life-Size Zoo* by Teruyuki Komiya (Seven Footer Kids 2010). Like the author's *Life-Size Zoo* (Seven Footer Kids 2009), this book shows life-size photographs of various animals, with fold-out pages and charts of interesting facts.

Or read *Biggest, Strongest, Fastest* by Steve Jenkins (Ticknor & Fields 1995). This book provides an introduction to the "world records" held by fourteen members of the animal kingdom, including the blue whale (the biggest animal).

Activity 12: Mighty Maddie

Key ideas: Comparing by weight; volume as an attribute
Learning trajectory levels: Volume Quantity Recognizer; Volume Quantifier (Comparing)

Essentials

Collect objects that are noticeably different in weight and that students can hold in their hands (e.g., a teddy bear, can of soup, pillow, piggy bank, various toys or books, plastic foam, paper clips, a toothbrush), a pan balance (if available), and Unifix cubes or a set of Cuisenaire rods.

Engage

Read *Mighty Maddie* by Stuart J. Murphy (HarperCollins 2004). Maddie has to clean up her messy room before her birthday party. As she cleans, she learns how to compare the weights of various objects.

Explore

Set out some of the objects in the story, such as books, toys, a piggy bank, a pillow, a can of soup, and a teddy bear. Allow students a chance to pick up the objects and compare their weights. Show the students two objects (e.g., a teddy bear and a can of soup). Which do they think weighs more? Have a student explain his or her answer and then pick up the objects to check. Having students compare objects by how heavy they feel when holding them is a good beginning for measuring weight.

Expect

- Students are often surprised to find that size and weight are not always directly correlated. Objects that are the same size may have different weights (e.g., a cubic foot of foam is much lighter than a cubic foot of ice), and a large object can weigh less than a small one.

- Students should be able to use gestures to indicate which of two objects is heavier by lowering the heavier object when holding one in each hand.

- Do students realize that we should not assume that size indicates weight? Can they explain this?

- After they have weighed the lightest and heaviest objects in their collection of four items, do students estimate the weight of the other two objects reasonably by assigning values between the two extreme weights?

- Later on in school and in their careers, students will need to distinguish between weight and mass. *Mass* describes the amount of matter something is made of, and *weight* is a measure of the object's force due to gravitational pull. The mass of a gorilla would be constant whether it is on the earth or the moon, but the weight of the gorilla on the moon would be approximately $1/6$ of its weight on the earth.

Extend

- Have a student stand with both arms outstretched to resemble a balance scale. Put a heavy object in one of her or his hands and see which way she or he tilts. Ask the student why it is more difficult to maintain her or his balance while holding a heavy object. Then ask the student to hold two objects of differing weights and have the other students predict which way she or he will tilt this time. What happens if you switch the objects? Can the students suggest two objects that would be about the same weight to balance the scale?

- Have students use a balance scale to compare pairs of Cuisenaire rods of varying lengths (or sets of Unifix cubes) to model number sentences for addition, such as $7 + 4 = 11$. To model this particular number sentence, ask students to place a rod that is 7 units long in one pan and then add a 4-unit-long rod to that pan. Ask them to find which rod is needed to balance the pan. The 11-unit-long rod would balance the 7- and 4-unit rods in the other pan.

- Have students use a pan balance to compare four objects of noticeably different weights. They should start by placing any two objects in the balance, one on either side. They will leave the heavier object in place and place a new object in the opposite pan. Students should keep repeating this procedure to check all four objects until they determine the heaviest one in the collection. They can then find the lightest object in the set of three remaining objects by repeating the procedure, starting with one of the three objects.

- After finding the heaviest and lightest objects, students should estimate the weight of these two objects in pounds or ounces and record their estimates. Next, have them weigh the two objects on a scale (pounds may be measured on a bathroom scale, and ounces may be measured on a postal scale, which may be available in the school office) and record their findings. Finally, have them estimate the weight of the remaining two objects on the basis of the weights of the heaviest and lightest ones.

Enrich

Read *Weight* by Henry Pluckrose (Children's Press 1995). A balance scale is shown as one of the tools used to measure weight.

Alternatively, read *Balances* by Adele Richardson (Capstone 2004). This book introduces the function, parts, and uses of balances and provides instructions for two activities that demonstrate how a balance works.

Activity 13: A House for Birdie

Key idea: Capacity as attribute
Learning trajectory levels: Length Comparer (Direct, Indirect); Volume Quantity Recognizer;
    Volume Filler; Volume Quantifier

Essentials

Gather a birdhouse, paper, tape, and cardboard boxes in a variety of sizes, such as a tissue box, a shoebox, a cereal box and a shipping box.

Engage

Read *A House for Birdie* by Stuart J. Murphy (HarperCollins 2004). Poor tiny Birdie has no house, but his friends help him find one that is not too tall, too thin, too short, too fat, too wide, or too narrow to hold him.

Explore

Show the students a birdhouse and talk about the fact that it has three dimensions. Give each student a sheet of paper, and ask them why a sheet of paper would not have worked as a house for Birdie. Explain that it is flat and has only two dimensions. Now have them try forming a birdhouse by using that sheet of paper and tape.

Expect

- Students may focus on a single dimension to compare a bird and a birdhouse, or they may coordinate two dimensions. To encourage them to focus on all three dimensions, review the drawings of birds and birdhouses on page 31 of *A House for Birdie*. For example, students may think that Spike's and Queenie's houses are the same size because both birdhouses are the same height, but this does not allow for the difference in width and depth.

- Ask students to compare the birdhouse for Birdie along all three dimensions at once. In particular, check whether they mention width, height, and depth.

Extend

- Have students construct a birdhouse out of a scrap box that would be a good place for Birdie to live.

- Ask students to write a new ending to Birdie's story. They should be sure to mention the width, height, and depth of the birdhouse that they imagine for their new ending.

Enrich

Read *Fine Feathered Friends: All About Birds* by Tish Rabe (Random House 1998). Dick and Sally find themselves on a bird-watching tour led by the Cat in the Hat after they learn what a bird is and where they live.

Another possibility is *The Best Nest* by P. D. Eastman (Random House 1968). Mr. Bird thinks his nest is the best in the world until Mrs. Bird tells him that is it all wrong. Their search for a "better" nest leads them to some peculiar spots.

Activity 14: The Mitten

Key idea: Capacity as an attribute
Learning trajectory levels: Length Comparer (Direct, Indirect); Volume Quantity Recognizer; Volume Filler; Volume Quantifier

Essentials

Gather leftover or used knitted mittens and socks of varying children's sizes, teddy bear counters (or Unifix cubes or other small, uniform items), and firm balls, including Ping Pong balls, golf balls, softballs, and basketballs.

Engage

Read *The Mitten*, adapted and illustrated by Jan Brett (Scholastic 1989). A small boy drops a mitten in the snow. When many animals decide it would make a warm home, they all crawl inside the mitten; but when one more animal crawls inside, there are too many, and they all lose their shelter.

Explore

Ask students to estimate and record which of several mittens would hold the most teddy bear counters. Next, stuff each mitten full of counters and ask students to record the findings. Which mitten held the most counters? Repeat the activity, using socks.

Expect

- Students may expect that the mitten would be overfilled only if a very large animal went inside, but in the story, it is a small animal that overfills the mitten. Explain this idea by using a cup of water that is filled to the brim. Ask students whether a small pebble would be enough to cause the water to overflow, or would we have to put in a larger object like a golf ball?

- Are students able to compare the capacity of mittens by relating how long or short and how wide or narrow they are?

- After students have measured the mittens by stuffing them with teddy bear counters, check whether they can use what they have learned from this activity to compare the capacity of various pairs of socks for holding other kinds of objects, like pebbles. Can students predict which sock can hold the most pebbles?

- Can students coordinate the attributes of long/short and wide/narrow simultaneously to describe *capacity*? Capacity is a measure of space. Asking students how much a container holds or how much "stuff" fits inside may help them focus on the attribute of capacity.

- Can students give examples of measuring units that would be more appropriate than a hand width for measuring something small, like a bug, or something vast, like the width of the room from corner to corner?

Extend

- Students might be able to hold the basketball in their hands, but this does not mean that they can completely surround it with just two hands. Holding a ball in your hands is different from surrounding it with your hands. Ask students to estimate and then check to see which ball would fit completely inside their hands.

- Have students try placing different balls in a mitten to see if any fit completely. If students found that the softball would fit completely in a mitten, even though it did not fit inside their two hands, ask them why they think that is. Students will probably note that a mitten can stretch to hold a ball bigger than their hand, but hands do not stretch.

- Have students use hand widths for measuring widths, heights, or depths of objects such as a cabinet or a bicycle. Then ask them to list some objects or spaces that would not be easy or practical to measure by using hands. For example, it would not be reasonable to use hand widths to compare different bugs. Likewise, it would be too tedious to measure a long expanse, such as the distance across the classroom from corner to corner, by using hands.

Enrich

Read *Capacity* by Henry Pluckrose (Children's Press 1995). The author includes real-life applications for finding capacity, such as how much water can be held in one object or another.

CHAPTER 3

GRADE 2: COMPARING AND UNDERSTANDING MEASURES

Big measurement ideas identified in CCSSM: Students recognize the need for standard units of measure (centimeter and inch), and they use rulers and other measurement tools with the understanding that linear measure involves an iteration of units. Students also learn to recognize that the smaller the unit, the more units they need to cover a given length.

Learning trajectory levels in this grade: Students move from making comparisons of lengths by counting end-to-end collections of nonstandard units to using measurement tools based on standard units. At this more advanced level, students are known as Consistent Length Measurers. This level incorporates understanding the relationship between unit length and the adaptive reasoning needed to use even a broken ruler to measure. As an example of one such transition, students initially compare the range of water shooters—water-projectile toys—by counting the total number of a set of sticks along the water path as the length. Later, they learn to iterate one or two measuring sticks (e.g., rulers), counting the iterations. A student's level of thinking can be assessed by checking whether she or he can measure effectively with only one or two sticks (Length Unit Relater and *Repeater* level; emphasis added). Otherwise, the student may need a complete set of sticks to span the total length (End-to-End Length Measurer level). Table 3.1 (following page) shows the learning trajectory levels for length, area, and volume for this grade.

Table 3.1. Grade 2 activities matched with Common Core State Standards and learning trajectory levels

Grade	Length LT levels	Area LT level	Volume LT levels
2	Length Direct Comparer End-to-End Length Measurer Length Unit Relater and Repeater Consistent Length Measurer	Area Unit Relater and Repeater	Volume Quantity Recognizer Volume Filler

As noted in chapter 2 (grade 1), rulers show us a careful and practical record of units that span a given length. In chapter 3 (grade 2), we help students see that the numbers along the ruler incorporate the concept of unit iteration. For example, in figure 3.1, the object labeled *YZ* might be measured using an end-to-end strategy. A student could find a length of three units by simply counting the three sticks above it. Eventually, the activities guide students to measure an object like *YZ* even if the object cannot be repositioned to the zero point on the ruler. They learn to recognize that the number labels at both ends of *YZ* are 5 and 2, and they can be used to calculate a difference of 3, the length of *YZ*.

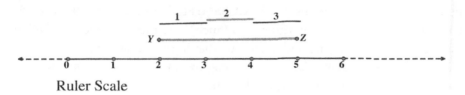

Ruler Scale

Fig. 3.1. Measuring an object with sticks and a ruler

An informal measurement post-assessment is the final activity in this chapter. Length measurement is the focus of the first eight activities, and we include one area and two volume measurement activities as foundations for work in later grades.

Table 3.2 provides an overview of the activities in the chapter. Each activity is linked to the relevant CCSSM standard and levels from a learning trajectory on length, area, or volume measurement.

Table 3.2. Grade 2 activities matched with Common Core State Standards and learning trajectory levels

General CCSSM	Learning activities	Activity-specific standards	Learning trajectory levels
Base-ten notation 2.NBT.A.1, A.2, A.3 Understanding place value 2.NBT.B.7 Add/subtract within 1,000	**Activity 1: The Long and the Short of It** Key idea: Measuring with different units	2.NBT.A.1 2.NBT.A.2 2.NBT.A.3 2.NBT.B.7	End-to-End Length Measurer
Building fluency with addition and subtraction 2.NBT.B.5 Add/subtract within 100 2.NBT.B.6 Add multiple two-digit numbers	**Activity 2: Surrounded!** Key ideas: Addition and perimeter	2.NBT.B.5 2.NBT.B.6	Consistent Length Measurer
	Activity 3: It's Time to Go! Key idea: Addition along time lines	2.NBT.B.5 2.NBT.B.6	End-to-End Length Measurer
Using standard units of measure 2.MD.A.1, A.2, A.3, A.4 Measure, estimate, and compare lengths 2.MD.B.5 Use length to model addition and subtraction	**Activity 4: X Marks the Spot!** Key ideas: Mapping and following directions	2.MD.A.1 2.MD.A.2 2.MD.B.5	Length Unit Relater and Repeater
	Activity 5: Third Time's the Charm! Key idea: Repeated measures reduce errors	2.MD.A.1 2.MD.A.2 2.MD.B.5	Length Unit Relater and Repeater
	Activity 6: The "Over a Wall" Challenge Key idea: Comparing lengths numerically	2.MD.A.1 2.MD.A.2 2.MD.B.5	Consistent Length Measurer
	Activity 7: Ridiculous Rulers Key idea: Measuring with a piece of a ruler	2.MD.A.1 2.MD.A.3 2.MD.A.4	Consistent Length Measurer
	Activity 8: Fetch the Flag! Key idea: Design and play distance games that are fair	2.MD.A.1 2.MD.A.3 2.MD.A.4	Length Direct Comparer

Table 3.2. continued

General CCSSM	Learning activities	Activity-specific standards	Learning trajectory levels
Describing and analyzing shapes 2.G.A.2 Column and row partitions of rectangles 2.OA.A.1 Using drawings to model addition and subtraction 2.OA.C.4 Quantifying arrays	**Activity 9: Is Bigger Always Better?** Key idea: Measuring area by covering with nonstandard units	2.G.A.2	Area Unit Relater and Repeater
	Activity 10: Box Up the Blocks! Key idea: Packing boxes with cubes to understand volume	2.OA.A.1 2.OA.C.4	Volume Unit Relater and Repeater
	Activity 11: Fill It Up! Key idea: Comparing capacity of containers by counting liquid units (cups)	2.G.A.2	Volume Quantity Recognizer
	Activity 12: Which Number Is Appropriate as a Measure? (Assessment)		

Activity 1: The Long and the Short of It

Key idea: Measuring with different units
Learning trajectory level: End-to-End Length Measurer

Essentials

For each student, gather paper and pencils and various measuring tools (e.g., ruler, cloth tape measure, yardstick, measuring cups, scale, thermometer) that might be used to measure classroom objects. A chalkboard, whiteboard, or chart paper also will be needed.

Engage

Introduce students to the idea of measuring length or distance with unusual end-to-end collections of objects. How many granola bars would it take to reach the top of a flagpole? How many umbrellas would reach as high as the top of a Ferris wheel? How many pieces of spaghetti would it take to reach from one corner to the opposite corner of a gymnasium? Ask students to propose some other wacky ways to compare length.

Next, read *How Long? Wacky Ways to Compare Length* by Jessica Gunderson (Picture Window Books 2014). How long is a dinosaur? How long is a ship? How long is a rocket's earth-to-moon trip? Other whimsical measurement questions are posed.

Explore

Help students make a connection between estimating and the process of measuring. First, ask them to estimate how many earthworms long a school bus would be. You may want to explain that even though you do not have a school bus available for them to measure, nor do you have an earthworm, they can still estimate and give a reasonable answer to the question.

In this case, we know something about the length of an earthworm: one earthworm is about as long as one child's hand. We also know something about the length of a school bus: if a child laid down in the aisle of the bus, the bus would be much longer than the child. The school bus would be longer than 5 students. On the other hand, it would not be as long as 30 students, even if they were kindergarteners. We might estimate that a bus is as long as 10 students if they were arranged in a line, lying from head to foot. Next, we need to relate the length of an earthworm to a child's length, and then relate the earthworm's length to the bus's length by translating through its fit with a child's length.

Ask students to work in pairs to find out how many earthworms (hands) long a child is. Next, have them find the bus's length in terms of earthworms by relating an earthworm's length to the child's length and then to the bus's length. If a child is about 10 earthworms long, a span the length of 10 students would require 10 sets of 10 earthworms. Students may need to skip-count by 10s ten times, or multiply 10×10 to find that a bus is about 100 earthworms long.

Expect

- Some of the students' estimates may be far-fetched, either much too small or much too large. Nonetheless, it is important to encourage students to make estimates without being concerned that they have to measure to produce a good estimate. Record all the estimates on a board so that the whole class can see the range. Be sure to accept all the estimates without comment, which will allow natural feedback—students will have a chance to look over the range of estimates and rethink their own.

- Check whether students match the unit to fit the attribute that they are measuring. If they intend to measure weight, they could use the weight of a stone as the unit, but they could not use a ruler. They might measure area by accumulating sheets of paper to cover the area and counting those paper sheets as units, but they could not use a thermometer. Having students include the unit label on each reported measurement supports their sense of consistency (i.e., using a weight unit to measure weight, using a length unit to measure length, or using a capacity unit to measure capacity).

Extend

- Read *Measuring Penny* by Loren Leedy (Henry Holt 1997). Lisa has an important assignment: to measure something in several different ways. She uses nonstandard units like paper clips and dog biscuits and standard units like inches and centimeters to find out the height, width, and length of her dog, Penny. Lisa also learns about measures of weight, volume, temperature, and time as well as cost comparisons, all related to her pet.

- Have students talk through attributes of the world around us that they would like to understand. How far? How cold? How big? How long would it take? How heavy? How much space does it fill? How much can it hold of something? How much does it cost?

- We may ask many similar questions to understand things in science, in engineering, or in technology.

- At the beginning of *Measuring Penny*, we learn that Lisa's teacher has asked her to measure something in as many ways as she can. She chooses to measure her dog to learn more about how her dog compares with other dogs, how tall she is in relation to Lisa's own height, how much food and water she needs, and even how much it costs to keep her. Pose the following questions to students: Let's say Penny weighs 16 pounds. What does that tell us about her? Knowing her weight may help us compare it to the weight of other animals, to Lisa's weight, or to the amount of food Penny eats each day.

- Have students brainstorm to see how many attributes of a chair one might measure. Try to measure each suggested attribute, if possible. Attributes might include the chair's seat height or the height of its back; the thickness of the seat; or its width, depth, weight, hardness, and temperature.

  For each measure, ask students to name and record an appropriate unit. They might record their work as follows:

  For the chair, we measured—

  16 inches for the height of the seat

  $3/4$ inch for the thickness of the seat

  8 pounds for its weight

- Next, ask students to share their own ideas for measuring two other items in the room (e.g., a book, a trash can, the class pet, a playground ball, a rug) by at least three attributes. Help students connect those attributes with appropriate units: weight fits with pounds and ounces; length fits with centimeters, meters, inches, feet, or yards.

Enrich

Read *Why We Measure* by Lisa Trumbauer (Yellow Umbrella Books 2003). This book explains why people take measurements by giving examples of ways that we can find out how tall, how far, how fast, or how heavy something may be. People measure to make comparisons of these attributes.

Activity 2: Surrounded!

Key ideas: Addition and perimeter
Learning trajectory level: Consistent Length Measurer

Essentials

Each student will need paper marked with large grids, at least 6 × 6 (e.g., 1-inch-square grid paper). Gather square plastic tiles that are uniform in size (inch tiles would work well); long pipe cleaners; a length of yarn (approximately 20 feet), string, or rope for the bulletin board border activity; and a tape measure that extends to 25 feet.

Note that this activity has two extensions and may require more than one class period if you choose to complete all the parts.

Engage

Read *Racing Around* by Stuart J. Murphy (HarperCollins 2002). It's a long way around Perimeter Path! Mike's brother and sister say he's too young to compete in the 15-kilometer bike race. If Mike gets a chance, he knows he can make it all the way around.

Explore

Have students design walking routes that are exactly 12 city blocks long. Hand out plastic tiles and the grid paper. Ask them to draw at least four different routes to scale on the grid paper, using the tiles to show city blocks.

Be sure to explain that walking a city block means walking from one corner of a block along the same street to reach the next corner. For example, if we walked from the corner of 2nd Avenue and Elm Street to the next corner at 3rd Avenue and Elm Street (see fig. 3.2 on the following page), we would say we had walked one city block, or just one block. Notice that we are not measuring in entire blocks but instead in block edges. So if we were to walk all the way around this block, first along Elm Street, then along 3rd Avenue and on around to return to our starting point at the first corner, we would have to walk four block edges; in mathematical terms, we would say that the *perimeter* of the block is four block edges.

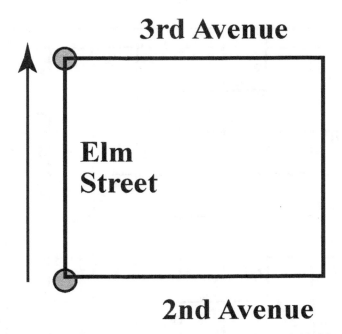

3rd Avenue

Elm Street

2nd Avenue

Fig. 3.2. Elm Street between 2nd Avenue and 3rd Avenue is one city block long.

Expect

- In the Explore activity, students may assume that their routes need to be convex in shape (without indentations), not concave, but routes with "dents" work just as well—see figure 3.3.

- In the first extension activity, can students explain why measuring for the bulletin board border with a piece of rope is best? Do they notice and see the importance of rounding once instead of rounding three times?

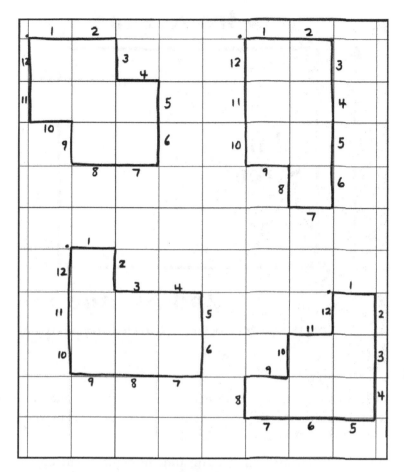

Fig. 3.3. Examples of walking routes with a perimeter of 12 city blocks

Extend

- Measuring paths along grid-paper routes makes it easy to count blocks. But if we must measure around an object without grid marks, we can measure in parts and add them up, or measure the object all together. Perimeter may be measured all at once as a continuous path or measured in steps by finding the length of all the parts separately and then finding the sum of those parts (see fig. 3.4, which shows three ways to measure a border around a bulletin board). Using this latter approach to measure a path introduces more error because any errors from each partial measurement accumulate. Instead, we recommend measuring the entire path at once by wrapping a string around the path and then finding the length of the straight-stretched string. This method can produce only one possible measurement error.

If we set out to measure around a bulletin board for a border to be placed along both sides and the top of the bulletin board, how many units long should this border strip be in all? (See fig. 3.4.) Encourage students to try measuring the entire path, as well as each side separately, and compare the outcomes. Discuss whether both approaches yield the same measurement in every case.

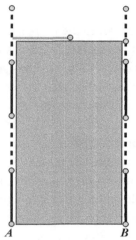

3 (side) + 2 (top) + 3 (side) = 8 units long

Here we rounded down to measure along each of the three sides. We would need 8 units of border.

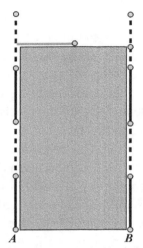

4 (side) + 2 (top) + 4 (top) = 10 units long

Here we rounded up to measure along each of the three sides. In this case, we would need 10 units of border.

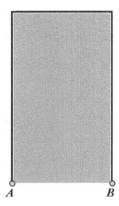

When we stretched a rope around the bulletin board from *A* to *B* and then measured the outstretched rope, we found that the border would need to be 9 units long to the nearest unit.

Fig. 3.4. Methods for measuring a three-sided border for a bulletin board

- Have students discuss two possible ways to report the length of the bike race in the story *Racing Around*. The length of the race was reported as 15 kilometers, but it might have been reported as 15,000 meters. Does it matter which way we report the length of the race? The first report of 15 kilometers tells us that the race course was longer than 14 kilometers but shorter than 16 kilometers. But reporting the length of the race course as 15,000 meters means the course is longer than 14,999 meters and shorter than 15,001 meters.

Which unit, the kilometer or the meter, provides the more accurate measure of the distance around the course? (The meter.) With regard to the bike race in the story, measuring to the nearest kilometer was good enough, and measuring to the nearest meter may have been unnecessary. Being accurate and precise with measurements requires more effort and is often costly.

Some situations require great accuracy and precision. For example, track and field events in Olympic competitions must be uniform in length from one field to another and over time so that records can be established and compared. When an Olympic sprinter breaks a world record in an official race, he can assume that he actually ran faster than the previous record holder because even if it is a different course, both courses were constructed to measure precisely 100 meters. In fact, they may even have been measured to the nearest centimeter, to allow careful comparisons like this one.

Enrich

Read *Ancient Greece and the Olympics* by Mary Pope Osborne (Scholastic 2004). This Magic Tree House Fact Tracker volume details the history of the first Olympic Games.

Activity 3: It's Time to Go!

Key idea: Addition along timelines
Learning trajectory level: End-to-End Length Measurer

Essentials

For the extension activities, gather large sheets of paper to draw time lines, a timer or alarm clock that can track intervals at least 30 minutes long, sticky notes, and adding machine or cash register tape. For the first extension activity, you will need at least two slices of bread, plates, and child-safe knives for each pair of students and enough peanut butter and jelly for the class.

Engage

Read *Get Up and Go!* by Stuart J. Murphy (HarperCollins 1996). Time lines and addition help a girl stay on track while she gets ready for school.

Explore

After reading the book, discuss with students the progress that the girl makes while she prepares for school. The story is told from the point of view of her dog, who helps her keep track of her progress by showing her time lines.

Look for several ways to help students connect the sequence of elapsed times (using numbers) with the time lines (visual displays). There are summary time lines on pages 10, 16, 23, and 29 of *Get Up and Go!* that can help students estimate the amount of elapsed time, count all the spaces between the minute marks on the lines, count the minute marks, or even skip-count by 5-minute spans. For example, the combined time line on page 16 shows a subtotal of 18 minutes, but skip-counting by 5-minute spans (by using hand motions to indicate repeating the 5-minute span along the entire time line) would indicate that approximately 20 minutes have passed. In another example, if students skip-count by 5-minute spans along the entire time line shown at the bottom of pages 22 and 23, they will count six 5-minute spans, which approximates the 31 minutes shown on the time line to have passed. Doing this may help students relate 30 minutes to half an hour.

It is important for students to visualize the passage of time both as a length (a time line) and as the collection of tick marks around half the clock face (between 12:00 and 6:00), with each tick mark showing the passage of 1 minute. A clock shows the passage of time overall, as well as the passage of single minutes.

Expect

Students may be inclined to use the numbers from the text to answer questions about the number of minutes that have gone by so far without relating those numbers to the time lines. However, we want students to learn to interpret multiple representations that record the passage of time in the story. At the end of the book (pages 30 and 31), the author shows how several representations of the girl's morning activities are connected: There is a list of the activities (e.g., snuggle, wash, eat), the corresponding number of minutes that each activity requires (e.g., 5, 3, 8), and the colored line segments (e.g., purple, orange, violet) that represent different events during the girl's preparations.

Extend

- Follow the snack-making suggestion on page 34 of *Get Up and Go!* Have students pair up to write out the steps required to make a snack, such as a peanut butter and jelly sandwich. (If there is any chance that any of your students have a peanut allergy, substitute another snack.) Next, one student in each pair should make a sandwich by following the steps, while the other student keeps track of the time in minutes. Finally, ask students to make a time line that shows how long it takes to do each of the steps in making and eating the sandwich. You may want to have students make posters to share their time lines and explain how long it takes to "cook" a peanut butter and jelly sandwich.

- Make a record of your class's morning activities. Use a timer (or alarm clock) that will ring every 30 minutes. As you go through the day, keep a cumulative journal of classroom activities that took place during those 30-minute segments. Record each successive activity along a time line on the board at the front of the room for the whole class to see. Sticky notes can be used to place events along the time line. The classroom schedule need not fit conveniently into these half-hour segments, but the regular timer alerts will help students notice the duration of various activities.

- Working from the class's time line, students can record the timing of classroom activities along their own time lines, using adding machine tape or another long, markable medium. Figure 3.5 shows a way to relate time on a clock face to the time in hours along a time line. This clock was "rolled," starting at the 6-hour mark, and leaves a dot at each hour mark along a flat surface, eventually returning to the 6-hour mark again.

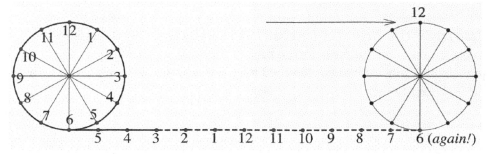

Fig. 3.5. Unrolling a clock face would make a line with hour marks like a time line.

- Ask students to imagine being part of a PE class that will be warming up, running laps, playing a game for 12 minutes, cooling down for 3 minutes, and then lining up for dismissal during the final 3 minutes of class. Use the time line shown in figure 3.6 to find the duration of the entire PE class.

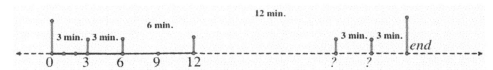

Get in squads during the first 3 minutes. Do warm-up exercises for the next 3 minutes.
Run laps for 6 minutes. Play a game that lasts 12 minutes. Walk to cool down for 3 minutes.
Line up during the last 3 minutes of the class.

Fig. 3.6. How many minutes long is this PE class?

- Use the time line in figure 3.7 to find the missing information, indicated by the blanks:

  The bus ride takes two times as many minutes as the walk to the bus requires. It takes _____ minutes. Shopping lasts three times as many minutes as the walk to the bus. That is _____ minutes. It takes _____ minutes to go from home to the store and back.

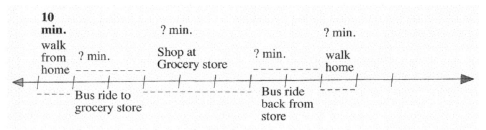

Fig. 3.7. How long does the shopping trip take?

Enrich

Read *Froggy Gets Dressed* by Jonathan London (Scholastic 1992). Froggy wants to play in the snow, but he has to go back in his house again and again to put on parts of his clothes until he is too tired to go out anymore. His preparations are detailed step by step.

Activity 4: X Marks the Spot!

Key ideas: Mapping and following directions
Learning trajectory level: Length Unit Relater and Repeater

Essentials

Make copies of figures 3.8 and 3.9 for each student (see Map of the Town and Mom's Directions to the Surprise Party at More4U). Gather #1 size paper clips (two for each student) and plain paper.

Engage

Read *Treasure Map* by Stuart J. Murphy (HarperCollins 2004). A map guides the Elm Street Kids' Club into a magical world—but it's real-life map-reading skills (like understanding distance, scale, direction, and symbols) and some guidance from Petey the parrot that will lead the kids to a buried treasure.

Explore

Ask students to imagine that they have been invited to a surprise party. They need to find their way to the surprise party by using a map of their town. Give each student a copy of the map (fig. 3.8) and the note from Mom with directions from their home to the party location (fig. 3.9). Remind students that they may travel only along the north-south streets and east-west streets shown on the grid. Also, explain that the grid is marked to show each block along each street.

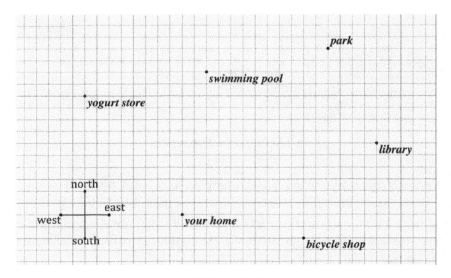

Fig. 3.8. Map of the town

From home, go north 4 blocks, then go 4 blocks east.

Next, go north 2 blocks, and then go 6 blocks east.

Now, go 6 blocks south, and then go 6 blocks east.

Next go 12 blocks north, 4 blocks west, and then 2 blocks north to finish your route. You should be at the surprise party location now.

Fig. 3.9. Mom's directions to the surprise party

Figure 3.10 shows the completed path. Ask students to tell how many blocks they traveled altogether.

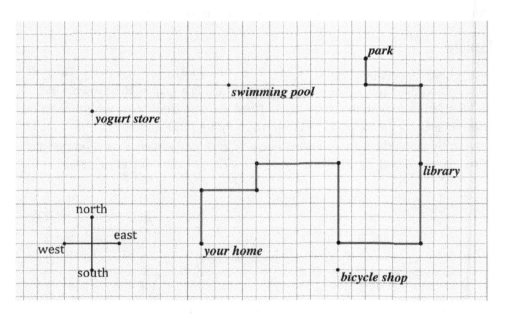

Fig. 3.10. Path to the surprise party

Next, ask students to map out a shorter path to get back home after the party. Write instructions for others to follow. How many blocks long is this path? How much shorter is it than the original path? Is it the shortest possible path? Some students may draw diagonal lines to create shorter paths, but these are not realistic unless you are flying as the crow does!

Expect

- Students often have a difficult time measuring with rulers because they misunderstand the zero point along the ruler and because they tend to count endpoints instead of the intervals between number labels on the ruler. Consequently, we designed the first extension activity to use paper clips instead of rulers to encourage students to relate the repeated image of paper clips to their image of the units along the ruler (either centimeters or inches). Paper clips, or any nonstandard linear unit, are a useful tool for helping students learn to measure and to anticipate the meaningful use of the ruler as a device that comprises iterated units along a single-scaled system of markings and number labels. Look for ways to help students relate their use of "trains" of paper clips to the "trains" of inch-long spaces along a ruler (see fig. 3.11).

Fig. 3.11. Coordinating a "train" of paper clips with a set of inch-long intervals along a ruler

- In the first extension activity, students may link, overlap, or allow gaps between the paper clips, producing inaccurate measures of path length. Some students might struggle to measure with only two paper clips if they are used to measuring paths by placing a complete set of unit objects and counting them all at once (end-to-end length measuring).

- Some students may struggle to follow the directions for north, south, and so on; and others may have difficulty keeping the angles between the direction changes at 90 degrees. The greatest challenge that students encounter as they learn to iterate units without having enough units to lay them out end to end is leaving gaps or overlapping the units. If they are struggling with this concept, it may help to have them measure a single part of the path (or object) several times, helping them work toward finding the same measure every time. This may help the student to see a persistent problem (either gapping or overlapping).

- To help students who miss the bull's-eye in the treasure-map activity, have them repeat their work, moving the paper clips and recording the location of each clip as they move along and form a path.

Extend

- Play a treasure-map game to give students practice in measuring paths by using just one or two units that are moved in a leapfrog manner, instead of having enough units to fill the entire length of the path. To play the game, give students a blank sheet of paper and exactly two paper clips (use #1 size paper clips). Use the paper clips to mark a starting point for the treasure-map activity, placing the starting location one paper clip north and one paper clip over to the east from the bottom left corner of the paper. Have students mark a compass rose near the starting point on their map drawing (see the compass rose in figs. 3.8 and 3.10 showing north, east, south, and west). Have students follow the treasure-map directions below, using one paper clip to represent each step taken in the treasure hunt. They will have to leapfrog the two paper clips to count steps along the treasure path. It may help if students see you step through the directions to demonstrate how to move the clips.

   Treasure-map directions:

   Begin by taking 5 steps and walking north.

   Walk to the east, taking 3 steps.

   Go south, taking 2 steps.

   Now, go east, walking 3 steps.

   Finally, go south just 1 step. Mark an X to show where you will dig for treasure.

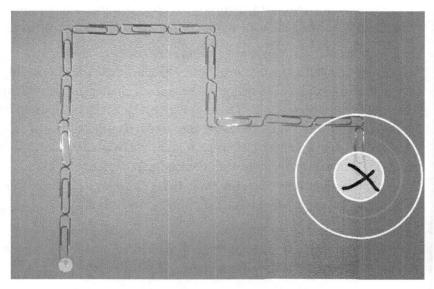

Fig. 3.12. A full set of paper clips showing the entire path to the treasure

Have students keep a record of their path as they step along it. Make a transparency similar to figure 3.13 to lay over the map drawings made by each student, and award points for accuracy in finding the treasure location. Perhaps hitting the inner ring merits 10 points, the second ring 5 points, and the outer ring 3 points.

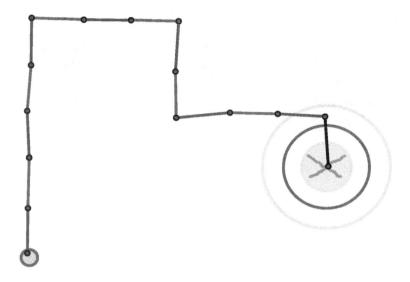

Fig. 3.13. A map showing a possible record of the paper-clip path taken to find the treasure

- When students have completed the treasure-map game, ask them to write out directions to backtrack along the same path, moving from the treasure back to the starting point on the map. This backtrack journey will begin by taking one step north.

- Ask students to design another treasure-map game based on a new path. They will write the directions and try out the steps to locate their treasure. They may measure with a unit other than paper clips. When the game is ready, have them try it with a classmate.

- Look back at the original map of the town (figs. 3.8 and 3.10), with the park as the place for the surprise party. Challenge students to mark the points that are 8 blocks away from home, traveling directly north, east, or west of the home point (8 blocks south is off the map). Ask students to show and explain which of these points is furthest away from the park.

- Have students make a three-dimensional model (using clay and cardboard) of the school playground or a nearby park. Suggest that they try to keep objects at the right distances in relation to other objects, but do not expect them to scale the models beyond using visual estimation.

Have them highlight their favorite piece of equipment on the playground and use their finger to trace a pathway from another spot to that piece of equipment. For example, ask them to trace a path from a drinking fountain to the slide. Talk about how far that is in their model and how far it really is on the actual playground or in the park.

Enrich

Read *Mapping Penny's World* by Loren Leedy (Square Fish 2003). Lisa's teacher says students can make a map of any place, so Lisa starts with her bedroom. She includes all the things people will need to read the map, including a scale and a key to the symbols she used. Lisa has so much fun making maps that she decides to map her dog Penny's world.

Activity 5: Third Time's the Charm!

Key idea: Repeated measures reduce errors

Learning trajectory level: Length Unit Relater and Repeater

Essentials

Gather rulers, measuring sticks (yard or meter), tape measures, masking tape, and sticky notes.

Engage

Ask students to find the distance across a large room (e.g., a gymnasium) by counting the number of steps needed to walk across the room, and have them record the distance. Counting steps while walking from one side of a room to the other is a way of measuring if it involves counting regular steps as units of distance (or length). Have them discuss their results with a classmate. Is one student wrong and the other right if their results differ? Note that students may not notice the effect of the varying lengths of their strides.

Next, ask students to walk across the same room again and record the number of steps again. Challenge students to compare their second measurement of this distance with their first measurement. Ask them to write both of their measurements on a sticky note and circle the better measurement. How should they decide which measurement is better? Encourage students to solve this dilemma by checking the distance one more time. This third measurement should sway them toward their first or second measure. The third measure is the charm!

Ask students to post their findings on the front wall and discuss the entire collection of measurements. What is the most common number of steps taken? It is OK if students struggle with this question before the data are organized. Posing the question before they have organized the data helps them realize the value of doing so.

Explore

Now ask students to help arrange the data from this set of measures in order along an empty number line on the front board (see fig. 3.14). Look for groups of data that cluster together along the number line. Can you find at least one such cluster of numbers? Which number is located at the center of that cluster? Are there extremely small measures or large measures posted along the number line? Mathematicians call the numbers that are isolated from the clusters at the middle *outliers*. These numbers may be ignored if we are interested in finding the best number to report the measurement of the distance across the room. Some numbers would not fit for this measurement. Encourage students to think of some numbers that would not have made sense. Perhaps they will say that $1/2$, 1, or 3 steps would be too few steps to get across the room. Similarly, they may suggest that 1,000 steps is not a realistic measurement.

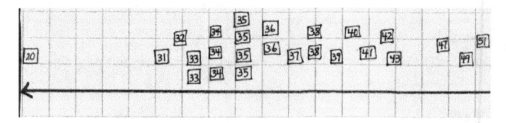

Fig. 3.14. A number line with clustered step-count data

It is important to discuss the reason that students' measurements were not all the same. What do students say about this? Explain that *variation* is a way to describe different results. Students may mention that they do not have the same foot size or shoe size, or that they take different strides. Maybe some took regular strides and others took longer strides (super steps!).

If a new student enrolled in the class tomorrow and measured the same distance in steps, how many steps would we expect him or her to take? Do students expect the measurement to be close to the center of a cluster?

Extend

- Ask students to estimate the distance along the longer dimension of the room and record their estimates. Encourage them to remember what they determined about the width of the room and use that information to make this estimate. How did they estimate the length as compared with the width? Did they estimate a number of steps that was larger or smaller than the width, or were the estimates the same? Now have them measure the distance to check their estimates.

- Ask students to use the measurement of the width of the room—shown in figure 3.15 as *GA*—to estimate and record the length of a path like *GB*. Then have them measure this path and discuss their estimates in relation to the length of *GA* and to their measurement of *GB*. Using what they learned from finding the length of *GB*, have them estimate and check paths *GC* and *GD*. Students should record their estimates and label them by the name of the path. Note that the placement of points *B* and *C* in the room does not have to be exact, but try to spread them apart somewhat evenly between the corners of the room, labeled *A* and *D* here.

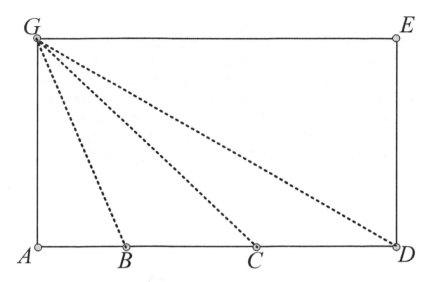

Fig. 3.15. If we know the length of *GA*, how long are *GB*, *GC*, and *GD*?

- Have students compare several (at least three) water shooters—water-projectile toys—by experimenting and collecting evidence to determine which is best (see the article listed below in the Enrich section for background information). First, students should predict the distance that each water shooter would cover. Will they compare the greatest distance reached by each one or the typical distance reached? Are some of the shooters more consistent than others, repeatedly reaching some distance? Then students should directly compare them by trying them. Encourage them to record measures by using iteration of a ruler or measuring stick, as well as a tape measure, to see which is more helpful. Which water shooter stores the most water? Does that affect how far it reaches? Have students summarize their findings in a mock report to a retail store that wants to promote the best products.

- As an adaptation of the water-shooter activity, have students crunch up sheets of paper to use as "snowballs" and then toss them to compare throwing distances. Measure the length of successive tosses.

Expect

On the basis of the second extension activity, how did students relate the estimation and measurement of one length to the next length, from *GA* to *GB*, *GC*, and finally *GD*? Did their estimates improve?

Enrich

Draw on "A Super Way to Soak in Linear Measurement" by Terri L. Kurz (*Teaching Children Mathematics* 18 [May 2012], pp. 536–41). A teacher discusses comparing different Super Soaker–style squirt guns to find how far they reach. The students observe differences in repeatability and check the squirt guns to see if they launch water as far as the manufacturer claims in the advertisements. What angle should you use to hold the gun? How fast do you pull the trigger? The article provides guidance on setting up an investigation of several shooters.

Activity 6: The "Over a Wall" Challenge

Key idea: Comparing lengths numerically
Learning trajectory level: Consistent Length Measurer

Essentials

Each student will need a 30-centimeter/12-inch standard ruler, a 14-centimeter paper strip marked at 2-centimeter intervals, an unmarked 14-centimeter paper strip, a printed paper version of a broken portion of a centimeter ruler (approximately 10 centimeters long), and a 14-centimeter paper strip marked at 1-centimeter intervals. Figure 3.16 shows the last four measuring tools in a smaller size; see More4U for a blackline showing them actual size.

Pairs of students will use several different tools: a pair of standard centimeter rulers (30 centimeters long), or a broken ruler (approximately 10 centimeters long, showing the 4-centimeter to 14-centimeter portion) paired with a standard ruler, or a pair of identical unmarked 14-centimeter paper strips, or a 14-centimeter paper strip marked at 2-centimeter intervals paired with a 14-centimeter paper strip with standard 1-centimeter markings.

Engage

Have the class watch a pair of students seated back-to-back as they compare a pair of line segments drawn on two separate sheets of paper. The line segment drawn on one sheet should be 7 inches long, and the other segment should be 7 centimeters long. At the top of the page with the segment that is 7 inches long, write "Measure with inches"; at the top of the other page, write "Measure with centimeters." Give each student a standard ruler that includes both scales. Ask students to try to compare the length of the two segments by talking but without turning around. Each student can measure only the segment on his or her page because he or she cannot see the sheet held by the other student. Ask the pair to discuss their strategies for measuring while the rest of the class listens.

Important: Without notifying the entire class, encourage both students to report their measure as a number value *without* reporting the unit type (that is, students should not say "7 inches" or "7 centimeters"). If one student measures the line segment in inches and the other in centimeters, as we expect, they will both say something like "The segment is 7 long." After they conclude that both line segments are equal (congruent) in length because both measure "7 long," have them turn around to compare the two line segments directly. They will "discover" that one is shorter than the other! Draw students' attention to the importance of measures having a reference unit (e.g., inches or centimeters) and to the value of careful communication about quantities. In this activity, we have dramatized the need for naming units to help students pay attention while they continue to explore.

Explore

Next, have students work in pairs to make comparisons between line segments. Give each pair of students an instruction card and the measuring tools described on their card (cards can be based on the examples in fig. 3.17 on p. 104). The students should work back-to-back, or on two sides of a visual divider so they cannot see each other's line segments and what they are doing to measure those segments. The goal is for the students to talk about their measurement actions by using common words.

Alternatively, this activity may be conducted with just one pair of students at a time; the pair sits where the first pair did, and the teacher asks the rest of the class to examine the pair's reasoning and the outcome of the task.

Expect

- Some students may not realize that every measure must be associated with a unit; counting alone does not allow comparison if we do not know the length of the units that are reported in the count. When measuring with a broken ruler, as in the extension activity, some students may report the number that falls at the end of the measured object without regard to the number of units that represent the difference between the starting and ending points along the ruler. Some students may not realize that a broken ruler can still be useful.

- If students are able to adapt to a variety of measuring tools, they are likely to have a well-developed conceptual foundation for measuring length. Otherwise, students may not yet understand that a line segment that is 6 centimeters can be measured by noting that it fits between the 0 point and the 6 point on a standard centimeter ruler or by noting that it fits between the 4 point and the 10 point on any centimeter ruler, even if the first portion of the ruler is broken and missing.

Extend

Have students measure pairs of line segments drawn on paper. See figure 3.17 again for suggested pairings that list which tool should be used to measure each segment. Students will then report which segment is longer or if they are the same length. Some of the suggested pairings are equal in length; others differ by at least 2 centimeters. The lengths to be compared should be equal in length to the paper strips (approximately 14 centimeters), longer by at least 2 centimeters, or shorter by at least 2 centimeters. You also could pair line segments that are twice or half the length of the paper strips (plus/minus 2 centimeters).

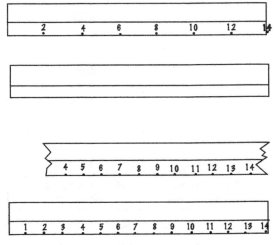

Fig. 3.16. Centimeter measuring tools

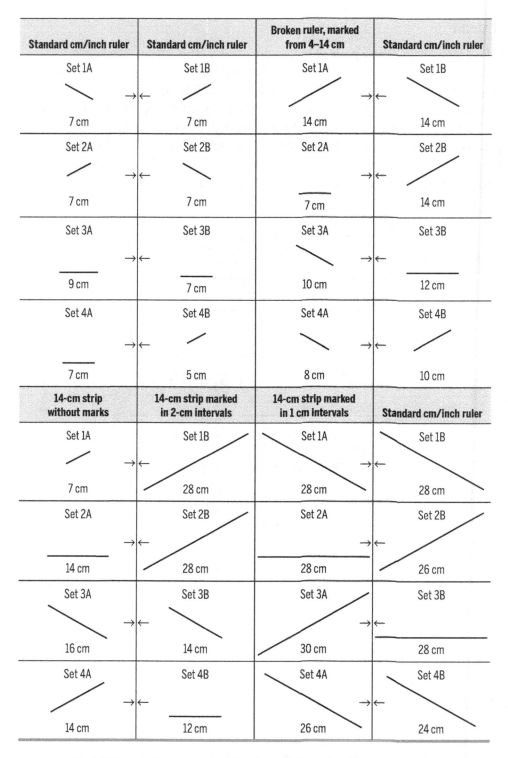

Standard cm/inch ruler	Standard cm/inch ruler	Broken ruler, marked from 4–14 cm	Standard cm/inch ruler
Set 1A — 7 cm	Set 1B — 7 cm	Set 1A — 14 cm	Set 1B — 14 cm
Set 2A — 7 cm	Set 2B — 7 cm	Set 2A — 7 cm	Set 2B — 14 cm
Set 3A — 9 cm	Set 3B — 7 cm	Set 3A — 10 cm	Set 3B — 12 cm
Set 4A — 7 cm	Set 4B — 5 cm	Set 4A — 8 cm	Set 4B — 10 cm
14-cm strip without marks	**14-cm strip marked in 2-cm intervals**	**14-cm strip marked in 1 cm intervals**	**Standard cm/inch ruler**
Set 1A — 7 cm	Set 1B — 28 cm	Set 1A — 28 cm	Set 1B — 28 cm
Set 2A — 14 cm	Set 2B — 28 cm	Set 2A — 28 cm	Set 2B — 26 cm
Set 3A — 16 cm	Set 3B — 14 cm	Set 3A — 30 cm	Set 3B — 28 cm
Set 4A — 14 cm	Set 4B — 12 cm	Set 4A — 26 cm	Set 4B — 24 cm

Fig. 3.17. Example line-segment pairings for measurement and comparison tasks

Enrich

Read *If You Were an Inch or Centimeter* by Marcie Aboff (Picture Window Books 2009). This book describes the usefulness of standard units of length measure and presents both English and metric systems.

Activity 7: Ridiculous Rulers

Key idea: Measuring with a piece of a ruler
Learning trajectory level: Consistent Length Measurer

Essentials

For this activity, collect the students' own rulers because they will be using special broken rulers to solve some measurement questions.

Cut strips from construction paper for students to measure. For the initial activity, each student will need one of the following: a 3-inch orange strip, a 4-inch blue strip, a 5-inch green strip, or a 6-inch yellow strip. For the first extension activity, provide each student with one of the following: a 7-inch black strip, an 8-inch red strip, or a 9-inch gray strip. For the second extension activity, each student will need a $3^1/_2$-inch brown paper strip, a $2^1/_2$-inch pink strip, or a $1^1/_2$-inch purple strip. Finally, make a copy of the broken ruler shown in figure 3.18 for each student (see More4U for a blackline master) and cut the rulers out.

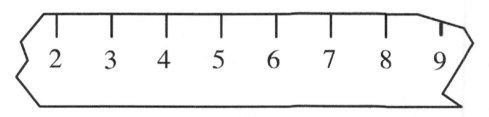

Fig. 3.18. A broken inch ruler

Engage

Imagine that a student closes her ruler into a drawer without having it entirely inside the drawer. Suppose that it is her only ruler, and now it is broken into two parts! But her friend says, "Good! Now we have two rulers, one for each of us!" This statement is confusing to the first student. "How can you measure with a broken ruler?" she asks. Ask students to recommend ways to do this.

Have students draw the broken ruler described, showing both parts and including the numbers and tick marks. Discuss their drawings of broken rulers. Next, give each student a copy of the broken ruler shown in figure 3.18, and ask students to compare their drawing to that ruler. Draw their attention to the spacing of the tick marks and the placement of numbers in relation to the tick marks. Afterward, collect their drawings and ask them to use the blackline version for the following activities.

Explore

Give each student one strip of colored paper from the collection you cut earlier. Each student will receive either a 3-inch orange strip, a 4-inch blue strip, a 5-inch green strip, or a 6-inch yellow strip. Ask students to record an estimate in inches of the length of their paper strips. Next, challenge students to use the blackline broken ruler to check the length of their paper strips. Be sure to avoid suggesting that students might use an unbroken ruler to measure their strips. Instead, help them find several ways to measure with the broken ruler, as shown in figure 3.19.

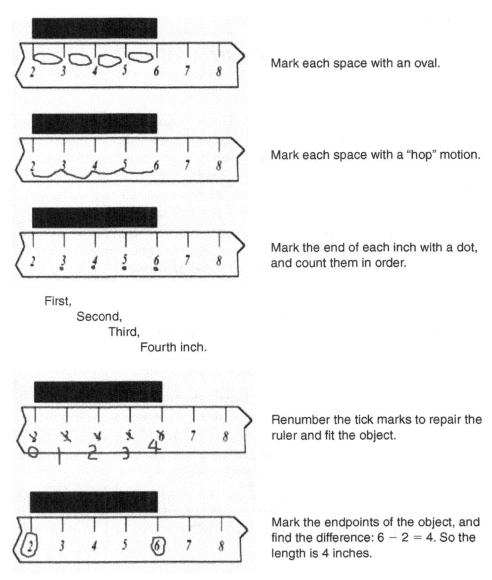

Mark each space with an oval.

Mark each space with a "hop" motion.

Mark the end of each inch with a dot, and count them in order.

First,
 Second,
  Third,
   Fourth inch.

Renumber the tick marks to repair the ruler and fit the object.

Mark the endpoints of the object, and find the difference: 6 − 2 = 4. So the length is 4 inches.

Fig. 3.19. Ways to use a broken ruler to measure length

After students have estimated and measured their strips, organize and report their findings, as suggested in figure 3.20.

Color of strip	Orange	Blue	Green	Yellow
Length estimates	3 in.	4 in.	5 in.	6 in.
	4 in.	6 in.	6 in.	8 in.
	3 in.	5 in.	6 in.	7 in.
	5 in.	4 in.	5 in.	7 in.
	5 in.	5 in.	7 in.	8 in.
	3 in.	4 in.	5 in.	6 in.
Actual lengths	3 inches	4 inches	5 inches	6 inches

Fig. 3.20. Sample strip-length estimates

Expect

- For the Explore activity, expect students to report a variety of measurements for their strips. They might, for example, line up a strip at the beginning of the ruler and report the number at the other end of the strip automatically. If the left edge of a 3-inch orange strip is aligned with the tick mark labeled 2, the other end will reach to the tick mark labeled 5, so these students would report the length as 5 inches. Others may count all tick marks along the object, including the first one, and report that it is 4 inches long. Finally, others will, correctly, count the spaces between the tick marks as inches and report a measure of 3 inches.

- How close are students' estimates to their measures? Can students measure with different starting positions along the ruler to find the length of a strip? For example, the 3-inch orange strip can be positioned between the tick marks labeled 2 and 5, 3 and 6, 4 and 7, or 5 and 8.

- In the second extension activity, students may report that the $3\frac{1}{2}$-inch strip measures $4\frac{1}{2}$ inches. They may explain that they saw the half inch between the 3 and the 4 and say, "So it is $4\frac{1}{2}$ inches." You can encourage them to see the length of the strip as more than 3 but less than 4; halfway between the two makes $3\frac{1}{2}$ inches. Another approach may be to relate length measurement to reporting their age after one birthday and before the next. For example, if a student has turned 7 years old but is not yet 8 years old, he is likely to report that he is $7\frac{1}{2}$ years old, not $8\frac{1}{2}$ years old.

Extend

- Hand out the 7-inch, 8-inch, and 9-inch strips, one for each student. Ask students to estimate and then find the length of their strips by using the blackline broken ruler and record their findings on a common section of the board according to the color of their strips. Ask the students in each group (by color) to review their measurements and reach a consensus to report. Look for ways to help them reach consensus by supporting their efforts to measure with the broken ruler, which is too short to measure any of these strips in a single step. Did anyone fold an 8-inch red strip in half, measure that, and then double the answer? Did anyone measure the first 6 inches of the 9-inch gray strip, mark that length on the strip, and then measure the 3-inch remainder of the strip by repositioning it?

- Hand out the 2¹/₂-inch, 3¹/₂-inch, and 4¹/₂-inch strips, one for each student. Again, ask students to estimate and then find the length of their strips by using the blackline broken ruler and record their findings on a common section of the board according to the color of their strips. Ask the students in each group (by color) to review their findings and reach a consensus to report. Look for ways to help them reach consensus by supporting their efforts to measure with a ruler that does not have increments smaller than an inch. Students might decide to add markings halfway between the tick marks on their broken rulers to help them measure these strips. Did anyone do this? Did anyone use visual estimates to report the half inch between number marks?

Enrich

Read *What in the World Is an Inch?* by Mary Elizabeth Salzmann (ABDO 2009). This author demonstrates the use of rulers, yardsticks, and tape measures and includes measurement scenarios involving mixed units—for example, both feet and inches are needed to measure a table that is 2 feet 6 inches long.

Activity 8: Fetch the Flag!

Key idea: Design and play distance games that are fair
Learning trajectory level: Length Direct Comparer

Essentials

Gather a piece of rope (about 20 feet long) and cones to mark lines on a field or open floor, tools for measuring length or distance such as metersticks or yardsticks or several jump ropes of the same length (6 to 10 feet), and notepaper and pencils for each student.

Engage

Display all three parts of figure 3.21 on the front board or a poster. Tell students:

> In each of these designs for a game called Fetch the Flag, each circle represents a player. Players must wait behind the line until a whistle is blown. Then they race to fetch the flag. Whoever fetches the flag is the winner.

Ask students to evaluate the fairness of each of these game designs and to support their reasoning.

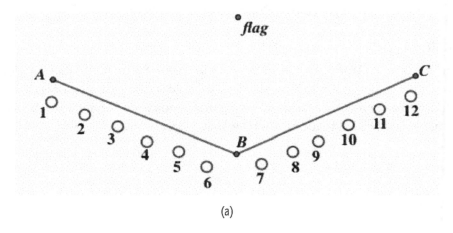

(a)

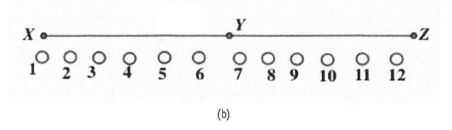

(b)

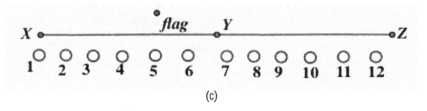

(c)

Fig. 3.21. Are these game designs fair?

Explore

Go outside (or to a large open-floor area indoors), and test the three proposed designs for a fair game, starting with the design in figure 3.21a. Have some students play the game while others observe and make written notes or drawings to evaluate the fairness of the game. If students struggle to evaluate the game, ask them to identify the starting positions offering the most and least advantage. If possible, have the observers play a second round of the game while the players from the first round observe, noting which positions have the most and least advantage.

Help students summarize their observations about this proposed design. If they have not yet measured the path lengths for various positions, ask them to make some measurements to support their analysis of the relative advantages of several positions. Suggest several options for measuring paths if necessary, such as using jump ropes, yardsticks, or their own steps. Arrange the cones to show where each player would begin the game for each game scenario.

Have students repeat the routine of playing, observing, and discussing the designs shown in parts (b) and (c) of figure 3.21. Continue to encourage students to measure paths to support their evaluation of the fairness of these designs. Have them summarize their work so far by asking them to write about their experiences, their observations, and their evaluations to select the fairest design.

Extend

Introduce several (at least three) other designs for the Fetch the Flag game (see fig. 3.22 for ideas). These designs should all involve a closed figure, as shown. Ask students to focus on the length of the paths shown for runners 1 and 2 in each of the designs. Compare the relative advantage for the two runners in each design. The sequence of triangle, square, and octagon shown in figure 3.22 would lead naturally to fair positions for all runners if they were all stationed in a circle. One definition for a circle itself is "the set of all points equidistant (the same distance) from a single point, the center." A circle arrangement would be completely fair for all players starting on the edge and competing to reach the circle center, so a circular design is a perfectly fair solution for a Fetch the Flag game.

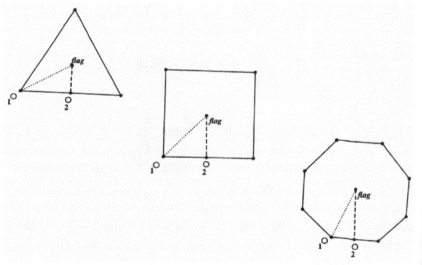

Fig. 3.22. Additional designs for the Fetch the Flag game

Expect

- Students may not see the differences that make a game fair or not unless they have moved beyond the level of merely counting steps. For example, students at such a stage might consider two paths to be the same length if two people take the same number of steps to traverse them, without taking step length into account. Encourage them to compare two paths by using very different step sizes and reconsider whether counting steps seems fair.

- The fairest starting situation for a group of runners whose objective is to reach a single object (as in Fetch the Flag) is to be stationed in a circle around the object. Ask students to explain why a circle provides the situation that is most fair for such a game. Eventually, students will learn that the definition of a circle is a collection of points (a locus) that are all equidistant from a single point (the center point of the circle).

When working with the closed shapes in figure 3.22, students may be comparing the angles rather than the distances that the two runners would have to cover. The angle of the lines between the runners and the center is not what makes the game more or less fair. Runners can be arranged at any angle within a circle design, but they will still be competing at a perfectly fair distance from the center.

Activity 9: Is Bigger Always Better?

Key idea: Measuring area by covering with nonstandard units
Learning trajectory level: Area Unit Relater and Repeater

Essentials

Gather 9-inch by 12-inch sheets of ledger paper, sheets of newspaper, playing cards or flashcards, graph paper, and sticky notes (3-inch by 3-inch).

Engage

Read *Bigger, Better, Best* by Stuart J. Murphy (HarperCollins 2002). Siblings Jeff and Jenny argue over everything, and their sister Jill cannot stand it anymore. In their new house, all three children must master the concept of area to figure out who will have the bigger room. The siblings compare window size and floor size. Is bigger always better?

Explore

As you review the story with students, have them count the pieces of ledger paper or newspaper sections that would be needed to cover the windows or floor in the illustrations. Explain to them that the children in the story are finding the area of the windows and floor to see which ones are bigger. Point out that they use paper of the same size when comparing the area of the two windows and then use newspaper sheets of the same size to find the area of the two bedrooms to determine which one is bigger. Suppose the children in the story had run out of newspaper before covering the entire floor. Could they have finished covering the floor by using sheets of ledger paper? They might have reported the combined number of newspaper and ledger sheets needed to cover each floor.

Discuss whether the children in the story might have used other objects to compare the floor spaces. What about using playing cards? Could they have used shoe boxes? Could they have used DVD cases? How about using various sizes of cereal boxes to cover both floors? Imagine what might have happened if they had tried cereal boxes:

> We wanted to compare the floor area of two rooms to find the larger room (see fig. 3.23). We used boxes to cover both areas and found that floor B takes more boxes. Does this mean that it is the larger room? This seems confusing because room B looks smaller, but our measurement indicates that it is larger.

Ask students if they can explain what happened during this measuring process. Did the children make a mistake? (The rectangular units of measure—cereal boxes—are not uniform in size or shape, so the counts are not comparable. Also, there is some gapping between units, and some units overlap.)

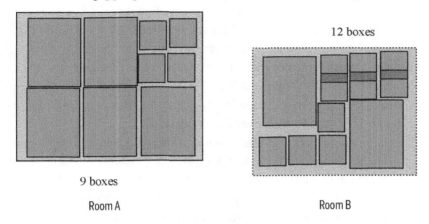

12 boxes

9 boxes

Room A   Room B

Fig. 3.23. Smaller room, more boxes: what happened?

Expect

Emphasize that a consistent unit of measure must be used to compare the area of shapes accurately. Students may not be aware that gaps or overlaps can lead to comparison errors in counts of the total number of sheets needed to cover different areas (e.g., of windows or floors). Some students may assume that using cereal boxes would work, even though it is not easy to tile with different-sized rectangles, and different-sized cereal boxes are not consistent units for measuring area.

Extend

- Ask students to use medium (3-inch by 3-inch) sticky notes to find the area of their desktop. Be sure to provide fewer sticky notes than would be needed to cover the desktop. This will prompt students to create a strategy for using what they have—say, 15 or 20 sticky notes. Emphasize the array of rows and columns that should naturally occur as students arrange the sticky notes.

  Next, challenge them to use sticky notes of the same size to find the area of a larger tabletop. This will probably seem like too much work and very tedious. Help students reduce the complexity of the task by using an intermediate unit and the operation of multiplication as follows: First, have them find and record the number of 9-inch by 12-inch sheets of paper that would cover the tabletop (arranging sheets in an array is an easy approach). Next, have them find and record the number of medium sticky notes needed to cover just one of those 9 × 12 sheets of paper (twelve 3-inch by 3-inch sticky notes). Suggest that these two findings can help them calculate the total number of sticky notes that would cover the entire tabletop. If students do not notice, show them that the number of sticky notes that would cover one sheet of paper (12) can be repeatedly added together to find the total area of the tabletop.

This situation can help illustrate the conceptual basis for multiplication. For example, if the tabletop required eighteen 9 × 12 sheets, and we know that each 9 × 12 sheet requires 12 sticky notes to cover it, then we can add together 18 sets of 12 sticky notes to find the total number that would cover the tabletop: 12 + 12 + 12 + . . . = 216. Thus, we would need 216 sticky notes to show the area of the tabletop.

The transition from the smaller unit (sticky notes) to the larger unit (sheets of paper) makes the calculation more efficient, and it shows the basis of multiplication. Adding up 18 sets of 12 is the same as multiplying 12 times 18. Both equal 216. Multiplication happens when we take a group of a particular size and repeat same-sized groups to find the overall quantity. Multiplication is often more efficient than addition.

- When students take a flyer home from school to put on their refrigerator, have them estimate how many flyers of the same size would cover the entire front of the fridge, and then have them find the solution based on the measurement of their refrigerator. When they share their findings with their classmates, can they explain why some students found different answers?

- Display one piece of student art in the middle of an otherwise empty bulletin board. Have students predict and record how many art pieces of the same size they would need to cover the bulletin board. Help them check their predictions by moving the piece already displayed into one corner of the board. Ask students to imagine an adjacent piece, using your hand to gesture and indicate where the next few pieces would fit. Ask students whether they want to change their predictions after seeing the art piece in the corner of the board. Discuss students' ways of forming their predictions. Be aware that some students may intuitively structure the region as several adjacent rows of artwork. This is a beginning level of thinking about rows and columns to form an array. This kind of reasoning eventually helps students understand the basis for the formula length × width = area.

Enrich

Read *Fraction Fun* by David A. Adler (Holiday House 1996). This book provides a basic introduction to the concept of fraction.

Activity 10: Box Up the Blocks!

Key idea: *Packing boxes with cubes to understand volume*
Learning trajectory level: *Volume Unit Relater and Repeater*

Essentials

Gather 1-inch wooden cubes, enough paper (or poster board) for students and the teacher to construct small boxes to hold the cubes, and enough clear tape for the class. For each student, make a copy of the template at More4U for a cubic-1-inch box, as shown in figure 3.24.

Engage

Remind students of the story of the toymaker Geppetto and his puppet Pinocchio. When toymakers finish their toys, they need to store them in packages to surprise children later when they open them. They also need to send them far away. It is important to make packages or boxes that fit the toys. Suppose you want to prepare a box that will hold 24 wooden cubes. How will you make one of these boxes? How long will the base need to be? How wide? How tall? We will answer these questions after we explore box-making basics.

Explore

We will focus on measuring volume by building boxes to fit specific sets of cubes. First, ask students how large a box is needed to hold just one cube. They may say a small box. Give each student a copy of the template for the 1-cubic-inch box shown in figure 3.24 on the following page. (See More4U for a blackline master of this figure.) Ask them to cut out the pattern along the solid lines and fold it along the dotted lines, then tape it into a box shape (without taping down the square for the lid). How many squares form the box? (Five, not including the lid.) You may mention that mathematicians would say the *surface area* of this box, including a lid, is 6 square inches. Explain that this same box has a *capacity* of one cube (it holds 1 cubic inch). Note that each edge is 1 inch long.

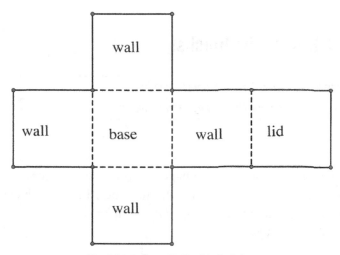

Fig. 3.24. Pattern for 1-cubic-inch box

Next, have students describe and make a paper box to hold two cubes. There are two ways to do this, so challenge them to find both ways (one way has a 1-inch by 1-inch base and requires the two cubes to be stacked; the other has a 1-inch by 2-inch base in a single layer). Then challenge students to construct two different boxes that will hold four cubes (one option measures 2 inches by 2 inches by 1 inch; and the other, 1 inch by 2 inches by 2 inches).

Now that students have explored ways of boxing up 1, 2, and 4 cubes, help them extend these experiences to deal with the challenge of boxing up large numbers of cubes. Consider another approach: start with an existing box (for example, a larger crayon box or pen box) and try to determine the numbers of cubes it can hold. Have students guess and then check its capacity in cubic inches.

Next, show students an empty box that measures 3 inches by 4 inches by 2 inches (fig. 3.25 shows the outline of such a box on a smaller scale; a template for the box in actual size is available at More4U). It is best to make the box while students watch, talking about the size of each flap as you work. Ask students to predict the number of cubes that will fill this box. Now have them take that number of cubes (the prediction) and arrange them at their desks to see if they fit in the box. Regroup as a class and have students talk about various ways that they arranged and counted the cubes on their desktops.

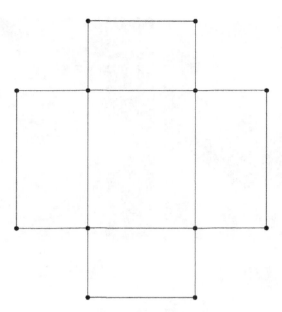

Fig. 3.25. Template for 3-inch by 4-inch by 2-inch box

You may want to pose a further challenge by playing a game that uses the set of photos in figure 3.26 as clues for finding how many cubes can fit in the paper box (or you might want to go directly to the guiding discussion that follows the figure). Ask students which of the photos (a–d) is most helpful for finding the number of cubes that would fill the box completely.

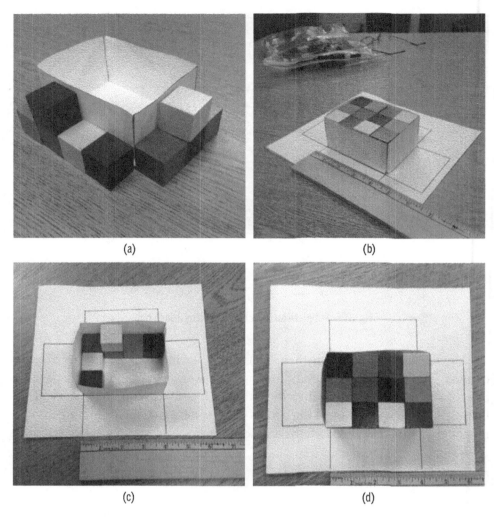

Fig. 3.26. Which of these photos can help us figure out how many cubes fit in the box?

Students may at this point realize that some number of layers of cubes, with 12 cubes in each layer, will fit in the box. Show them a layering strategy for arranging cubes (unless students already shared this strategy). First, make a layer of 12 cubes (3 × 4) on a tabletop and then place an open 3-inch by 4-inch box (with sides but no top or bottom) over that layer of cubes. Help students see that the layer of cubes fits exactly within the box shell. Then place the box next to the cubes and ask students to predict how many more layers of cubes would fill such a box (one more layer is needed). Now use 12 more cubes to create another layer, proving that the volume of the box is 24 cubes.

Extend

- Have students use the computer activity "Volume of Prisms by Unit Cubes" (go to https://www.geogebra.org/m/FgQVdDTb or http://www.childrensmeasurement.org/resources.html; click the first button on the Children's Measurement page) to find many ways to make a box that holds 24 cubes. They can use the buttons in the program to add or subtract cubes and groups of cubes until they have created a box with a volume of 24 cubes. Ask students to explain each solution that they find to their classmates and tell how many cubes the box contains along its front edge, its side, and along one wall.

- Ask students to pretend that they are package designers in a toy factory and they need to package 24 cubic wooden blocks. An arrangement of two layers of 12 cubes each works, but it requires a lid that is fairly large (3×4). Are there boxes in other shapes that would allow a smaller lid? Ask students to try to find another way to design the box. They should draw their ideas and then report to the class on the different designs they discover.

- Ask students to imagine packing one of these new box designs with smaller cubes—perhaps with 1-centimeter edges. How many of these smaller cubes do they think will fit in the box? Have them check their predictions. Ask them to determine whether the volume of the box has changed because the number of smaller cubes is larger than the number of inch cubes. Is the box *really* larger now?

- Show students a box that measures 5 cubes long by 3 cubes wide by 6 cubes high, and ask them to predict and check how many cubes can fit in this box.

Expect

- As students share their drawn designs, encourage them to label the dimensions and describe the base layer in their box design. They may draw designs such as a 24-block-long box ($1 \times 1 \times 24$ cubes), a 12-block-long box ($1 \times 2 \times 12$ cubes), or one that measures $2 \times 2 \times 6$ cubes, and so forth.

- Students may choose the dimensions of their boxes by finding a sum of 24 (e.g., they may say the box measures $10 + 5 + 5 + 4$) without actually building with the cubes to check their box design. We want students to build layer by layer to help them learn about arrays. Can students organize the 24 cubic-inch blocks into layers with the same number of blocks in each layer? If not, you may need to suggest breaking 24 into two, three, or four equal sets, then forming layers for each set. Can they form layers that are rectangular arrays? Did they use all 24 cubes, or did they create unused space? Students might build incomplete layers (e.g., five cubes per layer, leaving an empty corner).

- Can students explain why more cubes were needed to fill the box with the same volume when they used smaller cubes than when they filled it with larger cubes? If not, discuss the inverse relationship between unit size and the total number of units needed to fill a given volume.

Enrich

You can find additional resources online at https://lovewhatyouteach.com /2012/11/25/using-nets-to-develop-childrens-understanding-of-3d-shapes/. The author of the article, a teacher, discusses activities that she has done with her students to make virtual and physical nets and explain what shapes they produce.

Activity 11: Fill It Up!

Key idea: Comparing capacity of containers by counting liquid units (cups)
Learning trajectory level: Volume Quantity Recognizer

Essentials

Gather clear plastic containers in at least ten different shapes and sizes and enough liquid-measuring cups for each small group to have one.

Engage

Read *Room for Ripley* by Stuart J. Murphy (HarperCollins 1999). This story about a young boy who is getting a fish bowl ready for his new pet introduces various units of liquid measure: cups, pints, quarts, half-gallons, and gallons.

Explore

Go outdoors if possible (in warm weather!), and have students pour water between different measuring containers to learn about the relative *capacity* of containers in different shapes and sizes.

First, ask students to predict the number of cups of water that would fit into containers of various shapes and sizes. Next, ask them to arrange the containers in order of their capacity, from the smallest to the largest. Finally, ask students to check the order that they have proposed by counting and recording the number of cups of water needed to fill each container.

Extend

- Invite students to bring measuring cups or spoons for dry measure or liquid from home. It will be helpful if students bring a variety of measures that might include teaspoons, tablespoons, $1/4$ cups, $1/3$ cups, $1/2$ cups, pints, and quart measures. Ask students to look for differences between the dry measure and liquid measure tools. These are made differently to help with pouring (cup measures have spouts) or for filling (these do not have spouts).

- Make a bubble solution. We suggest the following recipe (adapted from the Busy Kids = Happy Mom website: http://www.busykidshappymom .org/giant-bubble-recipe/). The site also offers directions for making bubble wands by using two straws and string.

  Recipe for bubble solution:
  Place the following ingredients in a bowl or bucket: 12 cups water, 1 cup dish soap, 1 cup cornstarch, 2 tablespoons baking powder (not baking soda), and 2 tablespoons glycerin. Stir gently, taking care not to create bubbles now. Let sit for 1–3 hours before use.

  Note that the recipe calls for 12 cups of water. Challenge students to find more efficient ways of measuring out 12 cups of water (hint: they may use pints, etc., to measure the total amount).

- Ask students to write about the following scenario: What problems could arise if a baby food jar and a mayonnaise jar were used to measure volume instead of standard measures of cups, pints, quarts, and gallons when figuring how much punch to make for the queen's birthday party?

Expect

- Different container shapes can affect students' perception of capacity. For example, students often expect that taller containers will hold more liquid than shorter containers, without regard to the containers' other dimensions. Students may also be surprised that containers that are the same height but have different shapes may have exactly the same capacity.

- Check whether students understand that they can compare capacity by counting the number of units used to fill two or more containers.

- Check whether students are able to substitute a smaller or larger unit to duplicate a given measure. For example, ask students to place 3 cups of liquid in a large container without using a 1-cup measure (students may use 6 half cups, for example, to do this).

Enrich

Use *DK Children's Cookbook* by Katharine Ibbs (DK 2004), which offers quick and tasty recipes for young chefs with step-by-step, straightforward instructions and "look-as-you-cook" sequences of pictures for each dish.

Activity 12: Which Number Is Appropriate as a Measure? (Assessment)

Essentials

Read *Me and the Measure of Things* by Joan Sweeney (Crown, 2001). This introduction to units of measure helps students size things up—from a teaspoon to a cup, an ounce to a gallon, a pound to a ton, an inch to a mile, and a peck to a bushel. Questions like how much, how heavy, how tall, and how far may be solved by using tools such as rulers, scales, cups, and baskets.

Next, conduct the **assessment** as follows:

1. Measurement Facts about Me: Have students write and illustrate a journal entry that includes at least eight sentences with numbers and units that describe themselves. Challenge them to include and explain some unusual measures: How many months or weeks old am I? (Students can even state their age two ways, in months and weeks.) How tall am I if we measure me in yards or in millimeters? How many centimeters of string will wrap around my wrist? How long is my foot in inches? How many cups of water do I drink each day?

2. Work together as a class on the activities All About Jamal and All about Marie in *Navigating through Measurement in Prekindergarten–Grade 2* (Dacey et al. 2003, pp. 62–63 and 77–78), available at More4U. Ask students to work on the second activity on their own. Can students figure out what measures do not work in some contexts? For example, suppose we have the numbers 49, 6, 27, and 2 and we must guess which is appropriate for Jamal's grade in school, how tall he is in inches, the length of his pencil, and the weight of his dog.

4

GRADE 3: LENGTH, AREA, AND ANGLE MEASUREMENT

Big measurement ideas identified in CCSSM: Third graders are generally ready to compare regions of two-dimensional planes by identifying and organizing area units into arrays. They use area-measurement activities as models to understand the operations of multiplication and division. Students also use length and area activities to understand fractions, with special emphasis on the restatement of any fraction as a multiple of a unit fraction. For example, $9/15$ is the same as nine one-fifteenth unit pieces:

$$9\left(\tfrac{1}{15}\right) = \tfrac{9}{15}$$

This insight helps them understand that all fractions can be interpreted as a measure by repeating the unit fraction.

Learning trajectory levels in this grade: Students move from the Area Unit Relater and Repeater level into the Area Row and Column Structurer level, where they have some ability to structure area. The goal at this level is to support students' grasp of row-and-column structures for arrays while they measure area. Table 4.1 shows the learning trajectory levels for length and area for this grade.

Table 4.1. Learning trajectory levels by grade and topic

Grade	Length LT levels	Area LT levels
3	Consistent Length Measurer Conceptual Ruler Measurer Integrated Conceptual Path Measurer	Area Unit Relater and Repeater Initial Composite Structurer Area Row and Column Structurer

Table 4.2 provides an overview of the activities in the chapter. Each activity is linked to the relevant CCSSM standard and levels from a learning trajectory on length or area measurement.

Table 4.2. Grade 3 activities matched with Common Core State Standards and learning trajectory levels

General CCSSM	Learning activities	Activity-specific standards	Learning trajectory levels
Multiplying and dividing within 100 3.MD.C.5 Recognize and use area units to cover plane figures 3.OA.A.4 Determine unknown in multiplication or division equations	**Activity 1: Every Square Inch: Designing a Patio Space** Key idea: Connecting area to units and arithmetic	3.MD.C.5 3.MD.C.5a 3.MD.C.5b	Complete Coverer and Counter
	Activity 2: Patio Redesign Task Key idea: Determining unknown dimensions in area tasks	3.OA.A.4	Physical Coverer and Counter (with all needed tiles) Complete Coverer and Counter (with some tiles)
Understanding fractions, especially unit fractions 3.NF.A.1 Understand all fractions as multiples of a unit fraction 3.NF.A.2 Use number lines to model fractions 3.NF.A.3 Compare fractions	**Activity 3: Wraps and Sides** Key idea: Converting fractions	3.NF.A.3 3.NF.A.3a 3.NF.A.3c 3.NF.A.3d	Conceptual Ruler Measurer
	Activity 4: Wraps and Sides, Continued Key idea: Converting and comparing fractions	3.NF.A.1 3.NF.A.2 3.NF.A.2a 3.NF.A.2b 3.NF.A.3b	Integrated Conceptual Path Measurer
	Activity 5: To the Nearest Quarter Key ideas: Measuring to the nearest quarter inch; converting between units of measure	4.MD.A.1 3.NF.A.1 3.NF.A.3 3.NF.A.3.b	Integrated Conceptual Path Measurer
	Activity 6: More Ridiculous Rulers Key idea: Developing an understanding of number lines	2.NBT.B.7	Consistent Length Measurer

General CCSSM	Learning activities	Activity-specific standards	Learning trajectory levels
Structuring rectangular arrays 3.MD.C.5 Recognize and understand area measurement 3.MD.C.6 Measure areas by counting squares 3.MD.C.7 Relate area to multiplication and addition 3.MD.D.8 Geometric measurement: recognize perimeter	**Activity 7: Partial Arrays and Measuring the Area of Rectangles** Key idea: Developing an understanding of the structure of arrays	3.MD.C.5 3.MD.C.5a 3.MD.C.5b 3.MD.C.6 3.MD.C.7	Initial Composite Structurer
	Activity 8: Focus on Area and Conserving Area Key idea: Interpreting area as a count of unit squares	3.MD.C.5 3.MD.C.6 3.MD.D.8	Area Unit Relater and Repeater
Describing and analyzing 2-D shapes 3.NF.A.1 Understand all fractions as multiples of a unit fraction 3.MD.C.5 Recognize and understand area measurement 3.G.A2 Partition shapes into parts with equal areas and connect parts to unit fractions	**Activity 9: Comparison of Areas** Key idea: Composing and decomposing regions of area to compare	3.NF.A.1 3.MD.C.5 3.MD.C.5a 3.G.A2	Area Row and Column Structurer

Table 4.2. continued

General CCSSM	Learning activities	Activity-specific standards	Learning trajectory levels
Classifying geometric figures by attributes including angle 4.MD.C.5 Recognize and understand angle measure	**Activity 10: Angles and Arms** Key idea: Identifying the attribute of angle	4.MD.C.5	Angle Size Comparer

Activity 1: Every Square Inch: Designing a Patio Space

Key idea: Connecting area to units and arithmetic

Learning trajectory level: Complete Coverer and Counter

Essentials

Gather 11-inch by 14-inch (or 11-inch by 17-inch) paper; masking or painter's tape, jump ropes, or string; and 50 square-inch tiles for each desk station.

This is a two-part activity. In one part, groups of students work on the square-inch activity at their desks. In the other part, groups of students work on the square-foot activity at a station on the floor. Students should switch between floor and desk stations halfway through the lesson or on the following day.

For each student, make copies of the three sheets with rectangles A–F shown in scaled drawings in figure 4.3 on the next page as well as the recording sheets shown in figures 4.4 and 4.5 (on page 134; see this book's More4U page to download printable versions of these figures).

How to assemble a square-foot measuring tile

If you have access to 11-inch by 14-inch sheets of paper (or 11-inch by 17-inch sheets), start by cutting the 14-inch or 17-inch side down to 12 inches. Next, fold the sheet in half along the 11-inch edge and then in half again along the 5.5-inch edge. Open the sheet, and using a ruler, mark along the fold lines and then cut the sheet along each line, which should leave you with four 12-inch by 2.75-inch strips. Fold each of these strips in half along the short edge to make four strips that are 12 inches by 1.375 inches. (*Note:* The 2.75-inch and the 1.375-inch measurements need not be exact.) Overlap the strips and staple them at the corners to create a square-foot "tile" (a frame for such a tile), as shown in figure 4.1.

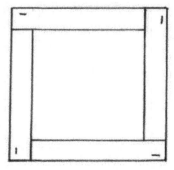

Fig. 4.1. Square-foot tile

How to mark a grid on the floor

Identify regions on the floor for your students to cover with their square-foot tiles. You can mark out regions (which should have integer side lengths) with tape, jump rope, string, or another material, or you may want to label points on the floor with letters. We suggest spacing these points 2 feet apart horizontally and vertically. The points can serve as the vertices of different figures. For example, the shaded rectangle *AILD* in figure 4.2 would have an area of 24 square feet, using our suggested spacing. If you have a large enough space, we recommend setting up two of these stations. If you do not have the necessary space, have half of your students work at your single floor station at the same time.

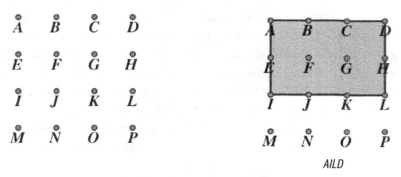

AILD

Fig. 4.2. Labeling points on the floor

How to prepare the desk stations

Each desk station should have 50 square-inch tiles and, for each student, a recording sheet similar to that in figure 4.5 (but without the data in the last three columns). Each student should also have copies of the three sheets showing rectangles A–F; these rectangles appear in scaled drawings in figure 4.3. Sheet 1 shows rectangle A (4 in. × 5 in.) and rectangle B (6 in. × 8 in.); sheet 2 shows rectangle C (3 in × 8 in.) and rectangle D (7 in. × 4 in.); sheet 3 shows rectangle E (5 in. × 8 in.) and rectangle F (5 in. × 7 in.).

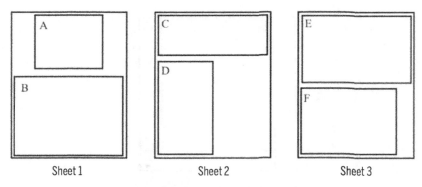

| Sheet 1 | Sheet 2 | Sheet 3 |

Fig. 4.3. Six rectangles, A–F (sheets 1–3)

Engage

Begin by explaining the scenario:

> Today we want to start thinking about building a patio for someone's backyard. Before we start, let's build as many different rectangular patios as we can, making each one exactly 12 square feet. Which of these patio shapes would you recommend and why?

Expect to discuss the benefits of different-shaped patios with the same area. For example, ask students whether they can think of a situation in which a 1-foot-by-12-foot patio would be better than a 3-foot-by-4-foot patio.

At this point, stop to have students build their square-foot measuring tiles, as described above. We suggest having each student make three or four squares so that they will have enough to work with in their groups. Ask students to use their square-foot tiles to lay out a few of their patio designs on the floor to help them decide whether the designs are big enough to be useful. (You can substitute 24 square feet or 30 square feet for 12 square feet as the area of the patio if you want students to build a patio that is more realistic in size. Each student will need to make several square-foot tiles for this variation.)

In groups at their desks, students should record the dimensions and area of all the patios that they build. Provide students with a sufficient number of square-inch tiles (about 30) to model the patios. The goal is for students to realize that the area is the same as the number of tiles used and thus constant. Draw students' attention to the connection between the factors of the number of tiles used and the number of patio designs that can be created. For example, the patios that can be created with an area of 12 square feet are determined by the factors of 12 (i.e., 1, 2, 3, 4, 6, and 12).

Explore

Activity for floor station: At the floor station, give students a recording sheet similar to that shown in figure 4.4 (but without the data in the last three columns). Ask students to make some additional patio designs on the floor based on the labeled rectangular regions named in the far-left column. Before letting students begin laying out their square-foot tiles, ask them to estimate how many tiles they think they will have to use to cover each region, and record their estimates on the sheet. Then have them check their estimates by covering each of the regions on the floor with the tiles. They should then draw the resulting figures and record the dimensions and area of each rectangle.

	How many tiles do you think it will take to cover the region?	Drawing	Length	Width	Area
AILD			6 feet	4 feet	24 square feet
AMPD			6 feet	6 feet	36 square feet
AIKC			4 feet	4 feet	16 square feet
AEGC			4 feet	2 feet	8 square feet
AEHD			2 feet	6 feet	12 square feet
AEFB			2 feet	2 feet	4 square feet

Fig. 4.4. Recording sheet for floor station

Activity for desk station: At the desk station, provide 50 square-inch tiles and a recording sheet for each student (see fig. 4.5) with the answers removed and the handout illustrated in figure 4.3. As in the floor station activity, students will estimate how many tiles they think they will have to use to cover each rectangular region and record their estimates on the sheet. Then have them check their estimates by covering each of the regions shown on the handout with the tiles.

	How many tiles do you think it will take to cover the region?	Length	Width	Area
Rectangle A		4 inches	5 inches	20 square inches
Rectangle B		6 inches	8 inches	48 square inches
Rectangle C		3 inches	8 inches	24 square inches
Rectangle D		7 inches	4 inches	28 square inches
Rectangle E		5 inches	8 inches	40 square inches
Rectangle F		5 inches	7 inches	35 square inches
Rectangle G		12 inches	12 inches	144 square inches

Fig. 4.5. Recording sheet for desk station

Expect

- The main misconceptions to anticipate in this task have to do with building the rectangular regions. Some students may allow gaps or overlaps (particularly with the frames of the square-foot tiles). Engaging students in these tasks will promote growth from Physical Coverer and Counter to the Complete Coverer and Counter level within the learning trajectory for area. Some students may still be operating at the Area Unit Relater and Repeater level; such students may iterate a single tile instead of covering an entire region with tiles. This method may not produce an exact measure of area, but it is an insightful method. However, students at earlier stages along the learning trajectory (e.g., Physical Coverer and Counter, Complete Coverer and Counter) may produce accurate measures if they are given access to enough tiles to fill the entire region.

- We expect that many students will be reluctant to give estimates or will make estimates that are too low.

- We encourage you to pay attention to the ways in which students count the number of tiles after they are laid out to cover a region. Do they count one by one or by the number in a row or a column, or do they use multiplication to keep track?

Extend

- Ask students to estimate and then check how many square feet will fit within a square yard after explaining the relationship between a linear foot and a linear yard. Students can cover a square yard with their square-foot tiles to confirm that 9 square feet are equivalent to 1 square yard.

- Next, challenge students to estimate and then check how many square inches it takes to cover a square foot. If you have 144 square-inch tiles, students can completely cover a square foot to check, but we anticipate that at least some students will suggest a shortcut. If students seem up to the challenge, you may finish this line of questioning by asking them to estimate and then check how many square-inch tiles it takes to cover a square yard.

- Ask students to find the area of other regions around the room in square feet. For example, what is the area of your whiteboard? What is the area of the door? What is the area of the entire floor? Again, we recommend asking students to estimate and then check.

Activity 2: Patio Redesign Task

Key idea: Determining unknown dimensions in area tasks
Learning trajectory levels: Physical Coverer and Counter; Complete Coverer and Counter

Essentials

Students will need blank paper and rulers. Depending on their success with the tasks, you may want to make grid paper and square tiles available.

Engage

Tell students,

> Imagine that you are helping me design a rectangular backyard patio made out of 1-foot-square paver bricks. I have purchased 36 bricks and want to use all 36 bricks to make my patio. I first laid out a design that was 2 bricks wide and 18 bricks long.

Ask students to make a scaled record (1 in. = 1 ft.) of this patio design and verify that the design is rectangular and that it uses all 36 tiles. (Note that students will have to tape two pieces of paper together to make the 2-inch-by-18-inch rectangle fit on the page.)

Explore

Continue:

> When I looked at this design, it seemed too long and skinny. I want to try a different rectangular design that uses all 36 bricks and is 4 (or 3, 6, 9, or 12) bricks wide. What will the length of the patio be? Make a scaled drawing (1 in. = 1 ft.) of the new patio design. Make sure to label the dimensions and draw in the bricks.

Assign different groups to record patios with widths of 3, 6, and 12 feet. Again, when needed, have students tape two pieces of paper together to make a scaled drawing of the patio fit. Encourage students to make their drawings on blank paper and use rulers, which will help strengthen the connection between the numerical and spatial representations (i.e., knowing that a width of 4 feet will contain four square bricks). If they need support to do this, consider allowing them to use grid paper, square tiles, or both.

Ask students to represent their ways of solving the problem both symbolically and verbally. For example, some students may divide 36 by 4 to find a length of 9, while others may reason by imagining $4 \times \underline{} = 36$. Still others may need to lay out rows of 4 tiles until they have counted out 36 tiles to discover that 9 rows of 4 are needed. If students are not using a division technique, encourage them to make connections between their own strategies and the division technique. For example, do they notice that 36 divided by 4 yields 9? These factors can be used as the length and width measures.

Expect

This activity is designed to reinforce the connections between multiplication and division in an area context. The CCSSM objectives state that students should be able to do this task without modeling or making a drawing. Keep in mind, however, that many students are still likely to struggle to create a 4×9 rectangular array in an efficient manner by using the edge lengths to constrain the placement of the square bricks. Some students may draw and repeat a single square (Area Unit Relater and Repeater level), some may repeat a single square to create a row and then make copies of that row (Initial Composite Structurer level), and still others may draw parallel row-and-column line segments to subdivide the region (Area Row and Column Structurer level). We anticipate that at least some students will demonstrate an Area Row and Column Structurer solution. If most students are not already using this strategy, it may be helpful to ask a student to demonstrate it to the class. If no students have used this strategy, consider modeling it at the board for them, using the ruler to find both dimensions of the region and drawing in the grid lines, first horizontal, then vertical, and counting the squares in row groups to find the area.

Extend

- As a class, students will have found the dimensions of and drawn four different patios, each with an area of 36 square feet. Ask students to choose which of these rectangles would be the best for a given purpose— for example, if you wanted to make a grilling station, a walkway from the garage to the house, or a space to place a table and chairs.

- Point out that a table and chairs might fit better in a space that is 36 square yards. Ask students to map out a space in the classroom that is 36 square yards. Is this space appropriately sized for a seating area?

Enrich

Read *Math on the Playground: Area and Perimeter* by Ian F. Mahaney (PowerKids Press 2013). Readers can figure out perimeters and areas from dimensions given to compare playgrounds shown in photographs, as well as solve other problems posed. The author includes helpful labeled diagrams.

Activity 3: Wraps and Sides

Key idea: Converting fractions
Learning trajectory level: Conceptual Ruler Measurer

Essentials

Gather square-inch tiles and 1-inch grid paper (printable from www.printable paper.net/category/graph) for students and a pipe cleaner, cut to a length of 4 inches, for your use in presenting the activity (you can also provide students with pipe cleaners, if desired).

Engage

Divide students into groups. Ask them to imagine that they are designing a community garden with separate plots made up of individual square sections. Each group will be allotted four square sections and must place them so that complete sides are joined. Give each group four square-inch tiles and a piece of 1-inch grid paper. Ask students to make all the different shapes that they can with the tiles and record them on the grid paper. You may want to check in with students before they make their records to avoid repetitions of shapes—for example, they should consider a J shape to be the same as an L—and cases where the sides are not touching completely. How many different garden plots are possible? Figure 4.6 shows the five distinct shapes that are possible.

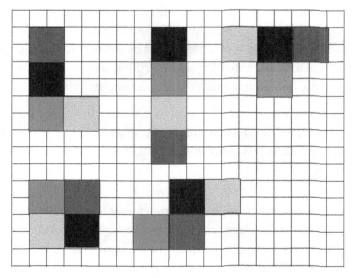

Fig. 4.6. Possible garden plot shapes

Explore

Tell students,

> Let's pretend that the border material for your garden plots will be this piece of pipe cleaner, called a *wrap*, because it can wrap around one tile completely. Notice that each wrap is made up of a total of four sides.

Demonstrate that the 4-inch pipe cleaner segment can be wrapped around a square-inch tile once, as in figure 4.7. Continue:

> How much border material (perimeter) would be needed to enclose each of the garden plots you designed? Give your answers in sides, wraps and sides, and finally wraps. For example, if you have two squares next to each other, the total perimeter will be six sides, which is equivalent to one wrap and two sides, and is also equivalent to $1\frac{1}{2}$ wraps.

(Note that giving answers in wraps will require students to reason about fractions, so you may decide to save this piece for a later date or for a subset of your students when differentiating instruction.)

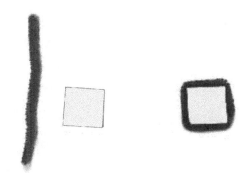

Fig. 4.7. Wrapping a 4-inch section of pipe cleaner around a square-inch tile

Expect

This activity is designed to encourage students to coordinate different relatable units (i.e., four sides = one wrap) and to understand and apply unit fractions (i.e., one side = $\frac{1}{4}$ wrap). We anticipate that some students may initially interpret the problem to include counting the internal, shared sides rather than the perimeter. We suggest clarifying this through the example above with two squares. When students are first asked to report the perimeter of the figures in wraps, they may struggle to equate two sides with half of a wrap. We recommend demonstrating with the pipe cleaner that two sides equal half of a wrap.

Extend

Give students a collection of tiles—six, for example. Ask them to build a garden plot that uses no more than six tiles and has a total perimeter of $3\frac{1}{2}$ wraps. Ask them how many different plots they can make whose borders will be $3\frac{1}{2}$ wraps? Using six or fewer tiles, how many different perimeters can they make?

Activity 4: Wraps and Sides, Continued

Key idea: Converting and comparing fractions
Learning trajectory level: Integrated Conceptual Path Measurer

Essentials

This is a continuation of Activity 3, so you will need the same materials.

Engage

Tell students,

> When we experimented with designing garden plots of different shapes, we realized that not all the plots that use the same number of squares required the same amount of border materials. For example, when we made five different garden plots with four square-inch tiles, four of these plots had perimeters of ten sides, but the fifth one had a perimeter of eight sides. Today we want to focus on comparing the perimeters of different garden plots. Imagine a garden plot that is just one square-inch tile. It would have a perimeter of four sides. How many tiles would you need to build a new plot with a perimeter that is twice as big? Any plot made of three tiles has a perimeter of eight sides, and so does a 2-by-2 plot of four tiles.

Explore

Pose the following problem to the class:

> Students in another class built some different garden plots and recorded the measures of the perimeters, but not always in the same units. Sometimes they reported the perimeter in sides, and sometimes they reported it in wraps—and sometimes they reported it in both sides and wraps! Unfortunately, I lost the pictures they made of the plots Your job today is to compare the perimeters of the different pairs of garden plots so that we can identify which perimeter is larger and by how much. To warm up, let's compare a garden plot with one square-inch tile to a garden plot with two tiles. List all the ways in which you could report the measure of the perimeters of these two plots. After listing all the measures, list all the ways that you can report the difference in the perimeters.

Table 4.3 shows some of the ways in which students might report the perimeters of the plots. As students compare these perimeters, they will find a difference of one-half of a wrap. This can also be stated as a difference of two sides (or even four half-sides).

Table 4.3. Ways to measure one- and two-tile plots

One-tile plot	Two-tile plot
4 sides	6 sides
1 wrap	1½ wraps
1 wrap and 0 sides	1 wrap and 2 sides
(other combinations are possible)	

Table 4.4 shows five examples of garden plot dimensions that you could give students for the activity, along with possible answers; feel free to make up additional examples.

Table 4.4. Comparing garden plots by perimeter

Plot 1	Plot 2	Perimeter differences
3 wraps	10 sides	Plot 1's perimeter is bigger than Plot 2's perimeter 2 sides bigger Half a wrap bigger
3½ wraps	14 sides	Plot 1's perimeter is equal to Plot 2's perimeter
3 wraps and 7 sides	5 wraps and 1 side	Plot 2's perimeter is bigger than Plot 1's perimeter 2 sides bigger Half a wrap bigger
7 half-wraps	7 sides	Plot 1's perimeter is bigger than Plot 2's perimeter 7 sides bigger 1 wrap and 3 sides bigger 1¾ wraps bigger 3½ half-wraps bigger
2 wraps and 3 sides	4 wraps and 5 half-sides	Plot 2's perimeter is bigger than Plot 1's perimeter 15 half-sides bigger 7 sides and 1 half-side bigger 7½ sides bigger 1 wrap and 3 sides and 1 half-side bigger 1 wrap and 3½ sides bigger 1⅞ wraps bigger 3¾ half-wraps bigger

Expect

We have designed this activity to lay the foundation for seeing all fractions as multiples of a unit fraction (3.NF.A.1) and comparing fractions (3.NF.A.3). Note that any time students work with the idea that four sides are equivalent to one wrap, they are also reasoning that one side is equivalent to $1/4$ of a wrap. Throughout this activity, students need to pay attention to the ever-changing units. Are they measuring in wraps? Sides? Half-wraps? Students are likely to forget to include the units in their answers at times. Additionally, they are likely to make mistakes when converting from one unit to another, especially when reporting or converting a measure given in half-sides or half-wraps. For example, students may double when they should halve or halve when they should double.

Extend

The comparison in the last row of table 4.4 deals with half-sides, which are $1/8$ of a wrap, so it lends itself to use as an extension. If your students can handle the introduction of half-sides, feel free to provide more examples, as they can be used to model eighths of an inch on a ruler. This can also be extended to quarter-sides, which can be used to model sixteenths of an inch.

Activity 5: To the Nearest Quarter

Key ideas: Measuring to the nearest quarter inch; converting between units of measure
Learning trajectory level: Integrated Conceptual Path Measurer

Essentials

Provide a wraps-and-sides ruler, shown in a reduced size in figure 4.8, for each student or each group (see More4U for actual-sized rulers). Include with each ruler the shapes shown below it. Each student will need three rulers if you do the follow-up activity. Print a page of the tools, cut the page into individual tools, and have students trim the tools carefully along the top edge. Prepare the line-segments handout described below and make a copy for each student or each group.

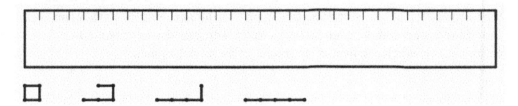

Fig. 4.8. Wraps-and-sides ruler

Engage

Tell students,

> Today we will be measuring with wraps and sides again, but we are going to use a different-sized wrap. Just as in our previous wraps activity, we assume that four sides together equal one wrap, but now, an unfolded wrap is 1 inch long, instead of 4 inches.

Explore

Give students or groups a handout showing a set of line segments with no markings. Students will measure these in sides, wraps and sides, and wraps, by using the wraps-and-sides ruler. (Tick marks on the actual-sized ruler are set to appear at ¼-inch intervals; likewise, segments between dots in the shapes below the ruler are intended to be ¼ inch long. Note, however, that when you create the line segments, you should use the ruler that students will use to ensure that the scale is the same, since printing processes and copy machines can slightly enlarge or reduce images.) Table 4.5 provides a sample list of line-segment lengths, but feel free to use your own ideas.

We suggest allowing students to modify their measuring tools as they see fit. For example, some students may decide to extend every fourth tick mark to indicate wraps, possibly labeling these extended marks as 1, 2, 3, and so on.

Table 4.5. Suggested lengths for sides, wraps and sides, and wraps

Length in sides	Length in wraps and sides	Length in wraps
28 sides	7 wraps and 0 sides	7 wraps
22 sides	5 wraps and 2 sides	$5\frac{1}{2}$ wraps
17 sides	4 wraps and 1 side	$4\frac{1}{4}$ wraps
3 sides	0 wraps and 3 sides	$\frac{3}{4}$ wrap 3 ($\frac{1}{4}$ wraps)
$8\frac{1}{2}$ sides	2 wraps and $\frac{1}{2}$ of a side	$2\frac{1}{8}$ wraps

Expect

- Note that because each wrap is 1 inch long, the numbers in the rightmost column of figure 4.4 also show the lengths of the segments in inches to the nearest quarter inch (with the last entry to the nearest eighth inch).

- This activity is designed to help students see all fractions as multiples of a unit fraction (CCSSM 3.NF.A.1). For example, giving students a segment with length 3 sides helps to elicit this understanding; as shown in table 4.5, students can think of this length in wraps in two different ways—as $\frac{3}{4}$ of a wrap, which emphasizes the wrap as the unit, and as 3 ($\frac{1}{4}$ wraps), which emphasizes that there are 3 quarter-wrap units. In inches, the segments measure $\frac{3}{4}$ inch or 3 quarter-inches.

- We expect students to struggle to discover the benefit of extending and labeling every fourth tick mark on the ruler. Most students will probably count the total number of sides each time, not taking advantage of the fact that every four sides are equivalent to one wrap. Some students will extend every fourth tick mark but fail to label them, whereas others may label them as 1, 1, 1 . . . (because every four tick marks equals one wrap) or as 4, 4, 4 . . . (because four sides equals one wrap).

- We also anticipate that some students will notice that each wrap is one inch long. If this happens, we suggest highlighting this observation and moving to the second extension activity.

Extend

- If no students have thought to extend every fourth tick mark and label them 1, 2, 3, . . . we suggest presenting this as an alternative strategy. (If a student does come up with this idea, have him or her present the idea to the class.) Discuss the efficiency of this idea with your students, then hand out new wraps-and-sides rulers so that your students can extend the tick marks and label them.

- Similarly, if a student has noticed that the wraps and sides can also be thought of as inches and quarter inches, have him or her present this finding to the rest of the class. (If no one mentions this, suggest it yourself.) Discuss this conversion with the class, noting that just as four sides = one wrap, 4 quarter inches = 1 inch. Hand out another round of new wraps-and-sides tools, referring to them now as inch and quarter-inch tools. Have students extend every fourth quarter inch and label them as 1, 2, 3, ... Then give students a new sheet of line segments to measure with their tools. Have students report their answers in quarter inches, half inches, and inches. (Remind them that this is the same as sides, half-wraps, and wraps.) At this point, you might have a class discussion about why this tool is more efficient than the earlier unlabeled version.

- Draw a large model of the inch and quarter-inch tool on the board with a line segment above the tool that is $1\frac{1}{2}$ inches long. Ask students to provide as many different labels for this length as they can. Answers might include 1.5 inches, 1 and a half-inch, 3 half-inches, $\frac{3}{2}$ inches, 3 ($\frac{1}{2}$ inch), 6 quarter inches, 6 ($\frac{1}{4}$ inches), and 12 eighth inches.

Activity 6: More Ridiculous Rulers

Key idea: Developing an understanding of number lines
Learning trajectory level: Consistent Length Measurer

Essentials

Create a poster or drawing on the board of a ridiculous ruler—one with numbers completely out of order, but with equally spaced tick marks. See figure 4.9 for an example. In this ruler, one problem is that two different lengths appear to measure 7 units because consecutive tick marks show inconsistent intervals.

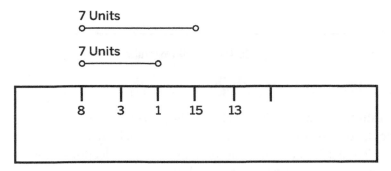

Fig. 4.9. A ridiculous ruler

Also, using the template at More4U, make each student a sheet showing the six ridiculous rulers displayed in figure 4.11 on page 149.

Engage

Display the ridiculous ruler in figure 4.9. Ask students what kinds of problems they would expect to have if they used this ruler to measure and compare several lengths. Students may notice that the number labels are not in order. Ask them to explain why that is a problem. You might point out that the line segment drawn between two points, 8 and 1, measures 7 units in length, whereas another line segment drawn between two points, 8 and 15, also measures 7 units in length. The problem here is that the line segments are different lengths, but this ridiculous ruler is reporting that they are equal.

Discuss a second ruler option (see fig. 4.10) that begins with a tick mark labeled zero that is not close to the end. Is this a correct ruler? Is it a useful ruler? Why or why not? (Note that the end of a ruler used by an engineer or a draftsman often becomes worn down, potentially leading to construction problems if measurements made with the ruler are too short. Thus, the scale on the ruler is sometimes shifted to the right to prevent inaccurate measures once the physical end of the ruler becomes worn. Rulers like this one still have a valid scale, with equally spaced intervals that are marked with consistent number labels beginning at zero. Students may find this type of ruler difficult to use. Try encouraging them to line up an object with the tick mark labeled zero, even if it is not at the end of the ruler.)

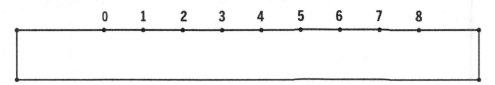

Fig. 4.10. Another ridiculous ruler

Explore

Give each student a copy of the sheet with the six rulers shown in figure 4.11. Ask students to compare the rulers to determine which are the most helpful for measuring lengths. Discuss students' reasons for their selections. Similarly, ask them to explain which ruler is the least helpful. Why?

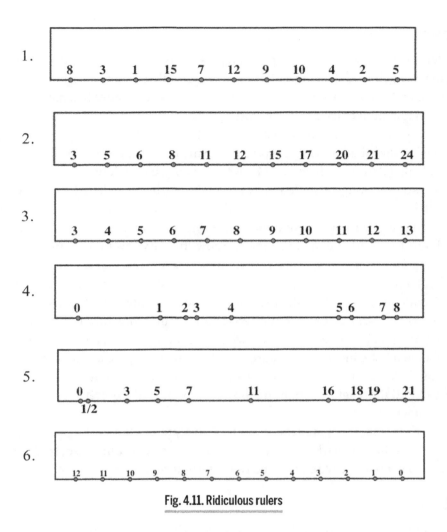

1.

| 8 | 3 | 1 | 15 | 7 | 12 | 9 | 10 | 4 | 2 | 5 |

2.

| 3 | 5 | 6 | 8 | 11 | 12 | 15 | 17 | 20 | 21 | 24 |

3.

| 3 | 4 | 5 | 6 | 7 | 8 | 9 | 10 | 11 | 12 | 13 |

4.

| 0 | 1 | 2 3 | 4 | 5 6 | 7 8 |

5.

| 0 | 3 | 5 | 7 | 11 | 16 | 18 19 | 21 |
1/2

6.

| 12 | 11 | 10 | 9 | 8 | 7 | 6 | 5 | 4 | 3 | 2 | 1 | 0 |

Fig. 4.11. Ridiculous rulers

Each ruler is problematic for a different reason:

1. Even intervals are marked but are labeled with nonsequential integer values.

2. Even intervals are marked but are labeled with inconsistent differences between label values.

3. Even intervals are marked and labeled with consistent differences, but the labeled values begin at 3 rather than 0.

4. Uneven intervals are marked but are labeled with integers increasing by 1.

5. Uneven intervals are marked, but the labels for each mark are based on an actual unit measurement between 0 and each mark.

6. Even intervals are marked but are labeled with integer values that sequentially decrease by 1.

Expect

Students may argue that all six options represent useless rulers. Ask them to look for the one that would be the easiest to fix. Suggest they find one that would be useful if they left the tick marks in place and either added more tick marks or changed the number labels for the existing tick marks.

Other students may argue that all the options are incorrect. Begin by asking them what they think of ridiculous ruler 3, which begins at 3 and has increments of one unit. Is this ruler incorrect? How? Can you use it to draw a line segment that is two units long? A student may respond, "No, because there is not a 2 on the ruler." Many students are accustomed to measuring an object by aligning the initial edge of the ruler with one end of the object and reading off the number label next to the other end of the object. Show students how to measure by counting unit intervals regardless of the number labels.

Still others may say that these drawings do not show rulers at all. Challenge these students to consider rulers as collections of unit intervals. The first two rulers in figure 4.11 do provide such collections of unit intervals. For example, ruler 1 has equally spaced tick marks to represent linear units, although the number labels are incorrect. Because the labels are wrong, we cannot simply read off the label matching the end of an object to find its length. Nevertheless, one can find the length by counting the intervals along the object, disregarding the number labels.

Be aware that many students expect "1" to represent the starting point of a ruler. Often the tick mark at the zero position on a ruler is unlabeled, so students may or may not understand that the ruler starts at zero.

Extend

Take your students through the following scenario:

- Imagine that Rumpelstiltskin has some gold bars that he wants to change into golden rulers. He asks several goldsmiths to submit their plans for helping him manufacture these rulers. He decides to have them indicate inch markings by notching the bars to create rulers that can measure any length between zero and the number at the end of the ruler to the nearest inch. But it is difficult and expensive to have a notch put into the bar at every inch, so he decides to have the rulers made with the fewest possible notches. He will check each of the three goldsmiths' plans to decide who will do the work. Imagine you are one of those goldsmiths, and you want your plan to be chosen.

Let's say that a bar is 5 inches long, and a notch along the bar indicates the first inch (see fig. 4.12). You may measure an inch by noting the distance between that notch and the left end of the bar.

Fig. 4.12. Five-inch gold ruler

How many more notches are necessary, and where should they be placed to build an effective 5-inch ruler? Remember, the ruler must measure every length from 0 to 5 inches, including 1-, 2-, 3-, 4-, and 5-inch lengths. With one notch, we can already measure or draw several lengths. Can you tell what lengths these are? (See fig. 4.13.)

We can already measure four different lengths with just one notch.

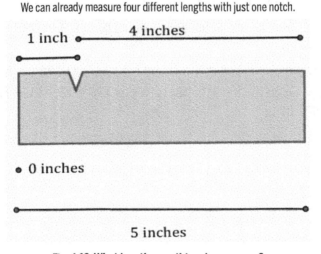

Fig. 4.13. What lengths can this ruler measure?

How many more notches will be needed to finish all the necessary lengths from 0 to 5? Let's track our progress. We have measured 0-, 1-, 4-, and 5-inch lengths but not 2- or 3-inch lengths. Can we make just one more notch? Where? Suppose we notch the second inch from the left. Would that allow us to measure both 2 inches and 3 inches? Yes!

If we mark a 2-inch interval out of a 5-inch total, we will have a 3-inch segment remaining, as we hoped. Could the mark just as well be placed 2 inches from the right end of the ruler? That would mark a 3-inch interval, but it would also leave a remaining segment of 2 inches. Either solution will allow us to finish the job with just two notches, even though we are building a 5-inch ruler. Will Rumpelstiltskin be pleased with your plan, or can someone solve this with just one notch? (No, it's not possible to solve this with only one notch.)

- Next, ask students to work on a similar problem with bars of a different length, perhaps a ruler between 6 and 10 inches. For example, ask students to find the lowest number of notches needed to build an 8-inch golden ruler. The number line in figure 4.14 shows the solution.

Fig. 4.14. Creating an 8-inch ruler with the fewest notches possible

We need to find all these lengths (cross off each integer as you find a notch that allows that length): 0, 1, 2, 3, 4, 5, 6, 7, and 8.

Notch the bar at 1: So far that gives us 0, 1 (1 − 0), 7 (8 − 1), and 8 (8 − 0).

Next, notch the bar at 2: Now we have 2 (2 − 0) and 6 (8 − 2).

Next, notch the bar at 5: That gives us 3 (8 − 5), 4 (5 − 1), and 5 (5 − 0).

Activity 7: Partial Arrays and Measuring the Area of Rectangles

Key idea: Developing an understanding of the structure of arrays
Learning trajectory level: Initial Composite Structurer

Essentials

For each student, use the Missing Tiles template at More4U to make a copy of the group of partial arrays shown in figure 4.16 on the next page.

Engage

Figure 4.15 shows a circular rug covering some of a tiled floor space. Project the image so that your entire class can view it. Explain what it shows, and ask students how many tiles this floor has in all. Remind them to be sure to include those that are hidden below the rug. How do they know that their answer is correct?

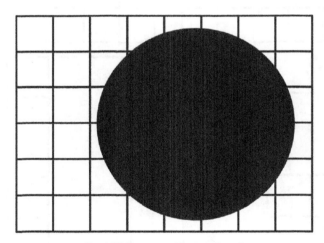

Fig. 4.15. How many tiles are there?

To check students' understanding of the connection between counting tiles and area, consider asking them to find the area of the floor. Assume that each square tile is 12 inches on a side. (When we measure area, we often assume that the unit for flooring is a square foot, but this is not necessarily true. We may choose to measure in units that are larger or smaller than a square foot.) Some students are likely to struggle to understand that the count of tiles represents the area of the floor in square feet.

Explore

Give each student a copy of the sheet showing the group of partial arrays in figure 4.16. Tell them that some square tiles have been drawn in each of these rectangles. Ask them to draw the rest, and then find and record the area measurement—how many tiles there are in each figure—for each of the four figures. Students may work in groups. When they have finished, ask them how they found the area of the figures.

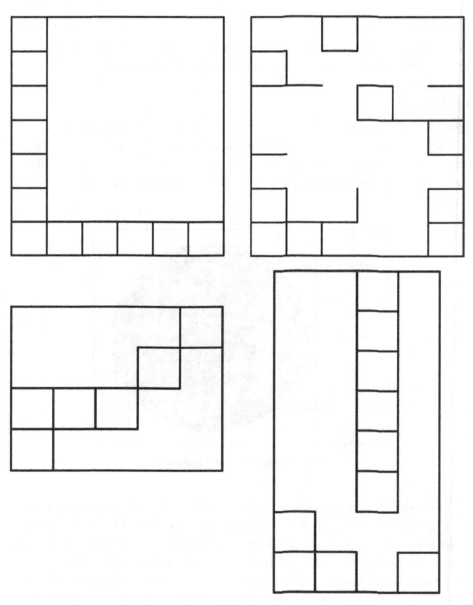

Fig. 4.16. Missing tiles

Expect

This task has two important parts. First, students will need to be able to complete the arrays when given partial structural support. Second, they will need to be able to count the number of tiles. Students will probably draw the tiles in many different ways. Many will draw individual squares when they fill the space, but others may construct a gridded array by drawing some horizontal or vertical lines with varying levels of sophistication. For example, some students may draw squares one at a time but still in rows (left to right) or columns (top to bottom), while others may draw all of the tiles around the border first. Even students who draw horizontal or vertical line segments to mark off rows or columns may revert at times to drawing individual squares, or they may draw horizontal line segments but not vertical ones.

There are likely to be differences in the ways that students count the number of squares as well. Some students will count individual squares with varying levels of sophistication (e.g., in concentric rings from outermost to innermost, in an S pattern, or in rows). More advanced students might begin to move toward a counting pattern that supports multiplication. For example, a student counting four tiles in a row may then skip-count by fours (i.e., 4, 8, 12, 16, 20). This thinking can be modeled by $4 + 4 + 4 + 4 + 4 = 20$ and eventually extended to $4 \times 5 = 20$.

Extend

- Show students a single square-unit tile and a rectangle that has been completely filled with square-unit tiles. Figure 4.17 shows an example: a 6×8 rectangle and a 1-inch $\times$ 1-inch unit tile. Ask students to find the dimensions and area of the rectangle.

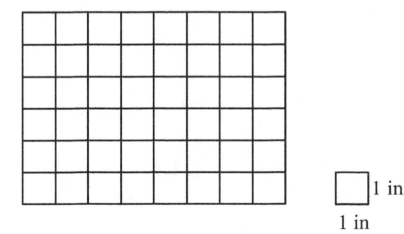

Fig. 4.17. What is the rectangle's area?

- Show students a rectangle with the side lengths labeled (see fig. 4.18 for an example) and ask them to draw in square tiles to fill the space and find the area of the rectangle in square inches. We anticipate that many students will struggle to make sense of how the number labels connect to the way in which the array would fill the rectangle.

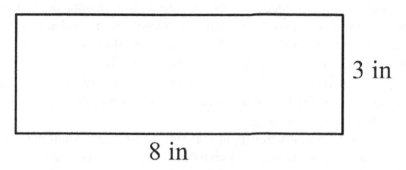

3 in

8 in

Fig. 4.18. Rectangle with labeled side lengths

Activity 8: Focus on Area and Conserving Area

Key idea: Interpreting area as a count of unit squares
Learning trajectory level: Area Unit Relater and Repeater

Essentials

For each student, gather two sheets of green paper, a dozen square-inch cubes, one-inch graph paper, and scissors. Optional: Square crackers such as Cheez-Its or chocolate bars containing eight square sections each.

Engage

Tell the following story to introduce the activity:

> Imagine that two farmers both have grassy grazing fields of the same size and shape on their farms. Suppose that both farmers build a barn on these fields, and the two barns are exactly the same size. The fields were the same size before the farmers built the barns. Will they still be the same size after the barns are built?

Give students time to respond and discuss their answers. Continue:

> Both farmers add another barn to the same fields, but one farmer places the second barn directly next to his first barn, and the other farmer builds her second barn away from the first barn. Will the two farmers still have the same amount of room for their animals to graze?

Have students discuss their answers and support their reasoning.

Show students the following scale drawings (fig. 4.19) of the farmers' fields and explain that the farmers are adding still more barns. The first farmer continues to place all of his barns so that one touches another, and the other scatters all of her barns around the field. Each farmer eventually builds six barns.

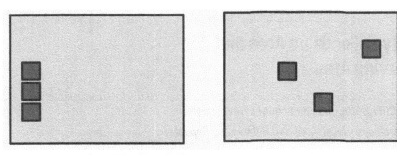

Fig. 4.19. Barn placement patterns for the two farmers

Explore

Give each student two identical sheets of green paper to model the fields and a dozen square-inch cubes to model the barns. Retell the story from the beginning, allowing students time to place the cubes on the sheets of paper to fit the sequence of events in the story. After students have placed six cubes on each sheet of paper, have them trace around the cubes and color the squares with a dark crayon to show that no grass is available there. When students are done, ask them to compare the amount of grassy field available to the farmers' animals.

Expect

- Students may start by trying to find the area of the green space rather than recognizing that the grassy areas can easily be compared because each has the same amount (three unit squares) removed. Ask students to imagine measuring the areas of both of the grassy fields with five barns on each, placed differently. What would they find? (They would find that the two fields have exactly the same area: the total field area, less the area covered by the five barns.)

- If students are struggling with the field comparisons and do not conserve area, you might modify the activity to involve crackers or chocolate bars. For example, removing two sections from one end of a chocolate bar that is divided into eight sections is the same as removing one section from one end of the bar and one more section from the other end. In both cases, six sections of chocolate bar will remain, although the shapes will be different.

Extend

Say the following to the class:

> Pretend that we need to build islands that have the same area but as many different shapes as possible to house our monkey exhibit at Zany Zoo. The islands are made of squares, and when they are made of more than one square, the squares join on a side.

Ask students to solve this problem first with islands with an area of 1 square unit, then proceeding to larger island sizes of 2 square units, and then moving on to 3, 4, and finally 5 square units. If possible, provide square-inch tiles for students to move around and experiment with in various combinations to form different island shapes.

Have students use 1-inch square sections of 1-inch ruled graph paper to research the possible variations of island shapes given exactly 1, 2, 3, 4, or 5 square units of area. Ask them to record their findings in a table, attaching the paper squares to the table. Avoid telling students how many different cases are possible with each number of square tiles; rather, if they believe that they have found all the cases, ask them to support their claim that they have exhausted the possibilities.

This task of looking for all the possible variations (especially with five squares) will be challenging. It will help encourage students to engage in systematic thinking. For example, consider the challenge of finding all the shapes that have an area of four square units. Think about all the addition facts that sum to four: 4 + 0 (four in a row); 3 + 1 (one square slides along the row of three, making a T shape and an L shape); 2 + 2 (first make a large 2 × 2 square, then let two squares slide away on one side to make an offset shape, like a Z). You may use a similar pattern of analysis to look for all the cases with 5 square tiles. See table 4.6 for a breakdown of all the ways in which islands with areas of 1 through 5 square units could be configured.

Table 4.6. Configuration possibilities for islands with areas of 1–5 square units

# of squares used	# of different cases (shapes)	Examples of various cases
1	1	
2	1	
3	2 cases	
4	5 cases	
5	12 cases	

After students grasp all the possible variations, ask them to write a recommendation to the superintendent of the zoo showing their favorite island shape with an area of 5 square units. Have them explain why they like this design best for the monkeys.

Activity 9: Comparison of Areas

Key idea: *Composing and decomposing regions of area to compare*
Learning trajectory level: *Area Row and Column Structurer*

Essentials

You will need to create a number line, preferably on a large scale. We suggest using masking tape on the floor to mark off and label 12 units that are a foot apart. Also, use the template at More4U to make each student a copy of the Area Comparison chart and accompanying shapes shown in figure 4.22 on page 162.

Engage

Create a collection of shapes out of construction paper. To start, cut out two squares, and then cut one of the squares in half diagonally to make a triangle. Have students watch you work with these shapes so that they understand that the ratio of the square to the half-square (triangle) is 2 to 1.

Put the square above the 4 on the large number line that you have created, as shown in figure 4.20. Tell the students that the square has an area of 4 and that is why it is placed above the 4 on the number line—not because it has four sides or four corners.

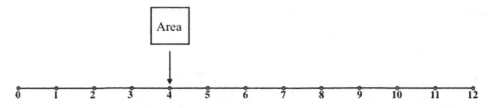

Fig. 4.20. Placing a square along a number line to indicate its area

Ask students where they should put the triangle on the number line to show its area compared with that of the square. If they say that the triangle should be placed above the 2, ask them to share their reasoning. If not, engage them in discussion to help them see that half of 4—half of the square—is 2. Ask students whether any other shape could have been cut from the square that also could be placed above the 2 on the number line. Several ways of cutting a square in half are possible, as shown in figure 4.21.

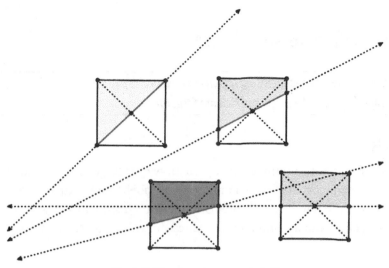

Fig. 4.21. Ways to cut a square in half

Next, move the square to 6 and ask students where the triangle should go now (at 3). Then choose a placement for the triangle (for example, at 5), and ask students to place the square correctly. When you believe that students grasp the game, move on to the activity.

Explore

Give each student a copy of the chart and shapes in figure 4.22. Using their understanding of area ratios, students should compare the area of shapes A–H and fill in the accompanying chart. (Assume that all the shapes are drawn to scale. See fig. 4.24 for a supporting hint.)

	A	B	C	D	E	F	G	H
Task 1	4							
Task 2					6			
Task 3			1					
Task 4	1							
Task 5		3						

Fig. 4.22. Area comparison

Figure 4.23 provides a completed chart as an answer key for the area comparison chart. Note that when possible the answers are given as fractions that use the same denominator to support and align with CCSSM 3.NF.A.1, "Understand all fractions as multiples of a unit fraction." To stress this idea, we recommend reading a non-unit fraction as some multiple of a unit fraction. For example, you would read "3/4" as "three one-fourths," and you might interpret this for your students as "three sets of one-quarter each," written as "3(1/4)" or "three one-quarter portions." It may be important for your students to read and write these numbers along with you to change the way that they think about them, rather than just saying "three-quarters" and writing "3/4."

	A	B	C	D	E	F	G	H
Task 1	4	2	2	1	3	1/2	1	3/2
Task 2	8	4	4	2	6	1	2	3
Task 3	2	1	1	2/4	6/4	1/4	2/4	3/4
Task 4	1	4/8	4/8	2/8	5/8	1/8	2/8	3/8
Task 5	6	3	3	3/2	9/2	3/4	3/2	9/4

Fig. 4.23. Student chart and answer key: Area comparison

Expect

To check students' understanding about parts of the same whole, consider asking them whether shape B or shape C in figure 4.22 has a bigger area. Some students are likely to think, on the basis of a visual comparison, that B is larger. This misconception may be influenced by the larger perimeter of shape B. You can anticipate same misconception when students are comparing shapes D and G. We encourage you to label shape F as a unit fraction, say 1/4, and use that shape to partition a larger shape, such as E, into a multiple of that unit fraction. Figure 4.24 illustrates how shape E equals six 1/4's, as represented by shape F.

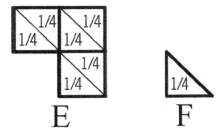

Fig. 4.24. Comparison of the area of shapes E and F, as 6:1

Extend

- Ask students to compare the perimeters of shapes A, C, D, and E in figure 4.22. For example, if the perimeter of A is 8, the perimeter of D is 4. (We suggest omitting all the triangles and the trapezoid to avoid answers that are irrational numbers.)

- Have students try working with much larger ratios by comparing the area and perimeter of a paper rectangle that is formed of six or eight unit squares with the area and perimeter of the original unit square and the half-unit triangle.

Enrich

Read *Hamster Champs* by Stuart J. Murphy (HarperCollins 2005). Three daredevil hamsters, a few alphabet blocks, a board, and a protractor show readers how to measure angles and escape a hungry cat.

Activity 10: Angles and Arms

Key idea: Identifying the attribute of angle
Learning trajectory level: Angle Size Comparer

Essentials

Gather sections of rope (or string or yarn) that are at least ten feet long, protractors, and ring-shaped objects such as bracelets.

Engage

Demonstrate with three students how to create an angle by passing a section of rope through a ring. One student should hold the ring while two others hold an "arm" of the rope. This arrangement serves as a model of an angle. Ask the rest of the students to put their wrists together and form a V shape with their hands to imitate the angle. Check students' understanding of angles measuring 90 degrees, less than 90 degrees, and more than 90 degrees by asking the students holding the rope and ring to create angles of those descriptions. The rest of the students should mimic with their hands the angle the demonstrators make.

Next, have the three demonstrators kneel on the floor and lay the rope out in an acute angle, as shown in figure 4.25. Use a protractor to check the angle at the vertex by Student B. The angle shown in the figure happens to be 33 degrees, but any angle between 20 and 60 degrees will be a good first example. Leave this angle on the floor for the Explore activity.

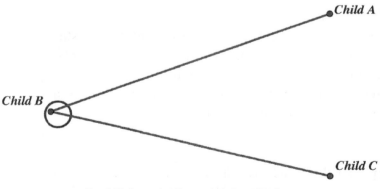

Fig. 4.25. Arranging the rope angle on the floor

Explore

Divide students into groups of three, and give each group a ring, a length of rope, and a protractor. Each group should try to copy the rope model on the floor. Check each group's angle by using a protractor to see whether it is close to the angle on the floor.

Next, assign two groups of three students to work together. Ask the three students in group 1 to start by forming an angle with their rope and ring that is less than 90 degrees but more than 30 degrees. Group members should remain standing while adjusting the size of the angle to their liking, and then place the rope on the floor for measurement with a protractor. The three students in group 2 should next guess the size of the angle and record their guess, measure the angle with the protractor, document the measurement, and then copy group 1's angle with their own rope and ring without using the protractor. Group 1 should then use the protractor to check whether the angle that group 2 built is a good copy.

Finally, the two groups should trade roles. The students in group 2 should start by creating an angle of their choosing that they expect to measure between 60 and 90 degrees. The students in group 1 should then respond by guessing the angle shown, recording their guess, measuring the angle with a protractor, and reporting the angle size. Group 1 should then copy group 2's angle, using their own rope and ring. Which group was able to copy the angle most accurately?

Expect

- Students may confuse the size of the angle with the length of the arms. The extension activity should help students distinguish these two aspects of angles.

- Protractor scales can be difficult for students to read, since two numbers appear at each tick marking. For example, the number labels 60 and 120 appear on the same tick mark and indicate two different angle measures. Students must decide whether an angle measures more or less than 90 degrees by visual inspection.

Extend

Select a group of three students and ask the class to watch while this group changes the arm lengths of their angle, leaving the angle itself at a constant measure (say, 45 degrees). Next, have groups experiment with changing the arm lengths of angles. After students try this several times (be sure to have them trade positions), regroup as a class and discuss students' findings about angle sizes in relation to arm length. Emphasize that the length of the arms of an angle may change without affecting the size of the angle. Have students document the angles they have produced while working in groups, labeling each angle with its measure in degrees.

Enrich

Read *Sir Cumference and the First Round Table* by Cindy Neuschwander and Wayne Geehan (Charlesbridge 1997). King Arthur is a good monarch, but he needs to find a good ruler. This math adventure uses humor to explain geometric concepts.

5

GRADE 4: LENGTH, AREA, VOLUME, AND ANGLE MEASUREMENT

Big measurement ideas identified in CCSSM: Throughout this chapter, we focus on two main ideas closely related to the grade 4 Common Core State Standards. We use measurement contexts to model and develop understanding and fluency with numerical operations. Specifically, we address multidigit multiplication and division, "fraction equivalence, addition and subtraction of fractions with like denominators, and multiplication of fractions by whole numbers" (CCSSM, Grade 4, Introduction). We also include an introduction to angle comparisons and measures.

Learning trajectory levels in this grade: Within the length learning trajectory, fourth graders are performing mainly at the Integrated Conceptual Path Measurer and Abstract Length Measurer levels. These two levels require students to work with bent paths as well as fractional length units. Within the area learning trajectory, students are growing from Area Unit Relater and Repeater (iterating individual units of area) through Array Structurer. This transition is the result of students' increasing ability to see and use groups of area units. In the final activity in this chapter, students are introduced to volume measurement, working at the Volume Quantity Recognizer and Volume Unit Relater and Repeater levels. At these levels, students will be expected to describe the attribute of volume more precisely and begin to reason about filling and packing space. Four activities also introduce angle and angle measure. The angle learning trajectory levels addressed are Angle Size Comparer and Angle Measurer. At these levels, students begin to compare angles by size and initiate the process of quantifying angles. Table 5.1 (following page) shows the learning trajectory levels for length, area, volume, and angle for this grade.

Table 5.1. Learning trajectory levels by grade and topic

Grade	Length LT levels	Area LT levels	Volume LT levels	Angle LT levels
4	Integrated Conceptual Path Measurer Abstract Length Measurer	Area Unit Relater and Repeater Initial Composite Structurer Area Row and Column Structurer Array Structurer	Volume Quantity Recognizer Volume Unit Relater and Repeater	Angle Size Comparer Angle Measurer

Table 5.2 provides an overview of the activities in the chapter. Each activity is linked to the relevant CCSSM standard and levels from the relevant learning trajectories.

Table 5.2. Grade 4 activities matched with Common Core State Standards and learning trajectory levels

General CCSSM	Learning activities	Activity-specific standards	Learning trajectory levels
Modeling multi-digit multiplication 4.MD.A.3 Apply area formula for rectangles 4.OA.A.2 Solve problems involving multiplicative comparisons 4.NBT.B.5 Apply area models to multiplication	**Activity 1: How Big Is This Room?** Key idea: Applying the area formula to determine area or a missing dimension	4.MD.A.3	Area Unit Relater and Repeater Initial Composite Structurer Area Row and Column Structurer
	Activity 2: Comparing Stacks Key idea: Comparing lengths additively and multiplicatively	4.OA.A.2	Abstract Length Measurer
	Activity 3: Why Is This the Same as That? Key idea: Connecting representations of area	4.NBT.B.5	Array Structurer

General CCSSM	Learning activities	Activity-specific standards	Learning trajectory levels
Operating on fractions 4.NF.A.1 Generate equivalent fractions using visual models 4.NF.B.4 Represent whole number fraction products using visual models	**Activity 4: Wraps and Sides Again** Key idea: Converting and comparing fractions	4.NF.A.1 4.NF.B.4a 4.NF.B.4b	Integrated Conceptual Path Measurer
	Activity 5: One-Third of What? Key idea: Multiplying a fraction by a whole number	4.NF.B.4	Array Structurer
Classifying geometric figures by attributes including angle 4.MD.C.5 Recognize and understand angle measure	**Activity 6: How Far Have We Gone?** Key idea: Connecting length and angle measure	4.MD.C.5	Angle Measurer Angle Size Comparer
	Activity 7: Where Do You Place Your Sprinklers? Key idea: Understanding and estimating angle measure	4.MD.C.5a 4.MD.C.5b	Angle Measurer
	Activity 8: Snowboarding Spins and Flips Key idea: Exploring turns and rotations	4.MD.C.5a 4.MD.C.5b	Angle Measurer
	Activity 9: Using Wedges to Focus on Angles Key idea: Discerning angle measure	4.MD.C.5a 4.MD.C.5b	Angle Measurer
Developing understanding of volume 5.MD.C.3 Recognize volume as an attribute of solid figures and understand concepts of volume measurement	**Activity 10: Capacity in the Kitchen** Key idea: Introduction to volume	5.MD.C.5a 5.MD.C.5b	Volume Quantity Recognizer Volume Unit Relater and Repeater

Activity 1: How Big Is This Room?

Key idea: *Applying the area formula to determine area or a missing dimension*
Learning trajectory levels: *Area Unit Relater and Repeater; Initial Composite Structurer;*
   Area Row and Column Structurer

Essentials

For each student, make a copy of the activity sheet shown in figure 5.2 on the next page (see More4U for a printable version).

Draw an image, or project one, that shows a scaled version of a rectangle with dimensions of 8 feet by 12.5 feet. Then draw a horizontal line segment scaled to approximately 10 feet, with dotted lines extending down from each end point. Label the rectangle and line segment as shown in figure 5.1.

Engage

Tell students,

> When Dave was a child, his family moved to a new house. Before he moved, Dave shared a room with his younger sibling, but each of them was going to have his or her room in the new house. Dave was excited about getting his own room and wondered how all his belongings would fit.

Working in groups, students should describe the dimensions of their ideal room and where in the room they would put all their belongings, including their bed, desk, and chest of drawers. Note that a variety of reasonable answers are possible and that students are likely to discuss typical bed size and other furniture sizes. Feel free to engage in this discussion as you see fit, keeping in mind that estimation has value. Then ask students to share their room sizes and what objects they would need to consider when setting up their rooms.

Explore

Explain that Craig moved to a new house as well. He remembers the event:

> When I moved, my younger sister and I had to pick our rooms in our new house. One room was 12.5 feet long and 8 feet wide, and the other room was 10 feet long (see fig. 5.1), but our parents assured us that both rooms were the same size (meaning the same area). When deciding which room I preferred, I remembered that I had two large posters (48 inches by 48 inches) that I wanted to hang side by side on the wall, but the 10-foot-long walls had either

doors or windows, so the posters would have to go on one of the
other two walls. I wondered whether the 10-foot-long room would
be wide enough to hold both posters? If so, how far apart could the
posters be spaced?

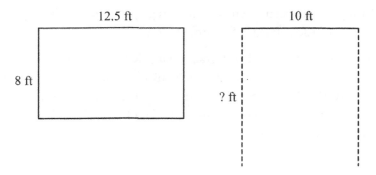

12.5 ft

10 ft

8 ft

? ft

Fig. 5.1. Dimensions of Craig's and his sister's rooms

Ask students, "If both rooms had the same area, how wide was the second
bedroom? Which room would you choose if you had your choice?"

Next, distribute copies of the sheet shown in figure 5.2. Have students work
through this collection of tasks. Note that item 4 is open-ended. Ask students
to find at least three different possible sets of dimensions for Room 2—without
switching the length and width. That is, a room that is 15 feet long by 8 feet
wide would be considered the same as a room that is 8 feet long by 15 feet wide.
Discuss which of these dimensions would yield a reasonable room design.

Both rooms have the same area. Find the missing dimensions.		
	Room 1	Room 2
1	Length: 16 feet Width: 6 feet Area:	Length: 8 feet Width: Area:
2	Length: 10 feet Width: 15 feet Area:	Length: Width: 12 feet Area:
3	Length: 12 feet Width: 12 feet Area:	Length: 9 feet Width: Area:
4	Length: 10 feet Width: 12 feet Area:	Length: Width: Area:

Fig. 5.2. Student activity sheet: What are the missing dimensions?

Expect

- Some students may use a missing-factor approach while others may use division to determine room dimensions. Because the distinction between the two strategies is subtle, it may be difficult for your students to distinguish between them. We encourage you to have students verbalize and record each strategy for comparison.

- If students have to deal with fractional side lengths, we anticipate that some may prefer to work with decimals while others may prefer fractions or converting between inches and feet. Watch to be sure that students don't inadvertently convert tenths of a foot to 1 inch—for example, calling 12.5 feet "12 feet 5 inches."

Extend

Challenge students by extending problem 4 from figure 5.1 to include all whole-number pairs for length and width that will result in an area of 120 square feet. Without switching the order of the dimensions, they can find a total of eight whole-number pairings (1 and 120, 2 and 60, 3 and 40, 4 and 30, 5 and 24, 6 and 20, 8 and 15, 10 and 12). Non-whole number solutions, such as 1.5 times 80, also are possible. Feel free to extend and explore as needed.

Enrich

Read *Math on the Playground: Area and Perimeter* by Ian F. Mahaney (PowerKIDS Press 2013). Readers can figure out perimeters and areas from dimensions given to compare playgrounds shown in photographs, as well as solve other problems posed. Helpful labeled diagrams are included.

Activity 2: Comparing Stacks

Key idea: *Comparing lengths additively and multiplicatively*
Learning trajectory level: *Abstract Length Measurer*

Essentials

For each student, make copies of the activity sheets shown in figure 5.3, below, and figure 5.5, on the following page (see More4U for printable versions of these figures).

Gather Unifix cubes of different colors and assemble stacks of cubes with heights of 1, 2, 3, 4, 6, and 12.

Engage

Present students with a stack of 2 cubes and a stack of 6 cubes by placing them side by side with the bottom cubes aligned. Ask students to compare the two stacks. Possible responses may include that the stack with 6 is higher or longer, the stack with 2 is shorter, the stack with 6 has 4 more, the stack with 2 has 4 fewer, the stack with 6 is three times as tall or as long, or the stack of 2 is one-third as tall or as long. All these comparisons can be interpreted as correct, depending on the type of comparison, what unit is used, and which object is chosen as the referent.

Explore

In a very real sense, all measurements are comparisons. Discuss all the different ways in which two objects can be compared—for example, the many ways in which the stacks of 6 and 2 may be compared. Help your students learn the vocabulary for additive comparisons (how many more than, or how many fewer than) and multiplicative comparisons (how many times as long as). Hand out copies of the student activity sheet in figure 5.3, and ask students to complete it. (Fig. 5.4 provides an answer key for the sheet.)

Stack A	Stack B	Additive		Multiplicative	
2	6				
3	6				
1	4				
4	6				
1	12				

Fig. 5.3. Student activity sheet: Find the additive and multiplicative comparisons

Stack A	Stack B	Additive		Multiplicative	
2	6	Stack A is 4 fewer than stack B.	Stack B is 4 more than stack A.	Stack A is $1/3$ as long as stack B.	Stack B is 3 times as long as stack A.
3	6	Stack A is 3 fewer than stack B.	Stack B is 3 more than stack A.	Stack A is $1/2$ as long as stack B.	Stack B is 2 times as long as stack A.
1	4	Stack A is 3 fewer than stack B.	Stack B is 3 more than stack A.	Stack A is $1/4$ as long as stack B.	Stack B is 4 times as long as stack A.
4	6	Stack A is 2 fewer than stack B.	Stack B is 2 more than stack A.	Stack A is $2/3$ as long as stack B.	Stack B is $3/2$ times as long as stack A.
1	12	Stack A is 11 fewer than stack B.	Stack B is 11 more than stack A.	Stack A is $1/12$ as long as stack B.	Stack B is 12 times as long as stack A.

Fig. 5.4. Answer key for the additive and multiplicative comparisons activity sheet

After students have completed the activity sheet in figure 5.3, hand out copies of the activity sheet shown in figure 5.5, which gives the additive and multiplicative comparisons for two unknown stacks and asks students to find the stacks that fit the descriptions. You might want to start with an example, perhaps completing the first row of the table as a class. (Have students who quickly complete this task find other pairs that fit the same descriptions.) Students may find it helpful to build models of the stacks with Unifix cubes. (Fig. 5.6 provides an answer key for the activity sheet.)

Stack A	Stack B	Additive	Multiplicative
		Stack A is 8 fewer than stack B.	Stack B is 3 times as long as stack A.
		Stack B is 2 more than stack A.	Stack A is $1/3$ as long as stack B.
		Stack A is 1 fewer than stack B.	Stack B is $4/3$ as long as stack A.
		Stack B is 2 more than stack A.	Stack A is $3/4$ as long as stack B.
		Stack A is 8 more than stack B.	Stack A is 5 times as long as stack B.

Fig. 5.5. Student activity sheet: Find the stack height

Stack A	Stack B	Additive	Multiplicative
4	12	Stack A is 8 fewer than stack B.	Stack B is 3 times as long as stack A.
1	3	Stack B is 2 more than stack A.	Stack A is ¹/₃ as long as stack B.
3	4	Stack A is 1 fewer than stack B.	Stack B is ⁴/₃ as long as stack A.
6	8	Stack B is 2 more than stack A.	Stack A is ³/₄ as long as stack B.
2	10	Stack A is 8 more than stack B.	Stack A is 5 times as long as stack B.

Fig. 5.6. Answer key for the stack height activity sheet

Expect

Keep in mind that there are other ways in which two stacks or numbers can be compared. Students may combine the additive and multiplicative approaches and report something equivalent to a percentage increase. For example, when comparing stacks that are 12 and 2 high, a student might report that 12 is "5 larger" by thinking of 2 as the unit and seeing that 2 goes into the 10 additional units in the 12-unit stack (12 − 2) 5 times, as shown in figure 5.7.

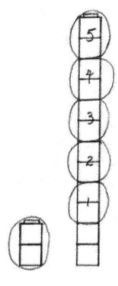

Fig. 5.7. Why a student might say 12 is 5 times larger than 2

It is common for students to take this approach in the simple case of comparing 2 to 1. Students will report that 2 is 1 times larger than 1, meaning 2 is 100 percent more than 1, rather than that 2 is 200 percent of 1 (or 2 is 2 times as large as 1).

Extend

Present students with challenges based on either additive or multiplicative comparison. For example, "I am thinking of two stacks that have an additive comparison of 3 more. Find two stacks that satisfy this rule." Answers might include a stack of 1 and a stack of 4 or a stack of 3 and a stack of 6. You can also encourage students to generate additional pairings that satisfy this comparison, all of which will have the form A:(A + 3).

This extension can be followed by similar multiplicative comparisons—for example, "I am thinking of two stacks that have a multiplicative comparison. One is 3 times as tall as the other. Find two stacks that satisfy this rule." Answers might include 1:3, 2:6, or 4:12. Again, you can encourage students to generate additional pairings that satisfy this comparison, all of which will have the form A:(3A).

Enrich

Throughout this activity, students have been thinking about the relationships between quantities; this is an essential part of algebraic thinking. For example, the relationships in the first row of the table in figure 5.3 can be represented as

(the number of cubes in stack A) = (the number of cubes in stack B) − 8

and

(the number of cubes in stack B) = 3 × (the number of cubes in stack A).

Or, more formally, they may be expressed as

$$A = B - 8 \text{ and } B = 3A,$$

with a solution of A = 4 and B = 12. The letter B represents the number of cubes in stack B, and likewise for the letter A. Consider having your students translate the rest of the rows in the table by using symbols that express the same relationships. In algebra, these relationships are modeled by a system of linear equations.

Activity 3: Why Is This the Same as That?

Key idea: *Connecting representations of area*
Learning trajectory level: *Array Structurer*

Essentials

Gather colored square-inch tiles, approximately 50 tiles per group. Alternatively, students can work on grid paper.

Engage

Tell students,

> Two students were working on different math problems and ended up getting the same answer. The first student was calculating 7×13, and the other student was calculating $(7 \times 10) + (7 \times 3)$, and both got an answer of 91. First, check to make sure both students calculated their answers correctly. Now create a similar problem by completing the equation $(7 \times \underline{\quad}) + (7 \times \underline{\quad}) = 7 \times 13$.

(You may want to encourage students to use whole numbers to create several of these examples.)

Continue,

> Now try this same approach to create an equivalent expression for 8×14.

Explore

Encourage students to explain what is going on with the problems that they just worked on. How could they best explain to a second grader why $5 \times 8 = (5 \times 5) + (5 \times 3)$? Students can use colored square-inch tiles to model the problems, as illustrated in figure 5.8.

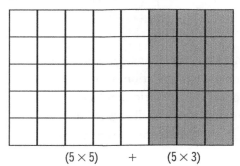
(5 × 5)   +   (5 × 3)

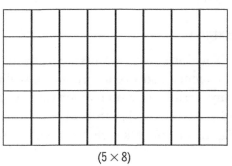
(5 × 8)

Fig. 5.8. Modeling equivalent multiplication problems

Keep in mind that we are trying to highlight the distributive property of multiplication over addition, and visual models like colored arrays of tiles help show that $5 \times 8 = 5 \times (5 + 3) = (5 \times 5) + (5 \times 3)$. We recommend asking students to use both representations—the numerical expressions and the physical representations of area measurement.

After presenting students with a numeric representation and asking them to provide the related spatial representation, show them a spatial representation such as the one in figure 5.9, and ask them to produce the accompanying numeric sentence. In this case, the sentence would be $(4 \times 7) = 4 \times (4 + 3) = (4 \times 4) + (4 \times 3)$.

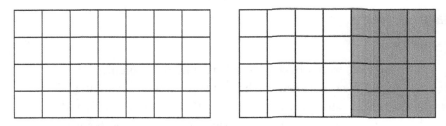

Fig. 5.9. Spatial representation of $(4 \times 7) = (4 \times 4) + (4 \times 3)$

Expect

Much of this activity assumes that students understand that a 5-by-6 array of 1-inch tiles models the operation 5×6 because it presents 5 sets of 6 tiles, or 6 sets of 5 tiles, but some students may need some guidance to make this connection. Note that this activity is meant to highlight 4.NBT.B.5 in CCSSM, which states that students should be able to apply area models to understand multiplication. Here we are using this modeling to draw out the distributive property of multiplication over addition. We think that urging students to provide and connect both the numeric and spatial representations is important, but we anticipate that some students will be more comfortable with one representation than the other, while others will fail to see how the two are related.

Extend

If you think your students are ready to progress further, consider extending the models above to incorporate distribution of multiplication over three terms. For example, you can give students the numeric sentence $(5 \times 4) + (5 \times 3) + (5 \times 2)$ or recreate the spatial model illustrated in figure 5.10 and ask them to provide the other representation as well as the equivalent product $a \times b$, with a and b being whole numbers. (In this example, the equivalent product is 5×9.)

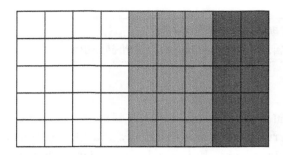

Fig. 5.10. Spatial representation of $(5 \times 4) + (5 \times 3) + (5 \times 2)$

Enrich

Read *Great Estimations* by Bruce Goldstone (Scholastic 2006). Strategies for estimating, such as eye training, clump counting, and box and count are presented. For example, if you need to estimate how many cherries are in a quart, it helps to see the space taken up by 10 cherries and 100 cherries.

Activity 4: Wraps and Sides Again

Key idea: Converting and comparing fractions
Learning trajectory level: Integrated Conceptual Path Measurer

Essentials

Use the template at More4U to make a copy of figure 5.11 for each student. On the board, draw a ruler, oriented horizontally, and a line segment above it, with its left endpoint aligned with the left end of the ruler, as shown on the left side of figure 5.15 on page 186. Make copies of the activity sheets in figures 5.12, 5.13, and 5.16 for each student (see More4U). (See activities 3, 4, and 5 in chapter 4 for background.)

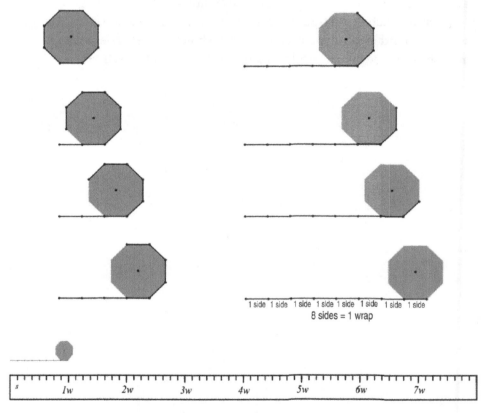

Fig. 5.11. Octagon wraps and sides display and tool

Engage

Tell students,

> Today we will be measuring by using units, "wraps," and sides with unique lengths. Imagine that you have a regular octagon whose perimeter is 1 inch (see fig. 5.11). Notice on the wraps-and-sides ruler that the regular octagon has been "unwrapped" and the sides are marked along the edge of the tool.

As a class, go over the example from the activity sheet (fig. 5.12), and then have students complete the rest of the sheet. When they have finished, ask students to convert given lengths to different units without providing drawings of the segments or the rulers. For example, how many wraps long is a segment if it is 16 sides long? 20 sides? 6 sides? How many sides long is a segment if it is 3 wraps long? $1^1/_2$ wraps? $^7/_8$ wraps? Finally, ask students which is longer, 3 wraps or 19 sides. How much longer? Have students explain their answers. (Note that this question is analogous to comparing lengths of 3 inches and 19 one-eighth inches, which can be solved by converting 3 inches to 24 one-eighth inches.)

Report the length of each segment in three
different ways: wraps and sides, sides, wraps.

Example

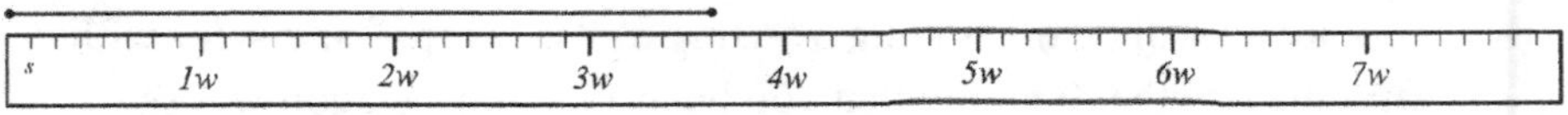

Wraps and sides:	Sides:	Wraps:
3w and 5s	29s	$\left(3 \text{ and } \frac{5}{8}\right)w$

1.

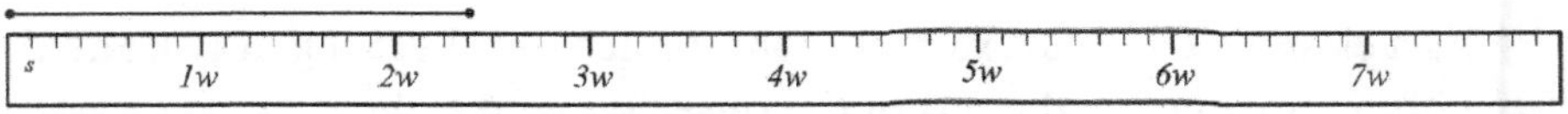

Wraps and sides:	Sides:	Wraps:

2.

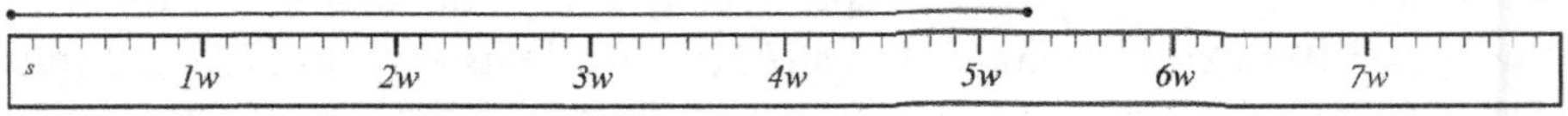

Wraps and sides:	Sides:	Wraps:

3.

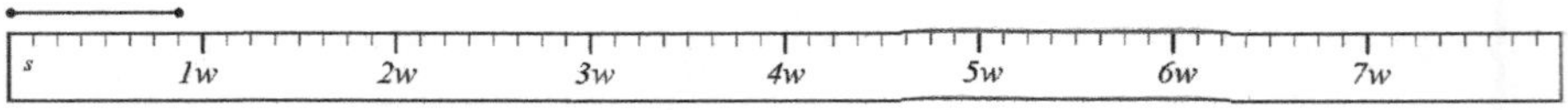

Wraps and sides:	Sides:	Wraps:

4.

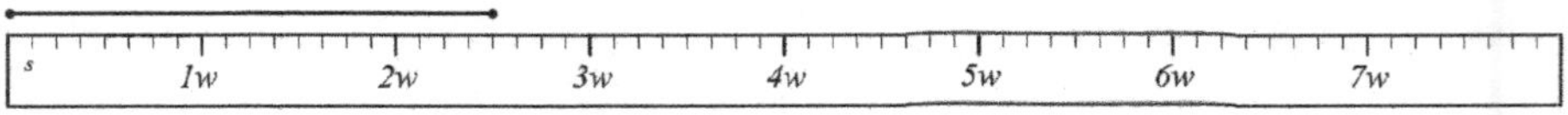

Wraps and sides:	Sides:	Wraps:

5.

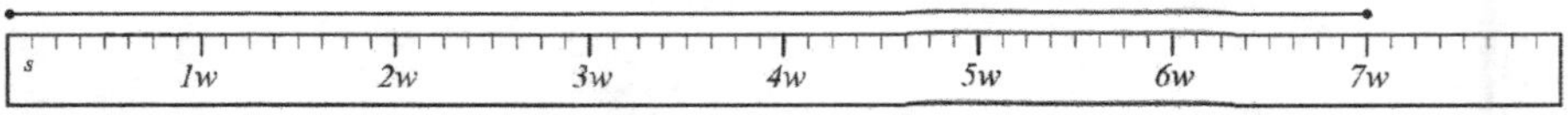

Wraps and sides:	Sides:	Wraps:

Fig. 5.12. Student activity sheet: Measuring wraps and sides

Explore

Tell students,

> I have a sheet with the measurements of some line segments on it.
> I lost the sheet that shows the line segments as well as their lengths,
> which were reported in different units. I think we can fill in the
> missing measures in the table (fig. 5.13), remembering that each
> side of the octagon was one-eighth of an inch long.

Lead students through a discussion to elicit the relationships between wraps
and sides. Assuming that the perimeter of the octagon is 1 inch, one side of the
octagon is $1/8$ inch long, two sides are $1/4$ (or $2/8$) inch long, four sides are $1/2$ inch
long, six sides are equivalent to $3/4$ inch, and eight sides are equivalent to 1 inch.
Record these measurements on the board.

Next, have students work on converting measures between eighths, quarters,
halves, and inches. Distribute the student activity sheet in figure 5.13. For each
example, ask students to draw a line segment of the given length, using their
wraps-and-sides measuring tool, and then use the tool to help them fill in the
values in the remainder of the table. (Fig. 5.14 provides an answer key.)

Example	Eighths ($1/8$ in)	Quarters ($1/4$ in)	Halves ($1/2$ in)	Inches
1	12 eighth-inches 12 ($1/8$ inches)			
2		14 quarter-inches 14 ($1/4$ inches)		
3			13 half-inches 13 ($1/2$ inches)	
4				7 inches

Fig. 5.13. Student activity sheet: Measurement conversions

Example	Eighths (⅛ in)	Quarters (¼ in)	Halves (½ in)	Inches
1	12 eighth-inches 12 (⅛ inches)	6 quarter-inches 6 (¼ inches)	3 half-inches 3 (½ inches)	1 and a half inches 1.5 inches
2	28 eighth-inches 28 (⅛ inches)	14 quarter-inches 14 (¼ inches)	7 half-inches 7 (½ inches)	3 and a half inches 3.5 inches
3	52 eighth-inches 52 (⅛ inches)	26 quarter-inches 26 (¼ inches)	13 half-inches 13 (½ inches)	6 and a half inches 6.5 inches
4	56 eighth-inches 56 (⅛ inches)	28 quarter-inches 28 (¼ inches)	14 half-inches 14 (½ inches)	7 inches

Fig. 5.14. Answer key for the measurement conversions activity sheet

After students have completed the activity sheet, ask them to compare the lengths of two of the segments at a time. For example, they should decide whether the segment in example 4 is longer or shorter than the segment in example 2 and how much longer or shorter it is. Encourage students to report these differences in eighths, quarters, halves, and whole inches. Record the measurements on the board for discussion.

Share the ruler from the left side of figure 5.15 (draw it on the board or project it for students to see), and ask students to compare lengths that do not appear in figure 5.13—for example, ask students to compare 1.5 and 2.5 inches. The difference between the two lengths can be given as 1 inch, 2 half-inches, 4 quarter-inches, or 8 eighth-inches. The rulers in figure 5.15 display the difference as 1 inch, 2 half-inches, and 4 quarter-inches.

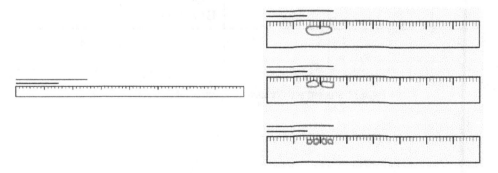

Fig. 5.15. The difference between two lengths, displayed three ways

Next, ask students to complete the activity sheet in figure 5.16 by drawing segments with the given lengths along the measuring tools provided in the figure. Encourage students to reason numerically (converting the measurements to a common denominator) as well as visually (displaying the segments along the measuring tool).

Length 1	Length 2	<, >, or =	Difference (larger length − smaller length)
$^3/_8$	$^2/_4$		
$^{12}/_8$	$^3/_2$		
$^{14}/_8$	$^9/_4$		
$2^3/_4$	$3^1/_8$		
$1^1/_2$	$^7/_4$		

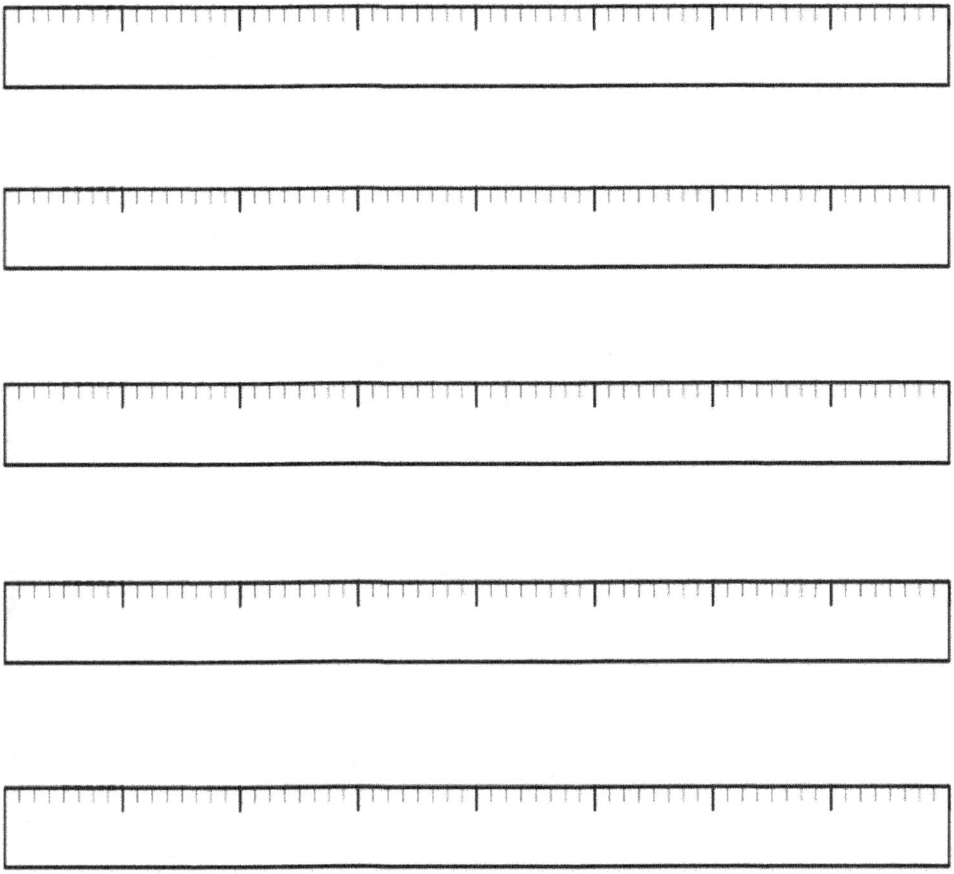

Fig. 5.16. Student activity sheet with measuring tools: Measurement comparisons

Expect

We anticipate that some students will compare fractions by their numerators without paying attention to the units. For example, they may claim that ⁵/₈ is larger than ³/₄. Students may also make mistakes in the use of units, either by not reporting the unit that they are using or by reporting the wrong units. Any time that a student struggles to compare lengths, encourage him or her to display the lengths along the measuring tool, connecting the denominator in the fraction with a different interval on the tool.

Extend

You might push students to measure lengths to the nearest half of an eighth of an inch (¹/₁₆ of an inch). Measuring to this level of precision will help students operate with a standard ruler marked to sixteenths of an inch. Students can also be encouraged to convert lengths such as ⁷/₈ to quarters or halves (3¹/₂ quarters or 1³/₄ halves).

Activity 5: One-Third of What?

Key idea: Multiplying a fraction by a whole number
Learning trajectory level: Array Structurer

Essentials

Make copies of diagrams in figure 5.18 and the activity sheet in figure 5.19 for each student (see More4U).

Engage

Figure 5.17(a) shows a shape that is 1 by 8, and figure 5.17(b) shows the same shape with shading to illustrate $1/2 \times 8 = 4$. Draw figure 5.17(b) on the board and tell students,

> Some fourth graders were asked to use this diagram to create a different diagram that shows $1/2 \times 8$.

Next, distribute copies of the four representations of $1/2 \times 8$ shown in figure 5.18, and say,

> These four diagrams were the four most common ways that the students represented $1/2 \times 8$. Which do you think is the best representation of $1/2 \times 8$? Why? Do any of these representations *not* show $1/2 \times 8$? If you find one that does not show $1/2 \times 8$, then what would you says that it shows?

This activity encourages students to notice and discuss the difference between the number $1/2$, taken to mean the decimal value 0.5, and the fraction $1/2$, taken to mean the part that indicates one of two possible identical parts. Representation (a) shows the number $1/2$, since it shows $1/2 \times 1$ unit square. In contrast, representations (b), (c), and (d) all show the fraction $1/2$ of an entire group of units—in this case, 8 unit squares. However, we prefer representation (c) to the other two. Although representation (d) shows 8 units of size $1/2$, the checkerboard arrangement of the colored pieces makes it more challenging to identify the overall effect of $1/2$ of the total area of 8 unit squares. Representation (b) is in an array, but unlike (c), it does not capitalize on the immediate correspondence between halves of unit squares. Instead, we might take it as a model of 1×4 or $2/2 \times 4$ if we disregard the white portion. In contrast, representation (c) creates an array that clearly shows $1/2$ by 8 because each colored half-unit corresponds directly to a half-unit that is white, so it models the problem $1/2 \times 8$ as a sum of 8 split units, showing that $1/2 \times 8 = (1/2 \times 1) + (1/2 \times 1) + (1/2 \times 1) + (1/2 \times 1) + (1/2 \times 1) + (1/2 \times 1) + (1/2 \times 1) + (1/2 \times 1)$.

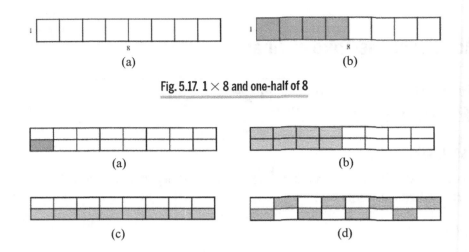

(a)   (b)

Fig. 5.17. 1 × 8 and one-half of 8

(a)   (b)

(c)   (d)

Fig. 5.18. Student representations of ½ × 8

Explore

Tell students that they will be creating pictures that will help them show multiplication problems. The representations that they just looked at helped them see that ½ × 8 = 4. The activity sheet shown in figure 5.19 presents five more examples. Each example gives one representation or the other—either the area model or the mathematical sentence. Distribute the sheet, and ask students to provide the missing representation. (Fig. 5.20 provides an answer key.)

	Area model	Mathematical sentence
1	$\frac{1}{3} \rightarrow$ 6	
2		$\frac{1}{3} \times 7 = 7(\frac{1}{3}) = 2\frac{1}{3}$
3	$\frac{1}{5} \rightarrow$ 7	
4		$(\frac{3}{4}) \times 4 = \frac{12}{4} = 3$
5	$\frac{2}{3} = 2(\frac{1}{3}) \rightarrow \{$ 5	

Fig 5.19. Student activity sheet: Area models representing mathematical sentences

	Area model	Mathematical sentence
1	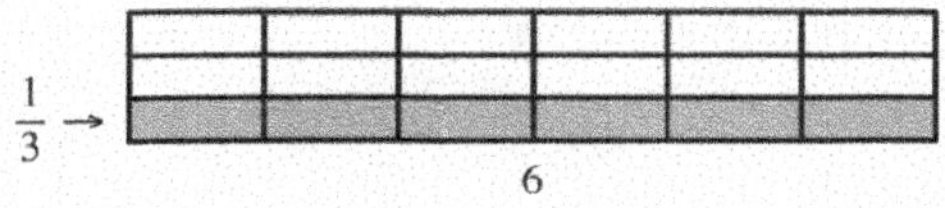 $\frac{1}{3} \rightarrow$ 6	$\frac{1}{3} \times 6 = 6(\frac{1}{3}) = 2$
2	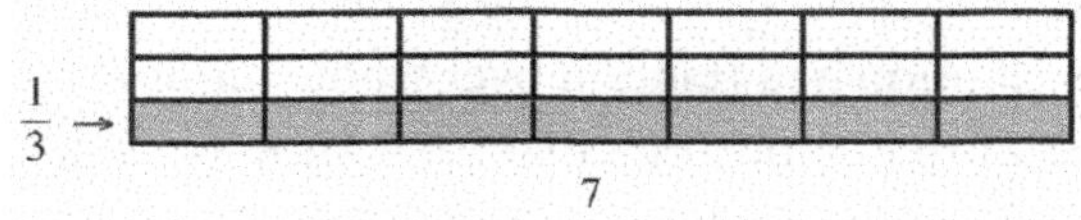 $\frac{1}{3} \rightarrow$ 7	$\frac{1}{3} \times 7 = 7(\frac{1}{3}) = 2\frac{1}{3}$
3	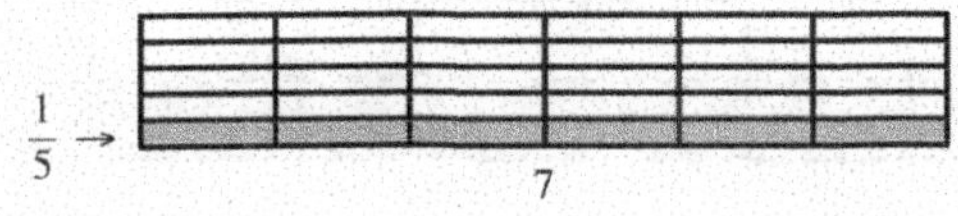 $\frac{1}{5} \rightarrow$ 7	$\frac{1}{5} \times 7 = \frac{7}{5} = 1\frac{2}{5}$
4	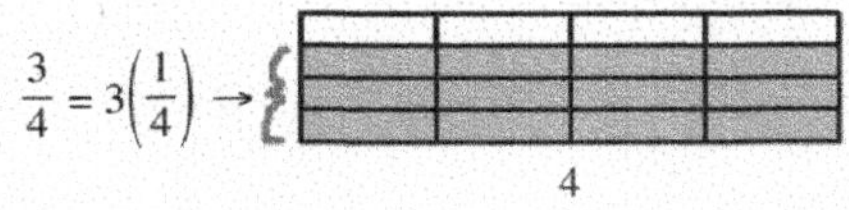 $\frac{3}{4} = 3\left(\frac{1}{4}\right) \rightarrow$ 4	$(\frac{3}{4}) \times 4 = \frac{12}{4} = 3$
5	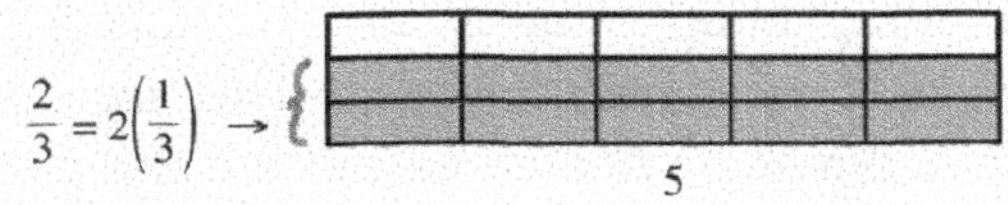 $\frac{2}{3} = 2\left(\frac{1}{3}\right) \rightarrow$ 5	$\frac{2}{3} \times 5 = \frac{10}{3} = 3\frac{1}{3}$

Fig. 5.20. Answer key for the activity sheet in figure 5.19

Expect

- This activity is designed to help students use visual models to apply and extend their understanding of multiplication to problems involving a fraction times a whole number (CCSSM 4.NF.B.4a, 4.NF.B.4b).

- We anticipate that some students will prefer to work with one type of representation over the other, and others will struggle to connect the two representations.

- The activity presents a notation challenge that can be confusing for students while they read or write mixed numbers ($3\frac{1}{2} = 3 + \frac{1}{2} = 3.5$) and whole number–fraction products: $3(\frac{1}{2}) = 3 \times \frac{1}{2} = \frac{3}{2} = 1.5$.

- When students are trying to draw area models to represent the mathematical sentences, they may have trouble creating the correct subdivisions. Drawing accurate fifths and thirds can be particularly tricky. Students can still model situations meaningfully even with imprecise drawings. However, the conceptual difficulties related to interpreting collections of unit fractions in different ways are likely to cause at least some students to struggle.

Extend

Combine this activity with activity 3 (Why Is This the Same as That?) to assist students in modeling the distribution of a fraction over whole numbers. For example, you can use figure 5.21 to demonstrate that $(1/2 \times 3) + (1/2 \times 5) = 1/2 \times (3 + 5) = 1/2 \times 8 = 4$. You also can create and use your own examples.

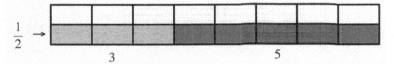

Fig. 5.21. Area model representation of $(1/2 \times 3) + (1/2 \times 5) = 4$

Enrich

Read *Great Estimations* by Bruce Goldstone (Scholastic 2006). Strategies for estimating, such as eye training, clump counting, and box and count are presented. For example, if you need to estimate how many cherries are in a quart, it helps to see the space taken up by 10 cherries and 100 cherries.

Activity 6: How Far Have We Gone?

Key idea: Connecting length and angle measure
Learning trajectory levels: Angle Measurer; Angle Size Comparer

Essentials

Make copies of the activity sheets in figures 5.22 and 5.23 for each student (see More4U).

Engage

Figure 5.22 shows four different paths along which a person has traveled. In each case the total length of the path is given. Ask students to determine how far each person has traveled along the path. (Answers: 1, 75 units; 2, 180 units; 3, 50 units; 4, 90 units.)

Example	Image of path and portion traveled	Distance traveled
1. Total path length is 100 units. How far has the person traveled at this point?	 *Start* *Finish*	
2. Total path length is 360 units. How far has the person traveled at this point?	 *Start* *Finish*	
3. Total path length is 100 units. How far has the person traveled at this point?	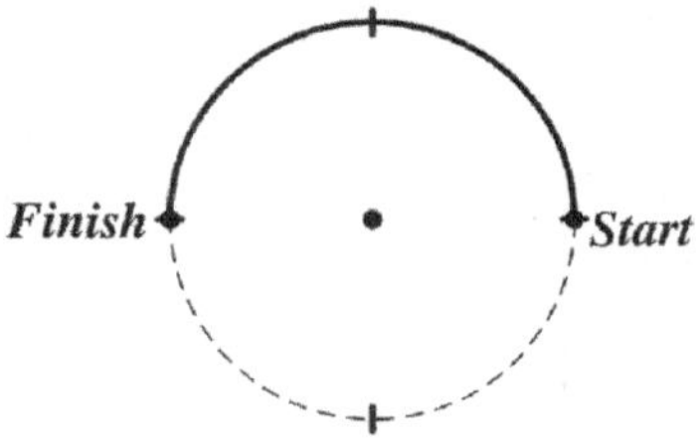 *Finish* *Start*	
4. Total path length is 360 units. How far has the person traveled at this point?	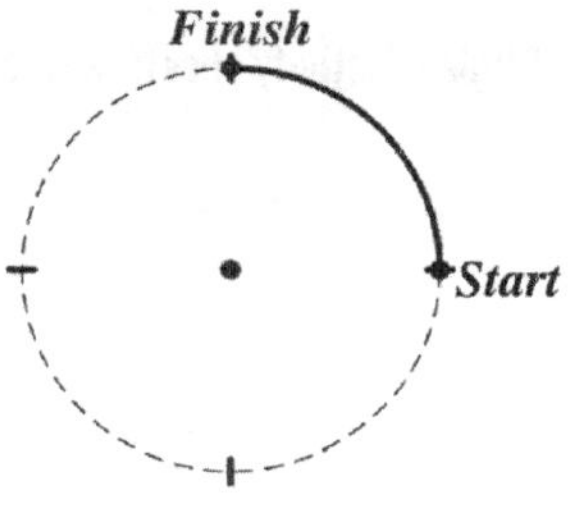 *Finish* *Start*	

Fig. 5.22. Student activity sheet: How far has each person traveled?

Explore

Figure 5.23 shows a circle with a starting and finishing point. (The two images depict the same circle.) Ask students to compare the length of the distance around the circle to the length of the path from start to finish, moving counterclockwise along the solid path. (Fig. 5.24 provides an answer key.)

	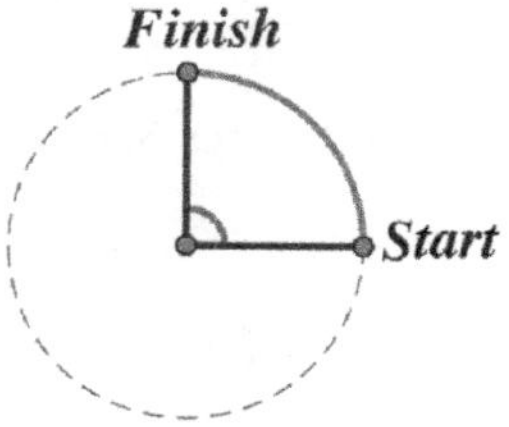	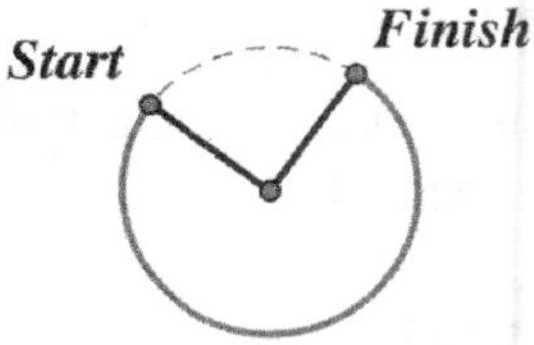
	Finish *Start*	*Start* *Finish*
1. Imagine that the distance around the circle (or the circumference of the circle) is 100 feet. What is the length of the path from start to finish?		
2. Imagine that the distance around the circle (or the circumference of the circle) is 1 foot. What is the length of the path from start to finish?		
3. Imagine that the distance around the circle (or the circumference of the circle) is 1 yard. What is the length of the path from start to finish?		
4. Imagine that the distance around the circle (or the circumference of the circle) is 360 miles. What is the length of the path from start to finish?		

Fig. 5.23. Student activity sheet: How long is the path?

Distance around the circle	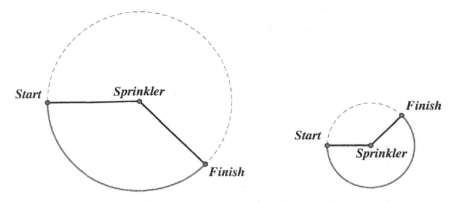...	
1. 100 feet	25 feet	75 feet
2. 1 foot	¼ of a foot, or 3 inches	¾ of a foot, or 9 inches
3. 1 yard	¼ of a yard, or 9 inches	¾
4. 360 miles	90 miles	270 miles

Fig. 5.24. Answer key for the activity sheet in figure 5.23

When developing the exercises in figures 5.22 and 5.23, we focused on part-whole comparisons of linear and curvilinear path lengths. Notice that we defined the whole as measuring 360 units several times to prepare students to work with angle measures. The remainder of this activity focuses on wholes measuring 360 units in an effort to connect this part-whole reasoning to quantifying amount of turn.

Draw or project the image in figure 5.25, which shows two different sprinklers on a golf course. Explain that the sprinklers have a turn adjustment; you can set them to turn through a larger or smaller part of a complete circle to water a larger or a smaller region. If the turn is set to 360 degrees, the sprinkler will rotate a complete circle. In the figure, the left sprinkler's turn adjustment is set to 135 degrees.

Fig. 5.25. The turn of two lawn sprinklers

Ask students:

- Which of the two sprinklers do you think turns more? Explain your reasoning. *Possible response:* "The sprinkler on the right turns more. I know this because the sprinkler on the left turns less than half a turn while the sprinkler on the right turns more than half a turn."

- How much more does one sprinkler turn than the other sprinkler? *Possible response:* Students' answers will depend on their understanding of angle. Expect approximate rather than exact answers. Students may be able to translate the sprinklers mentally, superimposing one on top of the other to reveal a difference of approximately 90 degrees. Alternatively, they may respond that the turn adjustment for the sprinkler on the right is set to approximately 225 degrees, so the difference is 90 degrees $(225 - 135 = 90)$.

Expect

CCSSM expects fourth-grade students to reason about angle measures "by considering the fraction of the circular arc between the points where the two rays intersect the circle" (4.MD.C.5.A). To interpret angle measures in this way, students need to be able to reason proportionally. With this in mind, we anticipate that students who do not have the ability to reason proportionally will struggle to deal with angle measure in a manner consistent with CCSSM.

Some students may confuse angle measure with the area of the region determined by the two rays. This misconception may be particularly prevalent in the sprinkler context, which may tempt students to focus on the amount of grass that will be watered instead of the amount of turn that the sprinkler makes. The next activity is designed to address this misconception.

The sprinkler context may prompt students to partition the arc to relate it to the circle. For example, figure 5.25 is far more helpful for answering the sprinkler comparison question if students think to partition the circle into fourths, eighths, or both, and reason that because the entire circle is 360 degrees, each fourth equals 90 degrees, and each eighth equals 45 degrees.

Extend

- The first task (fig. 5.22) gives students the total measure of a path and a diagram showing the portion of the path a person has traveled, and students use all this information to find the distance the person has traveled. Although this task features line segments and a circle, the procedure can be extended to regular polygons. For example, ask students to imagine a square with three of four sides traced out. If they know that the perimeter of the square is 360 units, then what would be the value of three sides? The same kind of exercise can be done with regular hexagons and octagons.

- The part-whole examples in figures 5.22 and 5.23 give students several wholes along with their measures and ask for the measure of an identified part. Consider having students work in the other direction— that is, giving them a part and its measure and asking them to find the measure of the whole.

- Many students associate the length of the depicted rays in an angle with the measure of the angle. To address this misunderstanding, reconsider the sprinkler context with an adjustment for the amount of turn and a separate adjustment for the distance that the sprinkler will reach. This idea is developed more fully in the next activity.

Enrich

Read *Sir Cumference and the Off-the-Charts Dessert* by Cindy Neuschwander (Scholastic 2013). When Sir Cumference and Lady Di of Ameter invite two bakers to compete for the honor of baking the annual Harvest Sweet, the bakers must figure out a way to show whose treats are the favorites. They introduce charts and graphs.

Activity 7: Where Do You Place Your Sprinklers?

Key idea: Understanding and estimating angle measure
Learning trajectory level: Angle Measurer

Essentials

You will need computer(s) with access to GeoGebra and the angle estimation file (see http://ggbm.at/Q4FujAr8). You will also use another GeoGebra file about sprinkler placement, angle, and distance (see http://www.geogebra.org/m/NjpjB7Uq?doneurl5%2Fmaterials).

Engage

Most sprinklers have two different adjustments on them, one for the amount of turn and the other for the length of the spray. Draw or project an image like that in figure 5.26, in which the sprinkler has its turn set to 90 degrees and its length adjustment set to 10 feet. Ask students to draw a picture showing what the sprinkler coverage would look like if you changed the settings to 180 degrees on the turn setting and 10 feet on the length setting. Next, have them draw a picture showing what the sprinkler coverage would look like if you changed the settings to 90 degrees on the turn setting and 20 feet on the length setting.

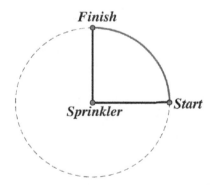

Fig. 5.26. Sprinkler with a turn setting of 90 degrees and a length setting of 10 feet

Explore

In this activity, students have an opportunity to interact with an interactive geometry file. This file has two main purposes. First, it gives students repeated feedback on estimating angle measures; second, it gives them repeated feedback on creating angles with a given measure.

Ask your students to go to a computer and open up the angle estimation file. Students can work individually or in groups; we suggest having them work in pairs (two students at one computer). You can also demonstrate the activity to the entire class and engage in a whole-class discussion, with students predicting and checking.

The file provides a dynamic image of an angle with a start and finish point representing the boundaries of the sprinkled region. Students will be prompted to enter an angle measure to try to match the sprinkler turn setting shown. The first four examples are 30 degrees, 45 degrees, 135 degrees, and 210 degrees. Figure 5.27 shows a correct solution for the first example.

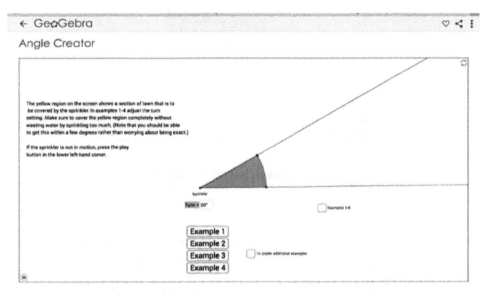

Fig. 5.27. Sprinkled region for a 30-degree angle (see http://ggbm.at/Q4FujAr8)

The next set of four problems contains examples for which the spray length (radius) is no longer constant. These four examples repeat the benchmark angles used above but with different spray lengths (radii) to help students understand that the length of the radius does not affect the measure of the angle. The four examples for this set are (30 degrees, 10 feet), (45 degrees, 30 feet), (135 degrees, 15 feet), and (210 degrees, 20 feet).

As a final task, draw on the board or project the image in figure 5.28, which shows a diagram of a lawn with eight sprinklers. Note that the length of the side of the yard is given as 40 feet. Ask the students to determine the angle and radius setting for each of the six sprinklers along the perimeter of the yard. (Sprinklers 1, 2, 4, and 5 are set to 90 degrees and 20 feet, and sprinklers 3 and

6 are set to 180 degrees and 20 feet.) Then ask students to give estimates for the settings for sprinklers 7 and 8. (The angle setting should be 360 degrees, with a radius setting of 5 to 10 feet. A more exact answer, which is not necessary, is approximately 6.3 feet.)

You may choose to discuss with your students the benefit of overlapping the sprinkled regions to avoid leaving sections of grass unwatered. You might pose a challenge task of changing the placement and setting of the sprinklers to create a "better" setup. For example, increasing the radius of sprinklers 7 and 8 to 20 feet would leave no grass unwatered. You might ask students, "Can you think of better setups that use fewer sprinklers or have less overlap? Is it OK to have the sprinklers spray outside of the edges of the yard?"

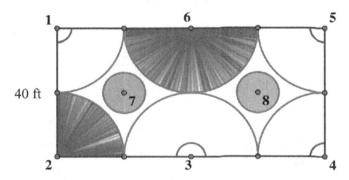

Fig. 5.28. Arrangement of eight lawn sprinklers

Expect

- A misconception that students commonly have about angles is the idea that the lengths of the sides of an angle affect the measure of the angle. To address this misunderstanding, the tasks in this activity include changes in both the angle and the spray length (radius).

- Accuracy and precision are important considerations in working on these tasks. Specifically, the issue of precision—"How close is close enough?"—should be addressed. We recommend expecting nothing more precise than estimates to the nearest foot and nearest degree; estimates within a few degrees are typically sufficient.

Extend

Ask students to make a sketch of their own yard, the school grounds, a community garden, or another plot of land and then design an efficient sprinkler layout that will water the areas that need it while minimizing the number of sprinkler heads, regions that get watered twice, or regions that don't require watering (e.g., sidewalks, driveways). Have students work in the GeoGebra file about sprinkler placement, angle and length, shown in the following link: http://www.geogebra.org/m/NjpjB7Uq?doneurl5%2Fmaterials.

Enrich

For a connection with another context, consider security cameras placed in art galleries. What is the minimum number of such cameras needed to protect a valuable art collection? Learn more by investigating the Klee Art Gallery Theorem; see https://en.wikipedia.org/wiki/Art_gallery_problem.

Activity 8: Snowboarding Spins and Flips

Key idea: Exploring turns and rotations
Learning trajectory level: Angle Measurer

Essentials

Gather construction paper, string, clear tape, and a protractor.

Engage

Read aloud the following news item from the Sochi Winter Olympics about a medalist in snowboarding. In the men's halfpipe snowboarding event at the 2014 Sochi Winter Olympics, everyone was surprised by the winning stunt performed by Iouri Podladchikov, an athlete widely known in the snowboarding world as "i-Pod":

> Having landed his winning run, which scored 94.75 and included his signature "yolo" cab double cork 1440—a flip that he invented and stands for You Only Live Once—Podladchikov went berserk, exchanging high-fives with the crowd and officials. (http://www.theguardian.com/sport/2014/feb/11 /winter-olympics-2014-shaun-white-halfpipe)

Ask students about the name of the stunt, "1440." What do they suppose it means? If they do not know, tell them that 1440 indicates that Podladchikov turned four complete spins in the air, landing back on his feet. The move is called 1440 because it equals 1,440 degrees of turning, with each full spin counting as 360 degrees (multiplying 4 by 360 results in 1,440).

Explore

Have students stand in an open space, allowing room for them to rotate without bumping into others or furniture. Begin by asking them to find a spot on the floor and then turn through one complete rotation while staying in that spot. Explain that this was one rotation of 360 degrees, but the snowboarder in the news report rotated *four* times. He rotated his body through 360 degrees four times in all, for a total of 1,440 degrees. Now ask students to rotate four complete turns, moving slowly to avoid dizziness. Ask students how many degrees they turned through just now (1,440 degrees).

Next, have students face the front of the room while standing and ask them to turn a half rotation to face the back of the room. Tell them that the measure of this half turn is 180 degrees. Ask them to continue turning in the same direction until they face the front of the room once again. Tell them that the second turn was also 180 degrees. In total, they turned one full turn of 360 degrees. Tell them this could also be described as two 180-degree turns.

Explain that, in mathematical language, we use the term *degrees* to describe the measure of turns and rotations. One complete turn equals 360 degrees, and this is the reference for angle measurement in degrees. Mathematicians show angles by drawing rays from the same starting point with some opening to show the angle. Figure 5.29 shows an example of an angle that measures 53 degrees. The angle starts at point *B* and has two "arms" that extend out, one called ray *BA* and the other ray *BC*.

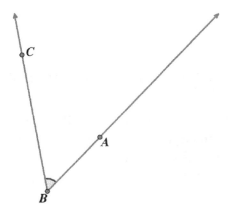

Fig. 5.29. Angle *ABC* measures 53 degrees

Expect

- Students may not realize that a *degree* is a measure of something other than temperature. The word actually has many meanings, one of which is the measure of an angle. As shown in figure 5.30, the measure 1 degree indicates one part of a full circle captured by an angle (*BCA*) with its vertex at the center of that circle and the arms of the angle cutting off $1/360$ of the circumference.

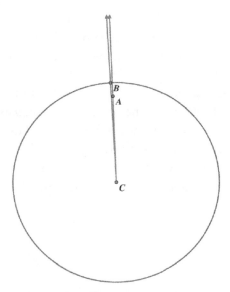

Fig. 5.30. A 1-degree angle, *BCA*, within a circle

- Students may also associate the term "a 180" with a skateboarding or ice skating stunt without seeing it as anything more than a name. We want to help them relate the number 180 to an action taken by the athlete, as a measure of his or her turn.

Extend

Have students stand on the floor, spaced as they were for the Explore activity. This time, they will use their arms to represent the rays of an angle, beginning with their arms together to indicate a measured angle of 0 degrees. It may help to refer to the right side of the room as the zero position for angles. Next, have students show an angle of 180 degrees as follows:

Start by facing the front of the room.

Put your arms together, pointing toward the right side of the room.

Keep your right arm pointing toward the right wall while slowly rotating your left arm across your body until your left arm is pointing to the left wall.

Remind students that this is half of a full turn, which they experienced before, but now they are showing the angle by using their arms.

At this point, stop to have a discussion about angles between 0 and 180 degrees. To make it easier for you to see the angles that students are making with their arms, have students start by putting their arms together pointing toward the right wall, but this time they should sweep the angle open by moving their left arm over their head. Ask students to demonstrate 0 degrees and 180 degrees and then ask them where 90 degrees would be. Next, ask students to create an angle between 0 and 90 degrees and then between 90 and 180 degrees.

As is often the case, students may benefit from making a record of their work. We suggest giving students a piece of colored construction paper and having them make a vertical mark near the middle of the bottom of the 12-inch side. Next, they can tape a length of string along the 12-inch side through the vertical mark, anchoring it in the middle with tape, and then tape one end of another piece of string on the vertical mark. They can use this string to mimic the movement of the students' arms, sweeping out angles between 0 and 180 degrees on the construction paper.

Invite one student to the front of the room and ask her or him to model 0 and 180 degrees. Have all the students at their desks mimic and label 0 and 180 degrees on their paper models. Now ask the student to display a 90-degree angle with her or his arms and have others copy it on their paper models. After checking for accuracy, have students tape down the other end of the second piece of string and label it *90 degrees*. Ask students to tape an additional piece of string at the vertical mark as before and repeat the process for angles of 45 and 135 degrees.

Enrich

Read *Hamster Champs* by Stuart J. Murphy (HarperCollins 2005). Three daredevil hamsters, a few alphabet blocks, a board, and a protractor show readers how to measure angles and escape a hungry cat.

Activity 9: Using Wedges to Focus on Angles

Key idea: Discerning angle measure
Learning trajectory level: Angle Measurer

Essentials

Gather colored paper (not construction paper because it is difficult to fold as needed) and scissors for each student. Provide at least three different-sized plastic lids (or cups or cans) for students to trace to make paper circles.

Engage

Talk about turns and angles as portions of a complete circle, as seen on the face of a compass or a clock (a digital clock display will not be useful for this activity). Focus on the second hand of the clock and its sweeping motion to illustrate the idea of the amount of rotation being captured by an angle. For example, as the second hand on a clock moves from the 12 to the 3, it has swept through 90 degrees. Similarly, we see a model of angles in the portions of a circle when one slices a whole pizza into eight same-sized sections; each section represents 45 degrees.

Ask students to give related examples of angles within other circular objects (e.g., cakes, pies, cross-sections of an orange or grapefruit, the face of a daisy, an open umbrella) and make sketches of them to show how they represent angles. Ask students to label the angles. Point out that the entire circle contains 360 degrees (by definition). If an object is divided into six parts, each part represents a 60-degree angle, because 360 divided by 6 is 60.

Explore

Read *Picture Pie* by Ed Emberly (Little, Brown 1984). This book shows how a circle divided like a pie (into halves, quarters, and eighths) can be used to make pictures of all kinds of things.

Have each student trace and cut out at least two different-sized circles from paper, using plastic lids (or cup rims or can rims) as templates (tasks adapted from Gayle M. Millsaps, "How Wedge You Teach the Unit-Angle Concept?" *Teaching Children Mathematics* 18, no. 6 [2012]: 362–69). The students will use these circles to model a single complete rotation. Explain that each paper circle represents exactly one complete rotation (if students completed activity 8, remind them of standing and rotating their arms to point in different directions). Then prompt students to fold their circles in half by folding the paper in a way that will show a half rotation, much like the change of heading from north to south. Next, have them fold that half in half again, resulting in a quarter section of a circle. Then have them fold the circle once more, resulting in a one-eighth section of a circle. Have them mark the very end of the sharpest corner of the paper wedge (the vertex) by using their pencils. Once unfolded, this mark will show the center of the entire circle. This wedge shape may look to them like a piece of pizza. They will use it to help measure angles.

Next, keeping their paper circles folded up into the wedge shape (one-eighth of a circle), students should compare the size of their wedge angle with that of three or four classmates. Some of the original circles may be different sizes (by radius), so it is important that students compare their circles with others that are larger or smaller to determine whether and how the wedge angles differ (they do not). The angles represented by the paper circle wedges are the same— about 45 degrees, or one-eighth of a full rotation, depending on the accuracy of students' tracing, cutting, and folding. Students can try placing different-sized wedges in a circle to confirm that their angles are the same, even if the arc lengths or areas of the wedges vary. The wedges will fit together in a circle (see fig. 5.31) as long as they are circles folded into eighths.

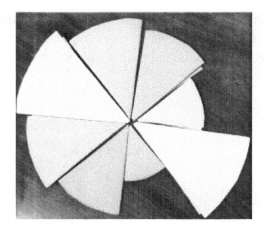

Fig. 5.31. Different-sized wedges arranged in a circle

Expect

Often students confuse the widest end (at the opening of the arms) of a wedge with the size of the angle for that wedge. The angle measure actually depends on what portion of a complete circle is wedged between the angle's arms. Figure 5.32 shows two wedges that have the same angle size but arms of different length.

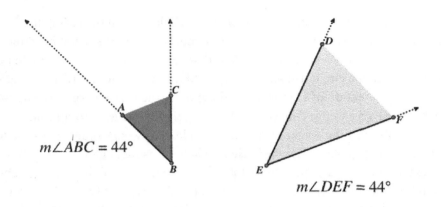

$m\angle ABC = 44°$

$m\angle DEF = 44°$

Fig. 5.32. Different-sized wedges can have the same angle

Enrich

Read *Apple Fractions* by Jerry Pallotta (Scholastic 2002). A variety of different apples are sliced in equal portions to show halves, thirds, fourths, . . . , all the way to tenths. Other illustrations show parts of a group. For example, out of every 10 apples picked, two are squeezed into cider and apple juice.

Another possibility is *A Fraction's Goal—Parts of a Whole* by Brian P. Cleary (Millbrook Press, 2011). Silly rhymes and illustrations demonstrate how fractions work: by splitting whole objects into parts. Cartoon cats divide everything from pieces of pizza to groups of people into halves, thirds, tenths, and more.

Activity 10: Capacity in the Kitchen

Key idea: *Introduction to volume*

Learning trajectory levels: *Volume Quantity Recognizer; Volume Unit Relater and Repeater*

Essentials

A copy of *Cook-A-Doodle-Doo!* by Janet Stevens and Susan Stevens Crummel (Voyager Books 1999).

Engage

Read *Cook-A-Doodle-Doo!* With the questionable help of his friends, Big Brown Rooster manages to bake strawberry shortcake, which would have pleased his great-grandmother, the Little Red Hen.

Explore

Reread the story and stop to talk with students about the details and explanations in the story, especially those dealing with measuring. For example, did you know there are 3 teaspoons in a tablespoon? Or notice that the iguana measures the flour by telling his companions that the pile of flour on the table is 4 inches tall? How will that information help the animals figure out the right amount of flour to put into the mixture? They decide to use the markings on the side of the measuring cup and put in enough flour to reach up to the $2/3$ mark.

Expect

Cook-A-Doodle-Doo! focuses on possible misconceptions. Notice the variety of ways in which one might misunderstand how to measure quantities of milk, time, flour, or heat in the oven. The book also gives examples to clarify the proper use of several measuring tools, such as teaspoons and tablespoons.

Extend

Have students name possible ingredients for a trail mix. List their suggestions. Possibilities include raisins, peanuts, chocolate chips, peanut butter chips, butterscotch chips, sunflower seeds, craisins, M&M candies, marshmallows, pretzels, goldfish crackers, dried banana chips, dried mango pieces, dried papaya pieces, and coconut. Have students vote to determine six or more favorite ingredients. Next, help students figure out how much of each ingredient they are likely to need to make the tastiest mix, and invite students to volunteer to bring particular ingredients to school.

On Trail Mix Day, have students put a cup of their ingredient in a very large bowl. Challenge them to do this without actually using a 1-cup measure. Students should come up with as many substitute measures as they can. If one student uses 2 half-cups to measure out a cup of chocolate chips, what could the next person use to add the same amount of coconut? Keep track of various combinations that students have used to avoid repetition as long as possible. Remember, sizes of measures can be mixed: using a $\frac{1}{3}$ cup and a $\frac{2}{3}$ cup is different from using a $\frac{1}{3}$ cup three times. Try using tablespoons and teaspoons if necessary.

After the mix has been made, ask students how much each person should get as her or his fair share. Talk about how they can reason back to figure how much trail mix was created altogether. Next, help them think about how many students will share it. Finally, hint that they should consider how much each person added into the mix, and see whether they realize that this is the same amount that they may get back.

Have students write about the experience of measuring whole cups without using the 1-cup measure. For example, ask them to explain the process of measuring out two cups' worth of pretzels using a $\frac{1}{4}$-cup, a $\frac{1}{3}$-cup, and a $\frac{1}{2}$-cup measure. (This would require using three $\frac{1}{3}$ cups to make the first cup, then one $\frac{1}{2}$ cup and two $\frac{1}{4}$ cups to make the second cup.)

Enrich

Read *Perimeter, Area, and Volume: A Monster Book of Dimensions* by David A. Adler (Scholastic 2012). A 3-D monster movie is used to introduce length, width, and depth. These dimensions are then used to figure out the perimeter, area, and volume of various things one can hold, pick up, or walk around— even monsters!

CHAPTER 6

GRADE 5: MORE LENGTH, AREA, VOLUME, AND ANGLE MEASUREMENT

Big measurement ideas identified in CCSSM: This chapter addresses two main measurement ideas closely connected with CCSSM. First, we use length and area models to support students' understanding of operations with fractions and decimals. Second, we present multiple activities designed to help students develop and deepen their understanding of volume measurement.

Learning trajectory levels in this grade: In the length and area trajectories, students are performing mainly at the highest levels of sophistication. We draw mainly from two levels, Integrated Conceptual Path Measurer (length) and Array Structurer (area). The major focus of this chapter is on volume. We present activities designed to promote student growth from Volume Quantity Recognizer to 3-D Row and Column Structurer. This transition is meant to highlight growth from dealing with individual volume units to dealing with groups of units in a way that lays the foundation for the volume formula (i.e., the number of cubes in a layer times the number of layers). Table 6.1 shows the learning trajectory levels for length, area, and volume for thise grade level.

Table 6.1. Learning trajectory levels by grade and topic

Grade	Length LT level	Area LT level	Volume LT levels
5	Integrated Conceptual Path Measurer	Array Structurer	Volume Quantity Recognizer Volume Unit Relater and Repeater Initial Composite 3-D Structurer 3-D Row and Column Structurer

Table 6.2 provides an overview of the chapter activities. Each activity is linked to the relevant CCSSM standard and levels from a learning trajectory on length, area, or volume measurement.

Table 6.2. Grade 5 activities matched with Common Core State Standards and learning trajectory levels

General CCSSM	Learning activities	Activity-specific standards	Learning trajectory levels
Operating on fractions (add, subtract, multiply, divide)	**Activity 1: Two-Thirds of One-Half of What?** Key idea: Multiplying a fraction by a fraction	5.NF.B.4 5.NF.B.4a 5.NF.B.4b	Array Structurer
5.NF.A.1 Add and subtract fractions with unlike denominators	**Activity 2: Wacky Races— Who Has Gone Farther? How Much?** Key idea: Adding and subtracting fractions	5.NF.A1 5.NF.A2	Integrated Conceptual Path Measurer
5.NF.A.2 Use visual fraction models for addition and subtraction 5.NF.B.4 Multiply a fraction by a fraction 5.NF.B.7 Divide unit fractions by whole numbers and vice versa	**Activity 3: Why Invert and Multiply?** Key idea: Dividing with fractional divisors	5.NF.A.1 5.NF.A.2 5.NF.B.7 5.NF.B.7b	Integrated Conceptual Path Measurer

General CCSSM	Learning activities	Activity-specific standards	Learning trajectory levels
Extending division to two-digit divisors and decimals 5.NBT.B.5 Apply standard multiplication algorithm 5.NBT.B.6 Apply area models for division 5.NBT.B.7 Model decimal operations with drawings 5.MD.A.1 Convert units within a measurement system	**Activity 4: The Larger Patio Redesign Task** Key idea: Dividing using a missing factor model	5.NBT.B.5 5.NBT.B.6	Array Structurer
	Activity 5: Base-Ten Multiplication Key idea: Multiplying two-digit by two-digit and decimal by decimal numbers	5.NBT.B.7 5.MD.A.1	Array Structurer
Developing understanding of volume 5.MD.C.3 Recognize and use volume units to measure solid figures 5.MD.C.4 Measure volume using various cubic units 5.MD.C.5 Find volume by packing and applying formulas	**Activity 6: What Is Volume Anyway?** Key idea: The attribute of volume	5.MD.C.5a 5.MD.C.5b	Volume Quantity Recognizer Volume Unit Relater and Repeater
	Activity 7: How Big Is a Cube? Key idea: Visualizing volume units	5.MD.C.3 5.MD.C.3a 5.MD.C.3b 5.MD.C.4	Volume Unit Relater and Repeater Initial Composite 3-D Structurer
	Activity 8: What Size Is Your Air Conditioner? Key idea: Applying volume with packing	5.MD.C.5a 5.MD.C.5b	3-D Row and Column Structurer
	Activity 9: Interpretation of the Volume Formula Key idea: Connecting volume representations	5.MD.C.3 5.MD.C.3a 5.MD.C.3b 5.MD.C.4	Initial Composite 3-D Structurer 3-D Row and Column Structurer

Activity 1: Two-Thirds of One-Half of What?

Key idea: Multiplying a fraction by a fraction
Learning trajectory level: Array Structurer

Essentials

Be prepared to draw the image in figure 6.1 on the board or to project it in the classroom. Use the templates at More4U to make a copy of the drawings in figure 6.2 and the chart in figure 6.3 for each student.

Engage

Tell students a story of a person looking back on the "journey" of learning multiplication (this may be your own story, or one about a fictional student):

> I remember that when I was a student, I had a hard time learning to multiply. One of the things I did to help myself when I was confused was to draw a picture. For example, when I was unsure of what 5 × 7 was, I would draw a picture (see fig. 6.1), then just count the total number of squares. It was easy to count seven 5's: 5, 10, 15, 20, 25, 30, 35. So 5 × 7 = 35.

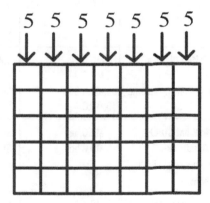

Fig. 6.1. 5 × 7 illustrated

> Eventually, these problems became easier for me, and I didn't have to draw the pictures anymore. However, later, when I was learning to multiply fractions, I started to have a hard time again. For example, when I was first asked to multiply ³/₅ × ⁴/₇, I was really

confused! To try to figure this problem out, I thought I would start with a problem with some easier numbers and see whether drawing a picture could help. I tried to draw a picture to help me calculate $\frac{1}{2} \times \frac{1}{3}$, which I was pretty sure should be $\frac{1}{6}$.

Give students the four drawings shown in figure 6.2, and tell them to work with a partner to examine these drawings to consider how they might be used to demonstrate that $\frac{1}{2} \times \frac{1}{3} = \frac{1}{6}$. (Note that the drawings show 1 square unit; $\frac{1}{2}$ of 1 square unit, indicated by hatching; $\frac{1}{3}$ of 1 square unit, indicated by hatching in a different direction; and the two square units with hatching overlapped to show that the portion of 1 square unit with crosshatching is equal to $\frac{1}{6}$ of the square unit.)

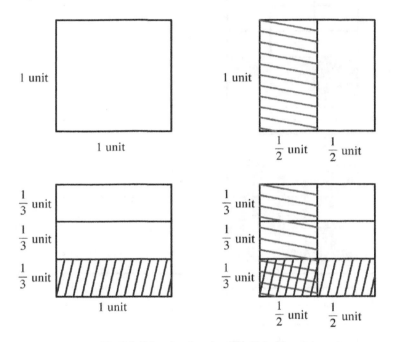

Fig. 6.2. Using drawings to solve $\frac{1}{2} \times \frac{1}{3}$

Explore

Students will model the multiplication of fractions with drawings and interpret drawings as models of fraction multiplication. They will work with a chart like that in figure 6.3. The chart for student use at More4U modifies the chart in the figure by removing either the visual representation or the symbolic representation. Distribute the modified version of the chart, and ask students to create the missing representation. You may provide additional numeric examples or offer examples verbally. Finally, you may present examples, either symbolically or verbally, without providing the answer.

	Visual representation	Symbolic representation
1	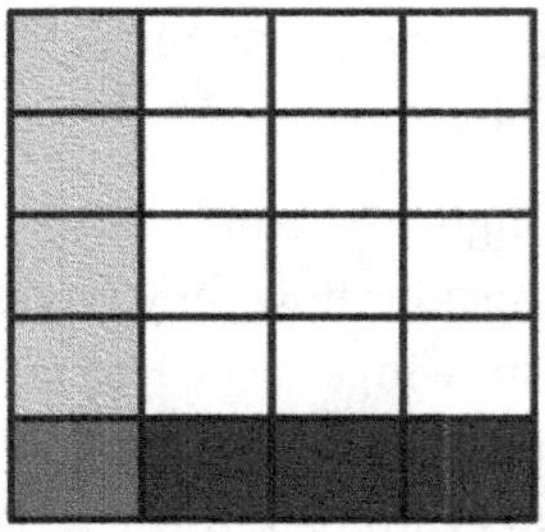	$\frac{1}{4} \times \frac{1}{5} = \frac{1}{20}$
2	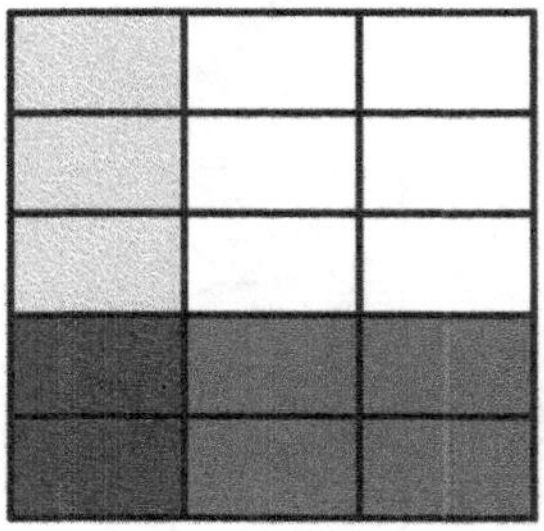	$\frac{1}{3} \times \frac{2}{5} = \frac{2}{15}$
3	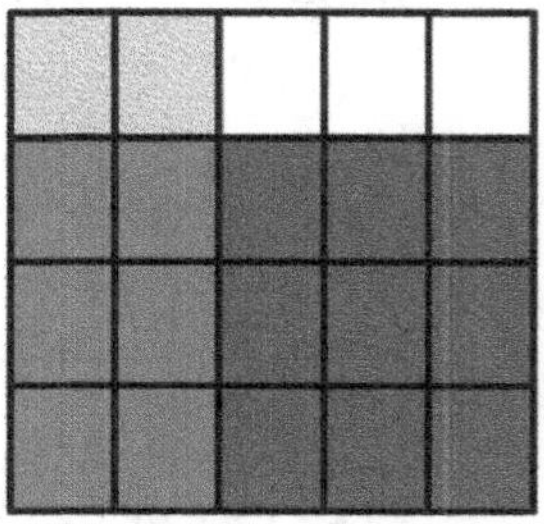	$\frac{2}{5} \times \frac{3}{4} = \frac{6}{20} = \frac{3}{10}$
4	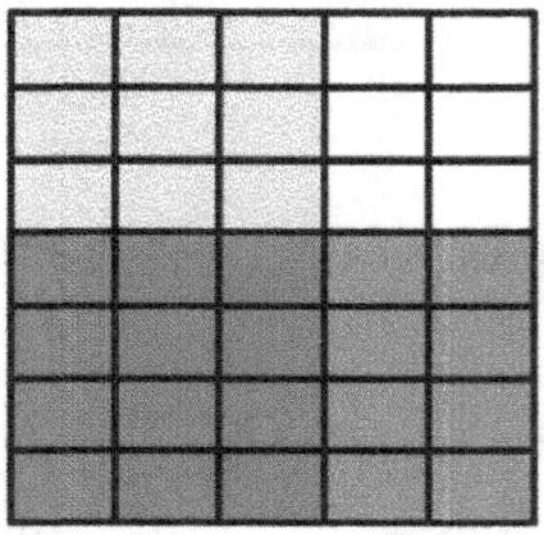	$\frac{3}{5} \times \frac{4}{7} = \frac{12}{35}$

Fig. 6.3. Showing multiplication of fractions visually and symbolically

Expect

- Some students are likely to recall or discover that they can find the answers to these fraction multiplication problems by simply dividing the product of the numerators by the product of the denominators.

Challenge these students to demonstrate or illustrate this procedure with a visual representation. For example, $3/5 \times 4/7 = 12/35$. We can see the 35 (5×7) as the total number of rectangles created in the 5-by-7 array. This means that each rectangle has an area of $1/35$ of the unit square. We can see the 12 (3×4) as the rectangles that are "double shaded" (like the crosshatching in fig. 6.2); thus, the visual representation shows that 12 (35ths) of the unit square are double shaded.

- This activity is designed to address CCSSM 5.NF.B.4 ("Apply and extend previous understandings of multiplication to multiply a fraction by a fraction"). Because students are asked to create drawings of arrays in some of these problems, it is expected that students will be at least at the Array Structurer level of the area learning trajectory.

Extend

Explain that "someone" has a cousin, somewhere, who owns a pizza shop, and she is designing a pizza in a new size. Continue,

> Her current pizzas are square and measure 1 foot on each side, and they sell for $10. For the new pizza, she is planning to increase the length by 50 percent and the width by 50 percent. She has set the price for this larger pizza at $20. She sells her current pizzas for $10 per square foot of pizza, and she wants her new pizza to be priced the same proportionally. Will her planned increases in length and width make the new pizza the right size for the new price that she has set? If not, determine dimensions for the new larger pizza so that the $20 price will be correct. Assume that she will definitely increase the length by 50 percent, so you should just determine a new width.

Note that the increases in length and width that she is planning will create a pizza that has an area of $2 1/4$ square feet. This size of pizza should cost $22.50. Instead, to achieve proportional pricing, she should increase the width by 33 percent, or $4/3$ of the original width. This will give a total area of $3/2 \times 4/3 = 2$ square feet, making a cost of $20.

Enrich

Read *Multiplying Menace: The Revenge of Rumpelstiltskin* by Pam Calvert (Charlesbridge 2006), a tale of how Rumpelstilskin causes disorder in the royal court by multiplying the kingdom's livestock and assets by fractions and making the resulting numbers of them disappear.

Activity 2: Wacky Races—
Who Has Gone Farther? How Much?

Key idea: Adding and subtracting fractions
Learning trajectory level: Integrated Conceptual Path Measurer

Essentials

Draw on the board the path images shown in figures 6.4, 6.5, and 6.6; or project them in the classroom. Make copies of the activity sheets in figures 6.7 and 6.8 for each student (see More4U).

Engage

Show students the two paths in figure 6.4, and tell them,

> Most of the time when people race each other, they travel along oval tracks. Today we are going to be comparing distances along some wacky racetracks. Imagine that two people are traveling along two different paths [indicate the paths shown in fig. 6.4]. In each case, the total distance all the way around the path, from "Start" to "Finish," is 1 mile. Which person has traveled a longer distance when he or she has reached the point labeled "Location"? How much farther has that person traveled than the other person? Who has a longer distance left to travel? How much farther does each person have left to travel?

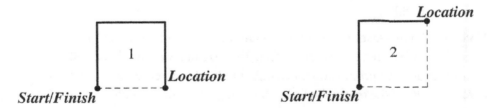

Fig. 6.4. Which person has traveled farther?

Note that on the first track the person has traveled $3/4$ of a mile; on the second the person has traveled $2/4$ (or $1/2$) of a mile. Therefore, person 1 has traveled $3/4 - 2/4 = 1/4$ of a mile farther than person 2. Similarly, person 1 has $1/4$ of a mile left to travel, whereas person 2 has $2/4$ of a mile left to travel. Thus, person 2 has $2/4 - 1/4 = 1/4$ of a mile more to travel than person 1.

Explore

Show students the two paths in figure 6.5, and tell them that one lap around each of these tracks is 1 mile, even though the shapes are different. Person 1 is running on track 1, and person 2 is running on track 2. Ask students to determine whether person 1 or person 2 has traveled farther by the point labeled "Location." Who has more distance left to travel, and how much farther does each one have to go? We suggest doing this problem together as a class or checking in with students after a short time to make sure that they are interpreting the task correctly.

We have chosen this example because we anticipate that some students might conclude that person 2 has traveled farther because he or she has traveled three segments, whereas person 1 has traveled two segments, ignoring that the segments are unequal in length. In the pentagonal track, each unit (side) is $1/5$ mile long, whereas each unit (side) of the triangular track is $1/3$ mile.

Fig. 6.5. Triangular and pentagonal wacky tracks

To help students visualize the benefit of a common denominator, you might suggest or model partitioning the sides of each of the shapes into the total number of sides of the other figure. In this case, each side of the regular triangle is subdivided into five equal subunits and each side of the regular pentagon is subdivided into three equal subunits (see fig. 6.6). The resulting figures each have 15 total subunits of equal length, making it easier to compare the tracks.

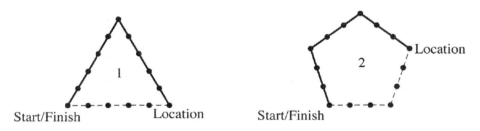

Fig. 6.6. Partitioning the tracks into equal subunits

Next, give students the activity sheets in figures 6.7 and 6.8, and ask them to complete the missing columns. Students may find it helpful to draw in subunits as suggested above. Feel free to include additional examples. (Fig. 6.9 provides an answer key for both parts of the activity.)

	1-mile wacky tracks	Who has traveled farther?	How much farther?
1	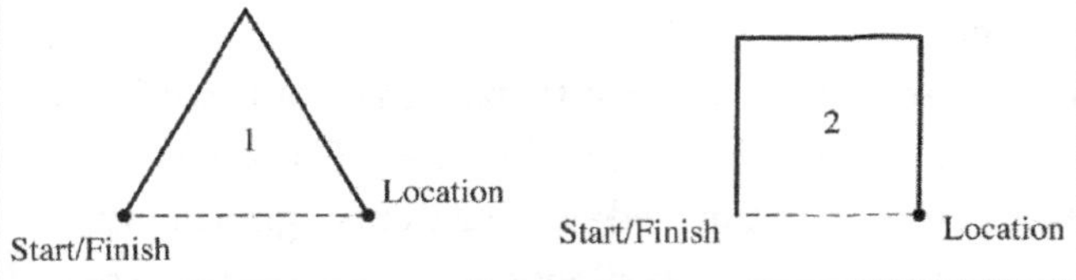		
2	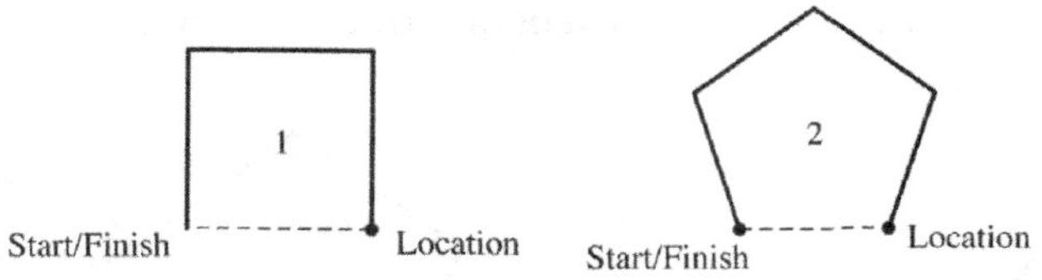		
3	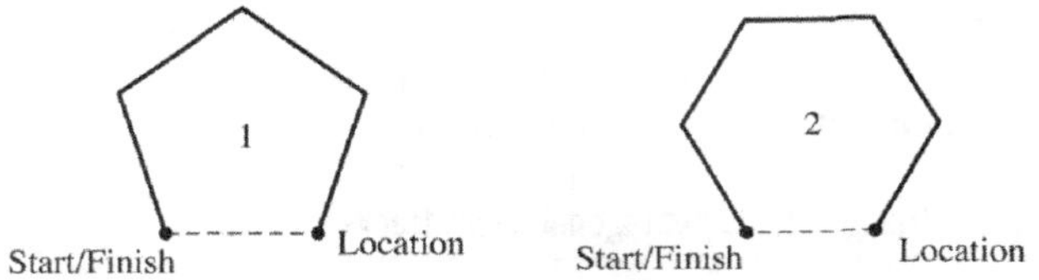		
4	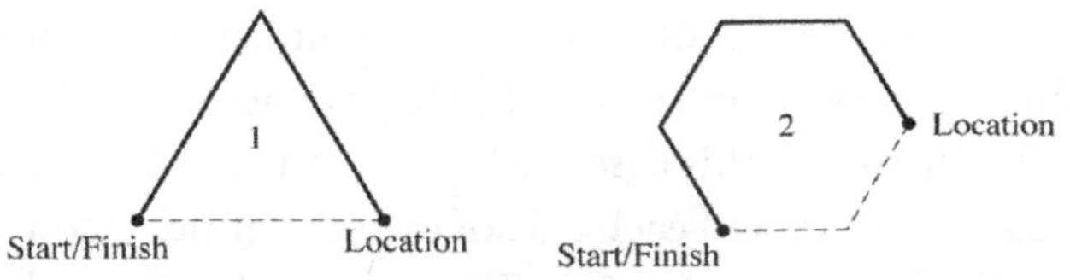		

Fig. 6.7. Part 1: Who has traveled farther? (Student activity sheet)

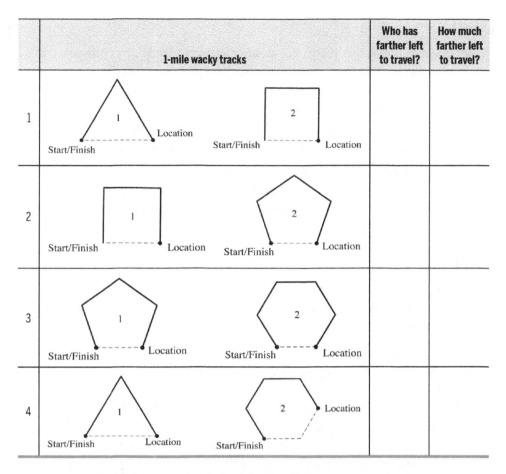

	1-mile wacky tracks		Who has farther left to travel?	How much farther left to travel?
1				
2				
3				
4				

Fig. 6.8. Part 2: Who has farther left to travel? (Student activity sheet)

Part 1: Who has traveled farther?

	Who has traveled farther?	How much farther?
1	Racer 2 has traveled farther. $^3/_4$ mi. $> ^2/_3$ mi.	$^3/_4 - ^2/_3 =$ $^1/_{12}$ mi.
2	Racer 2 has traveled farther. $^4/_5$ mi. $> ^3/_4$ mi.	$^4/_5 - ^3/_4 =$ $^1/_{20}$ mi.
3	Racer 2 has traveled farther. $^5/_6$ mi. $> ^4/_5$ mi.	$^5/_6 - ^4/_5 =$ $^1/_{30}$ mi.
4	Racer 1 has traveled the same distance as racer 2. $^2/_3$ mi. $= ^4/_6$ mi.	$^2/_3 - ^4/_6 =$ 0 mi.

Part 2: Who has farther left to travel?

	Who has farther left to travel?	How much farther left to travel?
1	Racer 1 has farther to go. $^1/_3$ mi. $> ^1/_4$ mi.	$^1/_3 - ^1/_4 =$ $^1/_{12}$ mi.
2	Racer 1 has farther to go. $^1/_4$ mi. $> ^1/_5$ mi.	$^1/_4 - ^1/_5 =$ $^1/_{20}$ mi.
3	Racer 1 has farther to go. $^1/_5$ mi. $> ^1/_6$ mi.	$^1/_5 - ^1/_6 =$ $^1/_{30}$ mi.
4	Both racers have the same distance left to go. $^1/_3$ mi. $= ^2/_6$ mi.	$^1/_3 - ^2/_6 =$ 0 mi.

Fig. 6.9. Answer key to parts 1 and 2 in figures 6.7 and 6.8, respectively

Expect

- Some students are likely to compare distances traveled by comparing the number of sides. For example, for the first problem in part 1 of figure 6.7, they may report that racer 2 traveled farther because she traveled three sides, whereas racer 1 traveled only two sides. Note that this strategy results in errors in part 2 as well: These students would conclude that the racers have the same distance left to travel—namely, one side.

- The process of finding common denominators is central to this task. Students may struggle to generalize that the product of the denominators serves as a useful common denominator even if it is not always the least common denominator.

Extend

- All the examples in figures 6.7 and 6.8 are comparing fractions with consecutive denominators (e.g., $1/10$ and $1/11$). Consider asking students to compare fractions with nonconsecutive denominators (e.g., $1/3$ and $1/7$), using the regular polygon models.

- Ask students to figure out how far the two racers have traveled altogether. In the first problem, they would have to calculate $2/3 + 3/4$. To challenge students, ask them to explain the following two observations. First, the entries for corresponding rows in the last column for both parts of the activity (see figure 6.9) have the same final answer, although we did not do the same calculations to arrive at the answers. Why does this happen? Will it always happen? Second, the statements in the middle column seem to be reversed from part 1 to part 2. Why does this happen? Will this always happen? Can your students generalize from the first three cases in part 2 (i.e., $1/3 - 1/4 = 1/12$, $1/4 - 1/5 = 1/20$ ...) to notice that

$$\frac{1}{n} - \frac{1}{n+1} = \frac{1}{n(n+1)}?$$

Enrich

Read *Fractions, Decimals, and Percents* by David A. Adler (Scholastic 2010). Lots of fractions, decimals, percentages, and their equivalents can be found at the county fair—gobble up a fraction of pie, boast about your batting average in the arcade, and take a percentage off the price of a toy.

Activity 3: Why Invert and Multiply?

Key idea: Dividing with fractional divisors
Learning trajectory level: Integrated Conceptual Path Measurer

Essentials

Each student will need a 12-inch ruler with markings at least down to $1/8$ of an inch and a copy of the activity sheet in figure 6.11 (see More4U).

Engage

Tell students,

> A fifth grader was looking over some math problems the other day and noticed a pattern. She noticed that $3 \div 1/4 = 3 \times 4/1 = 12$, and $5 \div 1/8 = 5 \times 8/1 = 40$. So she said that if you want to divide a number by a fraction, you can just flip the fraction over and multiply (invert and multiply). Create another example and test this method to see whether it works. Will this method always work? Why or why not?

Explore

Tell students,

> Today we need to try to figure out a way to help a second grader understand why the method that we just discussed for dividing by a fraction will work. Let's start by modeling the problem $8 \div 2 = 4$ by drawing a length that is 8 inches and a length that is 2 inches.

Sketch the image in figure 6.10a on the board, or project it in the classroom, and ask students whether they can use it to explain why $8 \div 2 = 4$. Figure 6.10b presents one possible student response.

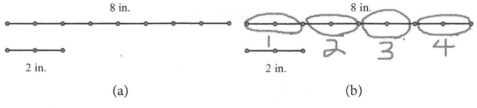

Fig. 6.10. Modeling $8 \div 2 = 4$

After discussing the task and the visual model in figure 6.10, distribute the activity sheet shown in figure 6.11. Ask students to create the missing number sentence or visual model. Note that students should be required to do something to show you the final result. For example, for problem 1 they should in some way display the 8 half-inches in the 4-inch segment. (Fig. 6.12 provides an answer key.)

	Number sentence	Visual model
1	$4 \div \frac{1}{2} = 8$	
2		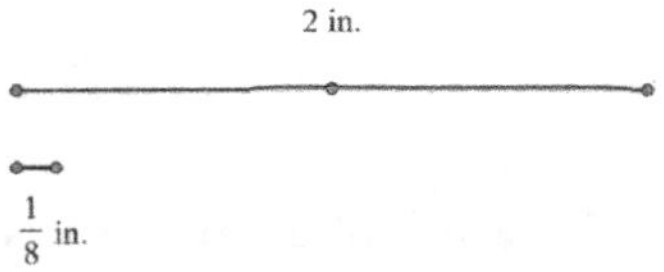 2 in. (segments) $\frac{1}{8}$ in.
3	$3 \div \frac{1}{4} = 12$	
4		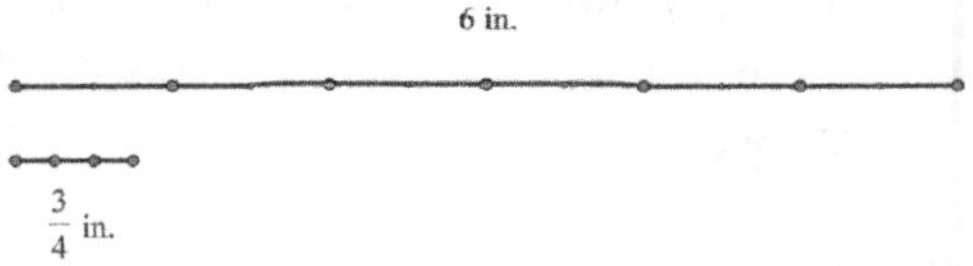 6 in. (segments) $\frac{3}{4}$ in.

Fig. 6.11. Student activity sheet: Showing division by fractions visually and symbolically

	Missing number sentence or visual model
1	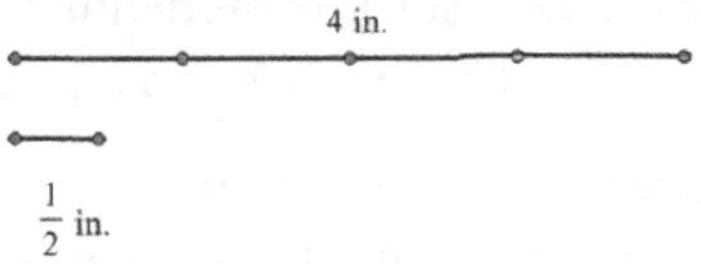 4 in. (segments) $\frac{1}{2}$ in.
2	$2 \div \frac{1}{8} = 18$
3	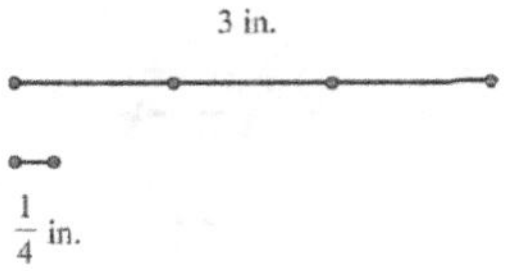 3 in. (segments) $\frac{1}{4}$ in.
4	$6 \div \frac{3}{4} = 8$

Fig. 6.12. Answer key for the activity sheet in figure 6.11

Expect

This task is intended to help students connect ideas of measurement to ideas of division. Measuring a length with different units results in different measures. For example, measuring a 3-foot length in feet results in 3, while measuring the same length in inches results in 36. Similarly, in the first example in figure 6.11, if we measure the 4-inch length in half-inches, we will get 8—that is, there are 8 half-inches in 4 inches.

Extend

Note that all the examples in figure 6.11 involve numbers that can be found on a standard ruler. You can extend this task to include numbers not found on a ruler. For example, consider modeling $5 \div 1/3 = 15$ with a visual model. You can also extend this task by including whole numbers divided by non-unit fractions (as shown in the last case in fig. 6.11). Consider that not all cases will result in an integer answer (e.g., $4 \div 3/4 = 5^1/_3$, which means that there are $5^1/_3$ three-quarters in 4).

Enrich

Read *The Hershey's Milk Chocolate Bar Fraction Book* by Jerry Pallotta (Scholastic 1999). This book creatively demonstrates the different parts of a whole and their equivalents. Adding, subtracting, and even simplifying fractions often seem easier to students when working with a candy bar.

Activity 4: The Larger Patio Redesign Task

Key idea: Dividing using a missing-factor model
Learning trajectory level: Array Structurer

Essentials

Students will need blank paper and rulers. Grid paper and square-inch tiles are optional but may be helpful if students are struggling with the task.

Engage

Tell students,

> Imagine that last year I designed a patio made of square tiles in my backyard. Since then, I have bought a new house with a bigger backyard, and I want a patio at my new house too. Imagine that you are helping me design a rectangular backyard patio made out of 1-foot-square paver bricks. I have purchased 168 square bricks, and I want to use all 168 bricks to make my patio.

Explore

Continue,

> When I was considering my options for designing a rectangular patio, I decided to make drawings to give to a landscape architect, who could make sure that the patio would fit into my landscape design. The first option that I considered was 12 feet wide. How long would the patio need to be if I wanted to use all 168 bricks? Make a scale drawing of this patio.

If you do not have paper that is large enough for students to use a scale of 1 inch = 1 foot, suggest that they use a scale of either 1 centimeter = 1 foot or 0.5 inch = 1 foot. Working with 1 centimeter = 1 foot will be easier for students, while 0.5 inch = 1 foot can be used to push students to use proportional reasoning.

Continue,

> I wanted to avoid having to rent a tool to cut the bricks. Find all the other rectangular patio designs that would not require any cutting. Draw each of these rectangular designs. Your drawings do not have to be very detailed.

There are eight design options in all (if designs that simply reverse length and width are regarded as equivalent—for example, a 12 × 14 patio and a 14 × 12 patio). The options are 1 × 168, 2 × 84, 3 × 56, 4 × 42, 6 × 28, 7 × 24, 8 × 21, and 12 × 14. Note that, depending on the scale you use, you may need to plan a way to accommodate drawings that are longer than a standard piece of paper. For example, you may consider marking out the region on the floor or taping several pieces of paper together.

In alignment with CCSSM, the purpose of these tasks is to develop students' abilities to reason abstractly about multiplication and division and connect these operations with area models. Encourage your students to explain how these area models connect with the operations. For example, 12 × 14 can be modeled by drawing (or at least imagining) a rectangle that is 12 centimeters by 14 centimeters and understanding that this rectangle would contain 12 sets of 14 squares or 14 sets of 12 squares. Similarly, to model division, all 168 bricks can be grouped into 14 sets of 12 bricks each.

Expect

This activity is designed to reinforce the connections between multiplication and division in an area context. Some students may still struggle with structuring the space (see activity 2: Patio Redesign Task in chapter 4), and others may struggle to make the connection between the length of a rectangle and the number of square units that would fit along that edge. For example, some students may mismatch a side length and the number of rows or columns along that side. The second extension task addresses this.

Extend

- Ask students to suppose that you do have a tool that will cut individual bricks. Ask students to create a 16-foot-wide rectangular patio using all 168 bricks. Students should be able to determine that the length of this patio would be 10 feet, with 8 bricks remaining. After some discussion, they should conclude that the length would need to be 10.5 feet to use all the bricks.

- If some students are not connecting the length of a side and the number of square units that will fit along that side, present a drawing like that on the right in figure 6.13 as the work of a student in a lower grade, and ask them to explain the student's confusion. Provide a hypothetical explanation that the rectangle is 2 units by 3 units and therefore has an area of 6 square units. Can students explain what the younger student did wrong? Notice that in the diagram on the left side of figure 6.13, the student has correctly used the length of the edge as an indicator of the number of area units that will fit along that edge. In the diagram on the right, however, the student has not done this.

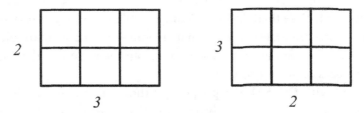

Fig. 6.13. What's wrong with the drawing on the right?

Enrich

Read *Math on the Playground: Area and Perimeter* by Ian F. Mahaney (PowerKids Press 2013). Dimensions given to compare playgrounds shown in photographs enable readers to figure out perimeters and areas, as well as solve other problems posed. The book includes helpful labeled diagrams.

Activity 5: Base-Ten Multiplication

Key idea: Multiplying two-digit by two-digit and decimal by decimal numbers
Learning trajectory level: Array Structurer

Essentials

Gather base-ten blocks: flats (hundreds-blocks), longs (ten-blocks), and units (ones-blocks).

Engage

Provide students with one flat, one long, and one unit (or one set per group). Tell the students that the *long* is 10 and ask them to decide what the *flat* and the *unit* are in this case. Next, tell students to consider the *unit* to be 10 and ask them what the long and flat should be considered to be in this new situation. Finally, tell students to consider the *flat* as 1, and ask them what they should consider the long and the unit to be now. Note that the purpose of this exercise is to help students see that they can use the base-ten materials to model different multiplication problems—even involving decimals—by redefining the unit.

Explore

Tell students,

> Two fifth graders were working on some computation problems. One of them found that $12 \times 14 = 48 + 120 = 168$ by using the standard multiplication algorithm.

You may want to put this work up on the board. Continue,

> Another student said that she found $12 \times 14 = 100 + 40 + 20 + 8 = 168$. Can you explain what the second student did? Will this method always give you the correct answer?

Ask students to use the base-ten materials to model the multiplication of 12×14, as illustrated in figure 6.14, and show the components of both students' work from above.

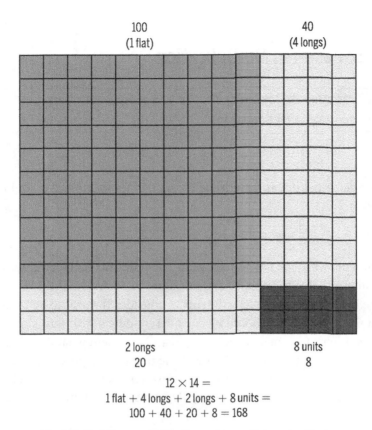

100
(1 flat)

40
(4 longs)

2 longs
20

8 units
8

$12 \times 14 =$
1 flat + 4 longs + 2 longs + 8 units =
100 + 40 + 20 + 8 = 168

Fig. 6.14. Modeling a multiplication problem with base-ten blocks

Expect

- Although breaking a multiplication problem down into four partial products is meant to simplify the computation, some students may have difficulty connecting the physical representation with the symbolic. If students struggle to see the four parts, consider modeling 12×14 as $12 \times (10 + 4) = 120 + 48$.

- Students may miss two of the partial products. For example, students often report that $(a + b)(a + b) = a^2 + b^2$, leaving out $ab + ab$. This difficulty tends to persist throughout many students' mathematics education. Encourage students to discuss this error and consider connecting the physical model with the symbolic one to help resolve this issue.

- In the extension task, students may have difficulties interpreting the changing unit, resulting in an erroneous placement of the decimal point in their products. Consider giving students the extension task on a different day so that they do not have to reconceptualize the unit in each problem so rapidly. Also note (and guide students in understanding) that when the unit (ones-block) is treated as having an edge length of 1 linear unit, then its face has an area of 1 square unit; however, when its edge is considered to have a length of 0.1 linear unit (for example, in modeling 1.2×1.4), then its face has an area of 0.01 square units.

Extend

Revisit the modeling of 12×14 and ask students to reinterpret the problem if they consider the flat to be 1. What does this new problem model, and what is the final product?

It should be noted that this example does not require students to deal with converting longs into flats or units into longs. Consider repeating the process above with 34×12. Model 34×12, and then explain how this model could also be used to describe 3.4×1.2 as a problem involving decimal multiplication.

Enrich

This task has important connections with later content that can be modeled in a similar fashion by using algebra tiles. For example, helping students understand $14 \times 12 = (10 + 4) \times (10 + 2)$ will enable them to make connections easily with $(x + 4)(x + 2) = x^2 + 2x + 4x + 8 = x^2 + 6x + 8$.

Activity 6: What Is Volume Anyway?

Key idea: The attribute of volume

Learning trajectory levels: Volume Quantity Recognizer; Volume Unit Relater and Repeater

Essentials

Each group of students will need twelve 1-inch cubes and sixteen 1-centimeter cubes. For the extension task, you will need sixteen 1-centimeter cubes and twelve 1-inch cubes for your use in the classroom.

Engage

Say to students,

> Let's talk about rectangular prisms. Start with two 1-inch cubes, and make all the different rectangular prisms you can.

This work can be done as a class, with your guidance, to help students learn the definition of rectangular prism. Repeat the process with three and then four 1-inch cubes, obtaining the results shown in figure 6.15. Note that if we consider horizontal and vertical arrangements to be different, there are two configurations with two and three cubes and four configurations with four cubes.

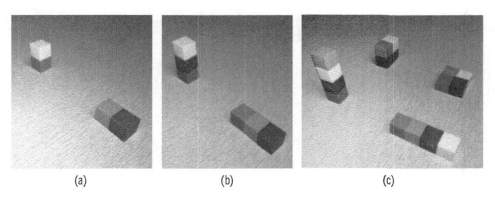

(a)   (b)   (c)

Fig. 6.15. Configuration possibilities with two, three, and four cubes

Explore

Continue,

> Now that we have an idea of what rectangular prisms are, let's see how many different rectangular prisms you can build by using all twelve of your 1-inch cubes.

Let students work until they have at least two different prisms to compare. Then draw the class's attention to these two prisms. Ask,

> Which of these two prisms has the larger volume? How do you know?

Depending on how your students react to this task, you can have them continue building prisms and comparing pairs of prisms to extend the discussion as needed to diagnose your students' misconceptions.

Expect

This activity is designed to elicit students' understanding of volume. It is likely that many will think that as they change the configuration of the twelve 1-inch cubes, they change the volume of the prism. Did you notice any students who treated the height (or the length) of the prism as the volume (thinking, for example, that taller prisms have more volume)? Did any students confuse the area of the base with the volume (supposing that the more space the prism takes up on the table, the more volume it has)?

To redirect students' attention to the attribute of volume, ask them to imagine that each of the different prisms is made from ice cubes. Then imagine that all the ice melts. Compare the prisms by the size of the puddle each creates.

Extend

After students have a sense of what volume actually is, another typical misconception can be probed. Some students may think that they can compare the volumes of two rectangular prisms simply by counting the number of cubes in their construction, even if the cubes in one prism are a different size from the cubes in the other. For example, when shown the setup in figure 6.16, many students will reason that the prism constructed of sixteen 1-centimeter cubes has more volume than the prism constructed of twelve 1-inch cubes because 16 is greater than 12. Again, this misconception can be dealt with by referring to the ice-melting metaphor.

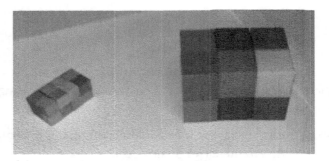

Fig. 6.16. Do more cubes always mean greater volume?

Enrich

Read *Perimeter, Area, and Volume: A Monster Book of Dimensions* by David A. Adler (Scholastic 2012). A 3-D monster movie is used to introduce length, width, and depth. These dimensions are then used to figure out the perimeter, area, and volume of various things one can hold, pick up, or walk around—even monsters!

Activity 7: How Big Is a Cube?

Key idea: Visualizing volume units
Learning trajectory levels: Volume Unit Relater and Repeater; Initial Composite 3-D Structurer

Essentials

Gather at least fifty 1-inch cubes, six sheets of 11-inch by 17-inch copy paper, a paper cutter (or scissors), a stapler, and a measuring tool.

Before beginning this activity, you will need to build a cubic foot, using the 11-inch by 17-inch paper. First cut eight 4-inch by 12-inch strips and four 4-inch by 14-inch strips. Take each of these twelve strips, and fold them in half twice to make eight 1-inch by 12-inch strips and four 1-inch by 14-inch strips. Now take four of the eight 1-inch by 12-inch strips, and lay them flat in a square. Interlace the corners of the strips and then staple them together at the corners. Repeat this process with the other four 1-inch by 12-inch strips. Fold 1-inch tabs at the ends of the 14-inch strips (make sure the strip without the tabs is 12 inches). Now connect the two squares with the four 1-inch by 14-inch tabbed strips by stapling at the corners. See figure 6.17 for the final product.

Fig. 6.17. Cubic foot made of paper strips

Engage

Tell students,

> Imagine that you are planning to purchase a portable air conditioner for your classroom. Before you buy the unit, you need to determine what size will be appropriate for the room.

Visit http://www.sylvane.com/tips-for-buying-airconditioner.html, and discuss the size recommendations with students (shown in fig. 6.18). Ask students to consider the options listed. Which air conditioner would they recommend for the room? Ask students to make predictions, and discuss them in small groups before sharing them with the class. Record the range of predictions on the board, and keep them to compare with students' final answers after completing activity 8.

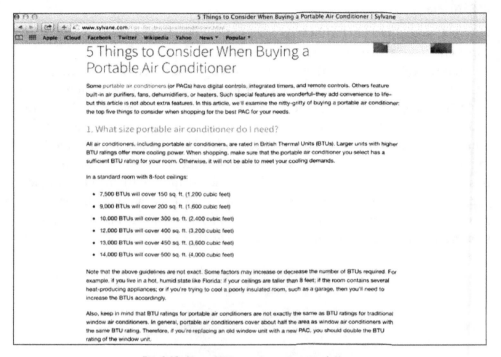

Fig. 6.18. Air conditioner size recommendations

Explore

Have students warm up by comparing a cubic inch with the cubic foot made of paper strips. Show the students a cubic inch (a 1-inch cube). How many of these would it take to fill the cubic foot? How do they know? Ask students to predict first, without using any tools or leaving their seats, and then make a record of the work that they did to find the answer.

Expect

Do any of your students give answers of 12 (12 inches in a foot), 144 (12 inches by 12 inches), or 864 (surface area), rather than the correct answer of 1,728? These common mistakes should be discussed and may be resolved by packing some 1-inch cubes along edges inside the cubic foot or by starting to fill the base of the cubic foot with 1-inch cubes, as shown in figure 6.19.

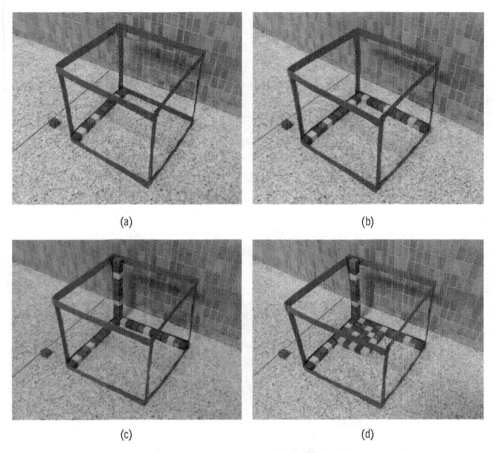

(a)

(b)

(c)

(d)

Fig. 6.19. Partially filling the cubic foot can help students calculate its volume

Focus on how students count or compute the total number of cubes needed. If a student says that she or he used the volume formula to get $12 \times 12 \times 12 = 1{,}728$, ask her or him to explain what that means and why it works. Ask her or him what the first $12 \times 12 = 144$ represents, and ask what the 144×12 represents, too.

As students begin working with volume, they apply the volume formula with varying levels of conceptual understanding. Thus, verifying that a student can accurately apply the volume formula does not always indicate that the student understands the meaning of the computation. Instead, we suggest focusing on three things: (1) working with physical representations of the volume units; (2) structuring space by iterating units and collections of units; and (3) connecting and interpreting components of the volume formula with these collections of units.

Extend

Continue to build and compare standard volume units within the American system of measures. Have students indicate the size of a cubic yard with yardsticks, string, measuring tapes, strips of paper, or jump ropes. Ask students to predict and then check how many cubic inches are needed to fill a cubic yard and how many cubic feet are needed to fill a cubic yard.

You can also do the same type of comparisons with metric volume units, using base-ten blocks. Compare a cubic centimeter to a cubic decimeter (1,000 cubic centimeters) and to a cubic meter. (Note that base-ten materials do not include a cubic meter. One can be constructed by laying out a square meter on the floor with four meter sticks, then having four students each hold two meter sticks to form the cubic meter. Alternatively, a cubic meter can be constructed by inserting 12 meter sticks into potting foam cubes as the corners. See fig. 6.20 for an example.)

Fig. 6.20. A cubic meter model

Enrich

Read *Perimeter, Area, and Volume: A Monster Book of Dimensions* by David A. Adler (Scholastic 2012), where a monster movie is used to introduce length, width, and depth. Or read *Millions to Measure* by David M. Schwartz (HarperCollins 2003), a story of a magician who introduces a group of children to the purpose and uses of measurement, including the metric system.

Activity 8: What Size Is Your Air Conditioner?

Key idea: Applying volume with packing
Learning trajectory level: 3-D Row and Column Structurer

Essentials

Gather staplers and precut sets of strips for each group: eight 4-inch by 12-inch and four 4-inch by 14-inch. It may be helpful to prefold and crease the 4-inch by 14-inch strips so that students can put their cubes together quickly (see Essentials, activity 7, p. 235, for detailed instructions on how to build a cubic foot).

Engage

Begin,

> Now that we have had some time to think about how cubes fill up space, let's revisit our original question about what size air conditioner we might need for our room. How many cubic feet would it take to completely fill the room? Before you start working, make a prediction without using any tools or getting out of your seat.

Give students time to predict, measure, and calculate.

> Now that you have determined the number of cubic feet that it would take to fill the room, use this information to select the appropriate air conditioner for your room [refer students to fig. 6.18 in activity 7 for their choices]. Next, find how many cubic inches you think it would take to fill the room. How many cubic yards do you think it would take to fill the room?

Explore

Recall some of the common mistakes and misconceptions mentioned in activity 7 (finding the length of one edge; finding the area of the floor; or finding the area of the floor, walls, and ceiling). These errors should be discussed and may be resolved by packing some 1-foot cubes along edges inside the room or by starting to fill the floor of the room with cubic feet.

Consider having students build cubic feet by following the process in activity 7, so that they can see a collection of cubic feet filling a portion of an edge of the room, a portion of the base layer, or a portion of the height.

If students use the volume formula ($V = L \times W \times H$), ask them to explain what it means and why it works. Ask them what $L \times W$ represents.

Expect

As students begin working with volume, they will apply the volume formula with varying levels of conceptual understanding. Thus, verifying that a student can accurately apply the volume formula does not always indicate meaningful understanding. Instead, we suggest focusing on three things: (1) working with physical representations of the volume units; (2) structuring space by iterating units and collections of units; and (3) connecting and interpreting components of the volume formula with these collections of units.

Extend and Enrich

Consider asking students to extend this activity by selecting a room at home and determining what size air conditioner (or space heater) would be needed to cool (or heat) that space.

Activity 9: Interpretation of the Volume Formula

Key idea: Connecting volume representations

Learning trajectory levels: Initial Composite 3-D Structurer; 3-D Row and Column Structurer

Essentials

Gather twenty-four 1-inch cubes.

Engage

Tell students,

> Today we are going to work to figure out what the volume formula
> ($V = L \times W \times H$) means and how it works. Verify that the volume
> of the prism [shown in fig. 6.21; build your own prism with the
> 1-inch cubes] is 24 cubic inches.

Fig. 6.21. Model for 24-cubic-inch prism

Explore

Ask students to look at how a few different students applied the volume formula
to the prism shown in figure 6.21. Match each student's work (student 1, 2, 3)
with the visual model (A, B, C) of their application of the volume formula, as
shown in figure 6.22. (Note that each layer is all one color, and all the layers
are different colors, though all the photos are black and white here. The correct
matching is student 1's written work with prism B, student 2's work with
prism C, and student 3's work with prism A.)

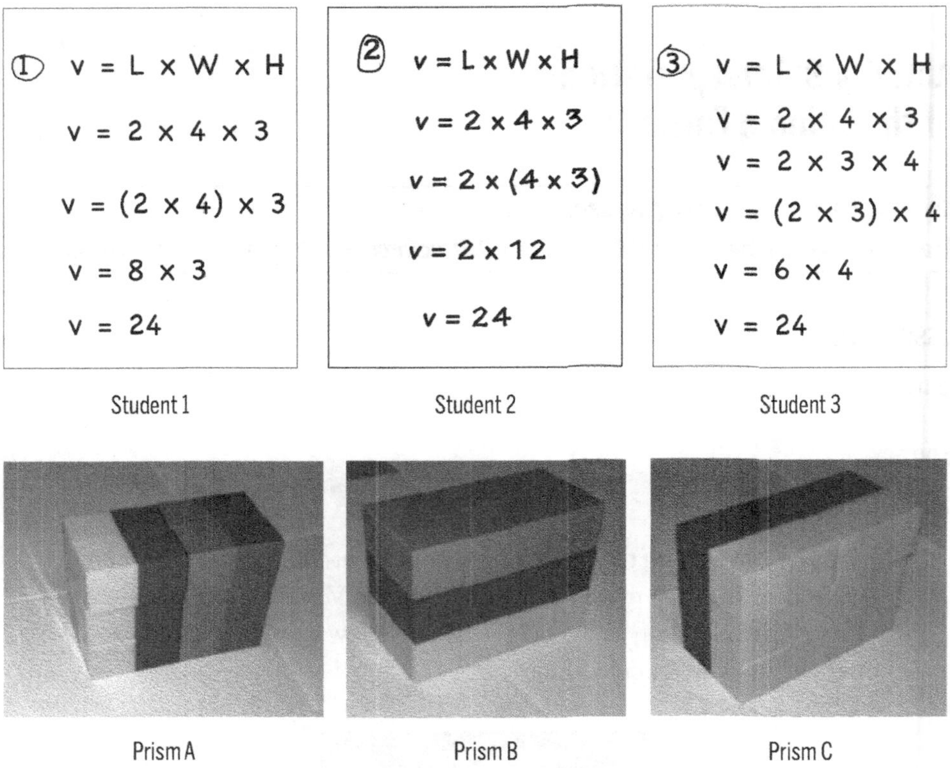

① v = L x W x H	② v = L x W x H	③ v = L x W x H
v = 2 x 4 x 3	v = 2 x 4 x 3	v = 2 x 4 x 3
v = (2 x 4) x 3	v = 2 x (4 x 3)	v = 2 x 3 x 4
v = 8 x 3	v = 2 x 12	v = (2 x 3) x 4
v = 24	v = 24	v = 6 x 4
		v = 24
Student 1	Student 2	Student 3
Prism A	Prism B	Prism C

Fig. 6.22. Volume formula represented three different ways

Expect

Some students may not realize that the formula and the physical objects are connected. To help them see this connection, students can build and manipulate the prisms, which can be used to model the different applications of the volume formula. Encourage students to describe and discuss how the models connect with the arithmetic work.

Extend

To continue working with students to connect the physical and symbolic representations of volume, present them with a physical model of a specific interpretation of the volume formula for a rectangular prism. Ask students to produce a symbolic representation along with a verbal description of that representation. For example, the prism shown in figure 6.23 would be symbolically represented as $3 \times (2 \times 5)$ and verbally described as consisting of 3 "walls" (vertical layers) of 10 cubes (2×5). Similarly, you can give students a symbolic representation (and the corresponding verbal description, as needed) and ask them to build the physical representation. For the prism in figure 6.23, you would give the symbolic representation as

3 × (2 × 5) and possibly a verbal description such as "3 'walls' (or vertical layers of 10 cubes, with each of the layers arranged in a 2 × 5 array." Note that if you describe the prism only as "3 layers of 10 cubes," other models can be produced, including figures that are not rectangular prisms (e.g., an L-shaped base with 3 layers).

Fig. 6.23. Prism that is 3 × (2 × 5), or 3 vertical layers of 10 cubes

REFERENCES

Barrett, Jeffrey E., Douglas H. Clements, and Julie Sarama, eds. *Children's Measurement: A Longitudinal Study of Children's Knowledge and Learning of Length, Area, and Volume. Journal for Research in Mathematics Education* Monograph Series, no. 16. Reston, Va.: National Council of Teachers of Mathematics, 2017.

Barrett, Jeffrey E., Graham Jones, Carol Thornton, and Sandra Dickson. "Understanding Children's Developing Strategies and Concepts for Length." In *Learning and Teaching Measurement,* 2003 Yearbook of the National Council of Teachers of Mathematics (NCTM), edited by Douglas H. Clements, pp. 17–30. Reston, Va.: NCTM, 2003.

Dacey, Linda, Mary Cavanagh, Carol R. Findell, Carole E. Greenes, Linda Jensen Sheffield, and Marian Small. *Navigating through Measurement in Prekindergarten–Grade 2.* Reston, Va.: National Council of Teachers of Mathematics, 2003.

Kurz, Terri L. "A Super Way to Soak in Linear Measurement." *Teaching Children Mathematics* 18, no. 9: 536–41.

Millsaps, Gayle M. "How Wedge You Teach the Unit-Angle Concept?" *Teaching Children Mathematics* 18, no. 6: 362–69.

National Council of Teachers of Mathematics (NCTM). *Principles and Standards for School Mathematics.* Reston, Va.: NCTM, 2000.

National Governors Association Center for Best Practices and Council of Chief State School Officers (NGA Center and CCSSO). *Common Core State Standards for Mathematics. Common Core State Standards (College- and Career-Readiness Standards and K–12 Standards in English Language Arts and Math).* Washington, D.C.: NGA Center and CCSSO, 2010. http://www.corestandards.org

CHILDREN'S BOOKS CITED

Marcie Aboff

If You Were an Inch or Centimeter (Picture Window Books 2009)

David A. Adler

Fraction Fun (Holiday House 1996)

Fractions, Decimals, and Percents (Scholastic 2010)

Perimeter, Area, and Volume: A Monster Book of Dimensions (Scholastic 2012)

Jez Alborough

Watch Out! Big Bro's Coming! (Scholastic 1997)

Jan Brett

The Mitten (Scholastic 1989)

Lisa Bullard

Big and Small: An Animal Opposites Book (Capstone Press 2006)

Fast and Slow: An Animal Opposites Book (Capstone Press 2006)

Long and Short: An Animal Opposites Book (Capstone Press 2006)

Pam Calvert

Multiplying Menace: The Revenge of Rumpelstiltskin (Charlesbridge 2006)

Eric Carle

The Grouchy Ladybug (Harper Trophy 1977)

Stephen Carpenter

The Three Billy Goats Gruff (Scholastic 1998)

Brian P. Cleary

A Fraction's Goal—Parts of a Whole (Millbrook Press, 2011)

Marilyn Deen

Big, Bigger, Biggest (Capstone Press 2012)

P. D. Eastman

The Best Nest (Random House 1968)

Ed Emberly

Picture Pie (Little, Brown 1984)

Paul Galdone

Goldilocks and the Three Bears (World's Work 1983)

Jack and the Beanstalk (Clarion 1974)

Bruce Goldstone

Great Estimations (Scholastic 2006)

Jessica Gunderson

How Long? Wacky Ways to Compare Length (Picture Window Books 2014)

Susan Hightower

Twelve Snails to One Lizard: A Tale of Mischief and Measurement (Simon & Schuster 1997)

Pat Hutchins

Happy Birthday, Sam (Penguin 1985)

Titch (Macmillan/McGraw Hill 1971)

Katharine Ibbs

DK Children's Cookbook (DK 2004)

Steve Jenkins

Actual Size (Houghton Mifflin Harcourt 2004)

Biggest, Strongest, Fastest (Ticknor & Fields 1995)

Steven Kellogg

Much Bigger Than Martin (Deal 1976)

Klutz Press (editors)

Everybody's Everywhere Backyard Bird Book (North American edition) (Klutz Press 1992)

Teruyuki Komiya

Life-Size Zoo (Seven Footer Kids 2009)

More Life-Size Zoo (Seven Footer Kids 2010)

Loren Leedy

Mapping Penny's World (Square Fish 2003)

Measuring Penny (Henry Holt 1997)

Seeing Symmetry (Holiday House 2011)

Patricia Lillie

When This Box Is Full (Greenwillow Books 1993)

Leo Lionni

Inch by Inch (Astor-Honor 1960)

Arnold Lobel

Frog and Toad Are Friends (Scholastic 1970)

Jonathan London

Froggy Gets Dressed (Scholastic 1992)

Ian F. Mahaney

Math on the Playground: Area and Perimeter (PowerKids Press 2013)

Joyce Markovics

Measure It! (Rourke Educational Media 2013)

Play with Sorting! (Rourke Educational Media 2013)

Rolf Mullar

How Big Is a Foot? (Dell 1991)

Patricia J. Murphy

Adding Puppies and Kittens (Enslow Elementary 2007)

Counting Puppies and Kittens (Enslow Elementary 2007)

Measuring Puppies and Kittens (Enslow Elementary 2007)

Subtracting Puppies and Kittens (Enslow Elementary 2007)

Telling Time with Puppies and Kittens (Enslow Elementary 2007)

Stuart J. Murphy

A House for Birdie (HarperCollins 2004)

Bigger, Better, Best (HarperCollins 2002)

Elevator Magic (HarperCollins 1997)

Get Up and Go! (HarperCollins 1996)

Hamster Champs (HarperCollins 2005)

Let's Fly a Kite (HarperCollins 2000)

Mighty Maddie (HarperCollins 2004)

Racing Around (HarperCollins 2002)

Ready, Set, Hop! (Scholastic 1996)

Room for Ripley (HarperCollins 1999)

Super Sand Castle Saturday (HarperCollins 1999)

The Best Bug Parade (HarperCollins 1996)

Treasure Map (HarperCollins 2004)

Cindy Neuschwander

Sir Cumference and the Off-the-Charts Dessert (Scholastic 2013)

Cindy Neuschwander and Wayne Geehan

Sir Cumference and the First Round Table (Charlesbridge 1997)

Mary Pope Osborne

Ancient Greece and the Olympics (Scholastic 2004)

Jerry Pallotta

Apple Fractions (Scholastic 2002)

The Hershey's Milk Chocolate Bar Fraction Book (Scholastic 1999)

Henry Pluckrose

Capacity (Children's Press 1995)

Length (Children's Press 1995)

Weight (Children's Press 1995)

Size (Children's Press 1995)

Sorting (Children's Press 1995)

Tish Rabe

Fine Feathered Friends: All About Birds (Random House 1998)

Margarette S. Reid

The Button Box (Dutton 1989).

Simone T. Ribke

A Garden Full of Sizes (Children's Press 2004)

Adele Richardson

Balances (Capstone 2004)

Marisabina Russo

A Very Big Bunny (Schwartz & Wade Books 2010)

The Line Up Book (Greenwillow 1986)

Mary Elizabeth Salzmann

What in the World Is a Foot? (ABDO 2009)

What in the World Is an Inch? (ABDO 2009)

David M. Schwartz

Millions to Measure (HarperCollins 2003)

Anne Schreiber

Slower Than a Snail (Scholastic 1995)

Tracey Steffora

Adding with Ants (Heinemann Library 2014)

Comparing with Cats (Heinemann Library 2014)

Measuring with Monkeys (Heinemann Library 2014)

Shapes with Snakes (Heinemann Library 2014)

Skip Counting with Meerkats (Heinemann Library 2014)

Taking Away with Tigers (Heinemann Library 2014)

Janet Stevens and Susan Stevens Crummel

Cook-A-Doodle-Doo! (Voyager Books 1999)

Joan Sweeney

Me and the Measure of Things (Crown 2001)

Simms Taback

There Was an Old Lady Who Swallowed a Fly (Scholastic 1997)

Lisa Trumbauer

Why We Measure (Yellow Umbrella Books 2003)

Scott Weidensaul

National Audubon Society First Field Guide: Birds (Chanticleer Press 1998)

Mo Willems

A Big Guy Took My Ball! (Hyperion 2013)